I highly recommend *Nobody Sees This YOU* as an explanation of being a spirit with understanding. Paul Renfroe has a great writing style. In the first chapter alone, he lays a great foundation of understanding for spiritual truths. Believers of all spiritual growth levels can grasp them because of his way of communicating. When we ordained Paul and Diane Renfroe for ministry, we knew they would help people come further in and higher up in the Lord Jesus. They have a gift for making spiritual things plain for you to grow in spirit.

Pastor Jane Hamon,
pastor with husband Tom Hamon of
Vision Church at Christian International, Santa Rosa Beach, FL

We know Paul Renfroe and his wife Diane quite well, and have been frequent guests in each other's homes. Therefore we are not surprised to read a book of such quality as *Nobody Sees This YOU*. Chapter Ten, "Church of Spirits," was especially insightful to us as pastors.

Jesus said that the spirit gives life and the flesh counts for nothing, and that God seeks worshippers in spirit and in truth. Our church is in the world but not of it. Paul's book gave us fantastic biblical guidance and will support anyone who wants to lead Christians into full function as living human spirits.

Pastors David and Alli Allen, New Covenant Church, Thomasville GA

I dare you to start reading this eye-opening primer on this "unseen" message. Paul Renfroe does a remarkable job laying the foundation and framework of the unseen realm for Christianity as a whole. I feel honored to have read and made suggestions to the manuscript of *Nobody Sees This YOU: How to Live as a Spirit in the Unseen Realm*. He is on to something bigger than he even imagined. We have much to learn from Paul's groundbreaking work. It will revolutionize the way the Church sees herself and operates.

Katie R. Dale, author of *But Deliver Me from Crazy: A Memoir*

There is more to our human existence than eating, sleeping, and working. Jesus spoke of it as living abundantly. It is life that transcends what is visible and yet touches everything we see. Paul Renfroe's writing will open the door to that life for you.

Chris Sutton, Burleson TX

NOBODY SEES THIS YOU

HOW TO LIVE AS A SPIRIT IN THE UNSEEN REALM

PAUL RENFROE

PARADIGM LIGHTHOUSE

Destin, Florida, United States of America

© 2022 Paul Renfroe

All rights reserved. No part of this publication may be reproduced in any form without written permission from publisher.

Published by Paradigm Lighthouse, PO Box 48, Freeport FL 32439 www.ParadigmLighthouse.com.

Nobody Sees This YOU: How to Live as a Spirit in the Unseen Realm
by Paul Renfroe

ISBN 979-8-9853944-0-5 paperback; 979-8-9853944-1-2 hardcover

LCCN 2021924277

BISAC: OCC019000, BODY, MIND & SPIRIT, Inspiration & Personal Growth
   REL012120, RELIGION, Christian Living, Spiritual Growth
   REL099000, RELIGION, Christian Living, Spiritual Warfare
   REL012070, RELIGION, Christian Living, Personal Growth

Cover Design by Hannah Linder

Editing by B. Kay Coulter

Interior Design by Michael J. Williams

Publication Consulting by Susan Neal

Except where indicated, Scripture quotations are from the New King James Version®. Copyright © 1982 by Thomas Nelson. Used by permission. All rights reserved.

Scripture quotations marked (NIV) are taken from the Holy Bible, New International Version®, NIV®. Copyright © 1973, 1978, 1984, 2011 by Biblica, Inc.™ Used by permission of Zondervan. All rights reserved worldwide. www.zondervan.com. The "NIV" and "New International Version" are trademarks registered in the United States Patent and Trademark Office by Biblica, Inc.™

Scripture quotations marked (ESV) are from The ESV® Bible (The Holy Bible, English Standard Version®), copyright © 2001 by Crossway, a publishing ministry of Good News Publishers. Used by permission. All rights reserved.

This book is for informational purposes only. While every precaution has been taken in the preparation of the book, neither the author nor the publisher shall have any liability to any person or entity with respect to any loss or damage caused by the content of this book.

Printed in the United States of America
First Edition

The Unseen Series

Prequel How to Unveil the Unseen and Live as a Spirit

Book 1 Nobody Sees This You:
How to Live as a Spirit in the Unseen Realm

Book 2 Nobody Sees This Unseen Realm:
How to Unlock Bible Mysteries

Book 3 Nobody Sees This Creation:
The Origin of the Devil and His Replacements

Book 4 Nobody Sees These Enemies:
How to Discern and Disarm Unseen Tempters

Book 5 Nobody Sees These Nations:
How Darkness Rules the Many Through the Few

Book 6 Nobody Sees This Israel:
God's Vanguard Against Darkness

Book 7 Nobody Sees This Warrior: God's Secret Ambush

Book 8 Nobody Sees This Church: Resisting Darkness

Book 9 Nobody Sees These Friends: Partners of the Unseen

Book 10 Nobody Sees This Victory: Defeating Darkness

Book 11 Nobody Sees This Time: Living in the Eternal NOW

Other Books by Paul Renfroe

Christian, What Are You? Removing the Blindfolds

Inadequacy

The Pains of the Christian: Desire, Glory, Joy

"So it is with everyone born of the spirit." (John 3:8)

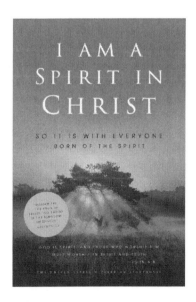

FREE GIFT TO READERS
The above full color 11X17 poster summarizes this book,
and you can get it for free.
Post it to encourage yourself, as well as all who see and ask about it.
Learn how you can receive one for free at *ParadigmLighthouse.com*.

Contents

Introduction 1
   What Is This Book? 1
   Foundations in Truth 2
   The Purpose of Everything 3
   The Mind and the Spirit 3
   About Capitalizations 3
   Format and Genre 4

Chapter One: *The Backing* 5

Chapter Two: *Getting to Know Your Spirit* 31

Chapter Three: *Spirit Defined* 45

Chapter Four: *Toward God* 59

Chapter Five: *The Capabilities of Spirits* 77

Chapter Six: *The Spirit, the Soul, and the Body* 93

Chapter Seven: *Living among Spirits* 113

Chapter Eight: *Darkness and Your Spirit* 131

Chapter Nine: *Discipleship of Your Spirit* 147

Chapter Ten: *Church of Spirits* 165

Chapter Eleven: *Spirits in the World of the Dead* 187

Chapter Twelve: *The Daily Life of Our Spirits* 205

Chapter Thirteen: *The Reality for Our Spirits* 237

Resources	249
About The *UNSEEN* Series	251
Works Referenced	259
Topical Listing of Books for Your Spirit	261
Reflection and Discussion Questions	263
Reader Engagement Resources	269

Foreword

Paul and Diane Renfroe have a long history of intense hunger for spiritual growth. With their leadership gifts, they have served in many churches. We have ordained them as ministers, acknowledging a clear love for people in both their past ministry and their writing. It is well-known that Paul and Diane have sought to be conformed to the image of Jesus Christ.

That's the subject of my book titled *Your Highest Calling*. I founded Christian International in 1968. For over fifty years, we have activated Christians globally in spiritual gifts, including prophetic ministry.

Paul learned about us in 2006, and quickly recognized Christian International as a welcoming home for their spiritual hunger. They attended our schools in Indiana and Florida, and became local residents so they could participate in our headquarters church, Vision Church at Christian International.

What Paul has produced in *Nobody Sees This YOU*—Book One of the nine-book *Unseen* Series—will enable any spiritually hungry reader to replicate his own discovery process.

Your church background gives you a foundation to build upon, and if you seek more, this is the book for you. Few churches pretend they can provide everything that a hungry Christian seeks. Every church and group of any kind has people who are on the forward edges, seeking more and not knowing where to look. You may be one such person.

What awaits you in these pages will satisfy many unsolved curiosities. I strongly encourage you to join Paul Renfroe in this book of discovery. You will advance your spiritual maturity in ways you never thought possible.

Bishop Bill Hamon
Bishop: Christian International Apostolic-Global Network
Author: *Who Am I & Why Am I Here; The Eternal Church;*
Prophets & Personal Prophecy; Prophets & the Prophetic Movement;
Prophets, Pitfalls, & Principles; Apostles/Prophets & the Coming Moves of God;
The Day of the Saints; The Final Reformation & Great Awaking;
70 Reasons for Speaking in Tongues; God's Weapons of War;
Your Highest Calling; and *How Can These Things Be?*

To The Reader

The test readers have asked me about the book's audience. It's you: curious, growing, unsatisfied, inquisitive, or charged to help such people. Like you, many now sense the unseen realm, and this book offers Christian explanations of that perception. Your own process of testing will reveal if these explanations are satisfying to you.

Nobody Sees This YOU is the first of the *Unseen* series, which explains the unseen influences on your life and on this world. Please see *About the Unseen Series* at the end of this book.

Many fields and authors attempt to explain the influences on us: philosophy, comparative religion, astrophysics, economics, history, ancient writings, and Christian literature. The explanatory power of the *Unseen* series unveils the origins of unseen forces and entities.

You might experience the same relief and delight of understanding. I say "might," because it is conditional upon responding to the King of the Unseen as He desires. It's possible that you don't think of yourself as a Christian, but that you are closer than someone who does. *About the Unseen Series* at the end of the book describes the protocol for becoming a living spirit and staying one.

Prior to publication, test readers from various age groups and walks of life reviewed and improved this book. Though unknown to you, their contribution has curbed or eliminated potential misunderstandings. Many thanks are due to them.

Churches often have study groups for books like this one that help us understand our faith. The Resources Appendix includes questions for discussion starters. In addition, a private online discussion group awaits you at ParadigmLighthouse.com. There you and other readers can discuss our discoveries about life as spirits. Each reader can request log-in credentials on that website.

Introduction

This book holds conversations with the Holy Spirit about the unseen world. The primary message: everything we want is possible when we become living spirits.

Every longing you have is obtained by maturing as a living spirit. And every obstacle you face in life serves that maturing process—by evil spirits to obstruct you, and by God's Spirit to develop, test, and prove you.

History confirms the only path for this: faith that pleases the King of the unseen realm, Jesus Christ. You may not be following Jesus but are curious about the world of spirit. Bible knowledge is not needed. I cite it throughout the book, with the location referenced. Any curious person is welcome, with one caution: spirit is not a matter of knowledge. Spirit is agreeing with God, THE Spirit, and with what He revealed in Jesus and the Bible that describes Him.

If you are already born as a spirit by following Jesus, your danger also is relying on knowledge. You'll gain knowledge, a new paradigm, and more effectiveness for the kingdom of God. Of that there is no doubt.

But though short for its topic, Book One is not a shortcut. If it is knowledge you seek, other books may be better. As eager as you are for the subsequent books in the *Unseen* series, remember what's at stake. This book is partially for your protection. Permit yourself the freedom to work through these activating reflections. You may choose to skim it. If so, remember that its greatest fruitfulness is your own reflection upon its truths.

WHAT IS THIS BOOK?

The *Unseen* series of nine books exposes the activities of an invisible evil kingdom. But though unseeable, this kingdom of darkness is not unknowable. It is known by its effects, spiritually.

The words ahead of you in this Book One of the *Unseen* Series are composed rationally—but they are not a book of the mind. Feelings are expressed, but it is not a book of the emotions. What you hold is a book of spirit for your spirit.

The title expresses the mysteriousness of your spirit. You will read of a secret intimacy possible for you with God Almighty. Wherever your spirit is in the maturing process, God sees you. The God of Jesus Christ calls you into a new intimacy with Him—and gives you the capability for that. As this maturity occurs, your fellowship as a spirit with other living spirits will render the title of this book a thing of your past. You will be seen, known, and loved. You will be safe.

This book will prompt many questions. Please be at ease; write them down in the margins if you want. Join our online discussion group for dialog with other readers. With the discussion questions in the back of this book, you and your study group can personalize each chapter's impact.

If you will look at your questions and their underlying motivations, you may find insecurity, fear, and even shame within yourself. Be at ease. In the following pages, your security with God the Father will grow. He orchestrated your intimacy with Him beginning before the foundation of the world. Make every effort to settle yourself on that fundamental issue of security with Him. Then your questions will gain a much different feeling—joy and discovery rather than shame and insecurity.

Such security with God will open your understanding as you proceed through this and the remaining eight books of the *Unseen* series.

FOUNDATIONS IN TRUTH

We follow Jesus Christ as Lord. He is the Savior, the Second Person of the Triune God. In His mercy and grace, He died on the cross, the substitutionary atonement for all our sins and offenses against our Creator. God makes each believer alive when we were dead in our trespasses and sins. He now saves anyone who believes and fills each one of us with His Holy Spirit. Everyone who believes in Him as Savior also follows Him as Lord.

Jesus is Lord of our entire being, including our thinking. He said, *"Everyone who is of the truth hears my voice"* (John 18:37). Truth includes historical facts, biblical thinking, logical connections, and true doctrine. The *Unseen* Series takes the Word of God as the truth. By the Bible we test every prophetic word.

This Book One will equip your activated spirit with such capability of thought.

Introduction

THE PURPOSE OF EVERYTHING

God is populating the unseen world of spirits with more living human spirits in His image. He first saves individual people from sin and makes them alive in spirit. He then proves these human spirits through the tests, challenges, and circumstances of mortal life. We thus develop over a process of time into mature spirits, in contrast to the angels whose spirit is part of their created nature.

God Almighty wants to enjoy eternal intimacy and effective agreement with us, involved as partner-kings in all He desires. Therefore this new royalty of living human spirits will function as His co-regents throughout existence.

THE MIND AND THE SPIRIT

The design of this Book One is not to satisfy your mind, but to stimulate your spirit to active function. To achieve its purpose, the following pages may even irritate your mind..

The visible order which our minds crave must subordinate to the invisible order governing the unseen world. Our minds know this visible world. Compared to what our spirit can know, that's a subset.

We don't know God with our mind. We know God spirit-to-Spirit. Our minds are important, but they are not lord. The mind is one member that the Bible says we must submit to our spirits. What makes sense to a living spirit in the unseen may not be sensible to our minds.

You who follow Jesus Christ are living spirits in an unseen world of creatures with angelic natures—both good and evil ones. The Holy Spirit expects our cooperation. For this we are woefully inadequate. Without a functioning spirit, mere knowledge of the unseen can be fatal. Understanding the Bible about your spirit is protective.

ABOUT CAPITALIZATIONS

The following pages are designed to help you identify and mature as a living spirit. Unfortunately, despite the versatility of the English language, our vocabulary for spirit is limited to a small assortment of words and phrases. These now carry religious connotations which hinder our freedom as living spirits in intimacy with God, who is spirit—not religious. Religious baggage has made its way into professional capitalization standards and obscures our nature as those who blow like the wind, as Jesus described us, in an unseen world populated by spirits.

To disarm the formal religious awkwardness of certain words, and to properly reflect the identify of personal participants in the unseen world, we have adopted the following guides for each book in the *Unseen* series.

We capitalize the first letter of each pronoun referring to God or a person of the Trinity. Current style guidelines regard this as archaic; I regard it as respectful. It also helps us keep the characters straight as we talk about the many spirits in the unseen world.

Because of the respect issue, I've chosen not to use an upper case first letter for the devil. Because satan means accuser in the Bible, it is the functional description and not capitalized. Originally created as a cherub, Lucifer does have a first letter cap as his given name prior to falling.

You'll learn that there are active personal entities that can't be seen but not completely revealed in the Bible, and when I refer to them, it is with an upper case first letter. Examples are Creation, Sin, and Earth. When they are lower case first letter, the reference is to the acts of creating and sinning, or to land, dirt or acreage.

FORMAT AND GENRE

The following pages contain several styles. Some I spoke into my recorder while riding on a long motorcycle trip. Other portions resulted from careful study. Yet more is from my journal. There are letters to others as well.

This fluidity of style portrays actual life as a living spirit. It balances observable facts of the mind and spiritual discernments. To see the backing of reality's tapestry, we need all our abilities. These stylistic variations should provoke your mind and shake up your expectations. If you will forge ahead through your mental irritation, it helps you submit it to your spirit.

The *Unseen* series of books concern the world of spirit. To derive the full benefit, you must be alive as a spirit. This book can help that happen within you.

May your spirit wake up to full function!

CHAPTER ONE

THE BACKING

IN OR OUT?

Record today's date. _____

You will find this useful in case this book has limited relevance to your life right now. But as your living spirit matures, its contents certainly will become more and more relevant with each rereading.

Readers' Online Discussion Group

As an owner of this book, you can request login credentials for a secure online discussion group at ParadigmLighthouse.com, to share your meditations and your progress. The group is limited to readers of the *Unseen* Series. There, you can share your reflections and discoveries. I am growing also and treasure your discoveries as you walk through this book and meditate on the scriptural principles.

With the correspondence and reflections our readers share there, we can all see how God is speaking to us, His body, about our spirits. I'm sure we will find patterns in God's speech to us. Doubtless we can use this book from our discoveries together.

THE NARROW GATE

Whether we look at our own lives and times, or the lives of ancients in the Bible and history, very few people live as spirits. Do you know anyone who identifies themselves as a spirit?

Jesus made our birth as spirits possible, everyone is eligible, and the gospel message tells how. Yet He said few would accept it, in Matthew's gospel chapter 7:13–14,

> Enter by the narrow gate; for wide is the gate and broad is the way that leads to destruction, and there are many who go in by it. Because narrow is the gate and difficult is the way which leads to life, and there are few who find it.

Why is the gate narrow? What is so hard to learn about our spirit? Why do so few people live as spirits?

Because we are so poor in spirit—so poor in fact that even the idea may make no sense yet. Only God, the Spirit, can make us spirits. Only He can supply the growth of our spirit. Few are those who want that. Fewer still are those willing to accept God's terms for it.

People take their poverty of spirit for granted because it's all they've ever known. Our entire environment codifies poverty of spirit; keywords and categories presume our inadequacy of spirit. Our period of history has conditioned us. The operating systems of our times also limit or hinder our perception of the unseen world.

A social penalty often follows our uncommon insights. The accepted protocols of behavior and relationship do not easily tolerate Christians' living spirits. Even in many churches, our leaders ask us to limit our inquiries to certain topics, or to restrict our exposure to their approved sources.

These topics and sources have their useful part to play. But while we mature as living spirits, we may outgrow our mentors and our church environment. My wife and I describe ourselves as Metho-Bap-Ter-Ic-Calia-Costal. We have been members and, in most cases, leaders in each of those denominations, described in Chapter Twelve, *The Daily Life of Our Spirits*. Why so many? Are we unstable? Those who didn't want to move on with us thought so.

No, our pursuit is quite steady, and our direction is very stable: further in and higher up. My wife and I aim at the narrow gate. At the Lord's request, we have released everything we prized. We laid every church relationship on the altar. Over our fifty years on this path, even our dearest friends and mentors have marginalized us. Have our sacrifices been worth it? Apostle Paul described the prize to the Philippians, chapter 3 verses 13–14:

> Forgetting those things which are behind and reaching forward to those things which are ahead, I press toward the goal for the prize of the upward call of God in Christ Jesus.

May you have a journey as passionate as that of my wife and me. May you enjoy the same reward: knowing Him more deeply all the way. We welcome your company.

THE BIGGEST OF THE BIG PICTURES

The Bible holds mysteries and puzzles. Bible students have yet to solve many after twenty centuries. To solve them we need a different frame of reference—like changing our definition of what direction "up" is.

Spirit Is Assumed

One of these puzzles is spirit. I cannot see it with physical eyes or hear it with physical ears. We do not move among the spirits of the unseen—they move among us. We cannot make ourselves see what is invisible to natural senses.

Jesus said, *"God is spirit"* (John 4:24). One result: only God can reveal the unsee-able to us, because we are poor in spirit. He uses the Bible to reveal it to us, which is full of certainty about the spirit world.

After Jesus said *God is spirit*, He indicated who God sought to worship him: people worshipping in spirit and in truth. Jesus also said, *"the words I speak to you are spirit and they are life"* (John 6:63). It's quite clear: for us to follow Jesus most effectively, we have to understand what He meant by "spirit."

He titled His earliest followers *apostles*. They knew what Jesus meant by spirit, and lived it. They wrote what we call the New Testament, after Jesus' ascension. It reveals the new covenant God offers to everyone who desires to live as a spirit. In it, the original apostles convey the truths about this unseen world to us. One of them was John. Late in his life, he wrote four books of the New Testament in the Bible. The first is John's gospel, a genre that encapsulates the message and three-year ministry of Jesus.

Apostle John recorded Jesus' many statements about spirit. In one conversation with a famous teacher, Jesus used a simple metaphor to describe people who are born as spirits.

> The wind blows where it wishes, and you hear the sound of it but you do not know where it comes from or where it is going. So it is with everyone born of the spirit. (John 3:8)

Apostle John wrote three brief letters that you find in the back of the New Testament. In chapter 4 of the first one, he exhorted the Christians to *"test the spirits."* In order to do this, we must understand spirit.

John divided the unseen origin of people's confession about Jesus into only two spheres of influence: *"the Spirit of God"* and *"the spirit of antichrist"* (1 John 4:1–3). Either way, we must recognize spirits. But how do we do that? This book and the *Unseen* Series can activate that ability in you. John taught with our living spirits we can know the unseen world God lives in. He wrote we know all things and we know all truth (1 John 2:20, 27). But what's puzzling is that so few people experience this.

Clearly John was not describing a mental knowing of all facts or principles. Rather, you can know the unseen world as a living spirit yourself. The Spirit of God, who knows all things, lives in you and what He knows is available to your spirit.

Apostle John recorded Jesus' original promise of this in his gospel, 16:12–14.

> When He, the Spirit of truth, has come, He will guide you into all truth. All things that the Father has are Mine. Therefore I said that He will take of Mine and declare it to you.

Paul, another apostle of Jesus, wrote two letters to the church of Corinth, in Greece. In the first, he says the same thing: Christians are living spirits who know God, the Spirit who knows and shares all things.

> For the Spirit searches all things, yes, the deep things of God.... No one knows the things of God except the Spirit of God.
> Now we have received, not the spirit of the world, but the Spirit who is from God, that we might know the things that have been freely given to us by God.... We have the mind of Christ. (1 Corinthians 2:10–16)

Jesus and His apostles all agree about this: When we follow Jesus, we are privy to what God thinks, because the Spirit of God lives in us. If He sees the unseen world, then we can see it too, because He lives in us and shows us what He sees. God is spirit, and we Christians are too.

We are living spirits in the unseen world of spirits. Many of the Bible's mysteries are unlocked. It is a point of view question. By gaining the frame of reference that Jesus had, the spirit world will be primary. It unlocks puzzles about ourselves, as well as puzzles in the Bible.

The Bible's Tapestry of Spirit

God revealed Himself to many people over fifteen hundred years. Forty of them wrote it down. Leaders from several cultures affirmed these writings in one highly attested collection in 397 AD—our Bible. This collection is contextual. It does not give theological outlines. The Bible's variety has consistent background truths and facts, but identifying them requires hunger and effort.

Consider the tapestries commonly hung on Britain's castle walls. Each has two sides. The room-facing side has different fabrics, colors, and textures. This variety forms images of distinct individuals, times, places, and events. The event and its participants are what you see—not the materials.

The wall-facing side is unseen—a backing which is not visible. Touring Cardor Castle in 2017, I looked behind a tapestry to see what it looked like. It was uniform and unchanging. On the room side were scenes, people, and events—but the backing was one fabric. The visible variety on the room side had no impact on the backing.

The truths about spirit are the backing of the Bible tapestry. God revealed Himself in the Bible—both sides. The variety of life is presented to us in the room side. One fabric holds it together. Like the castle's tapestry, the backing is unaffected by culture, times, people, or events. Elements of change in this mortal life do not affect the backing.

That fabric is the spirit world.

God did not give us outlines or theological formulations. He didn't give us outlines about Jesus, about salvation, about Himself, about existence, or frankly about anything. The Bible has no outline of spirit. Why not?

Although God is love, He is not cheap. Anyone desiring any relationship with Him must pay a price for the privilege and pleasure. Jesus described that price with two stories, or parables, in the thirteenth chapter of the first New Testament Gospel, Matthew.

> Again, the kingdom of heaven is like treasure hidden in a field, which a man found and hid; and for joy over it he goes and sells all that he has and buys that field.
>
> Again, the kingdom of heaven is like a merchant seeking beautiful pearls, who, when he had found one pearl of great price, went and sold all that he had and bought it. (Matthew 13:44–46)

God's habit of concealing mysteries is how He proves whether we would be kings in His kingdom.

It is the glory of God to conceal a matter,
But the glory of kings is to search out a matter. (Proverbs 25:2)

A Process of Testing

Such spirit-to-spirit intimacy with God is beyond imagining for most people. If we truly follow Him, we automatically go that direction. You can't make it happen, but you can yield yourself to Him. God tests us to pull us forward into our maturity as spirits.

I pass some tests. I also fail some tests and get to retake them. A person can be born as a spirit yet can fail tests and live in the flesh. Scripture says that one sign we are born in the spirit is the war between our spirit and flesh (Galatians 5:17). Jesus Christ the perfect shepherd of our souls redeems even our worst failures and troubles if we will persist with Him. Our troubles are a significant part of God's tests. Think about Jesus—He had extreme troubles.

First, He was born fully God and fully man. Then at age thirty, the Holy Spirit filled Him—when He met John the Baptist in the river and heaven opened upon Him. Those qualifications should be enough, right? He's fully prepared, right? No, in fact. Despite His apparent readiness, that same Spirit of God drove him into isolation, deprivation, and temptation for forty days.

We think of this as Jesus' temptation when we read it in the fourth chapter of Matthew's gospel. Much more was occurring, no doubt. Think of its effect on you. Imagine yourself those forty days—with your thoughts, prayers, hunger, desperation, confusion, weakness. Mark's gospel reports that angels cared for Jesus afterwards, and wild animals were with Him.

These events signify Jesus' effective unseen citizenship—not to mention face-to-face temptation by the devil. Testing like this definitely changes your outlook to the new paradigm of the unseen. And you would certainly be more attentive to your spirit after such an experience.

The alteration to your outlook on life would be permanent. You would stand out. Your thoughts and speech would be strange to everyone around you without such testing. No one could refute what you experienced. Your confidence would be unassailable. That is exactly what people saw in Jesus after those forty days.

The Spirit Summary of the Bible

The Bible's creation account causes much discussion about our origin. Genesis, the Bible's first book, reveals clearly that God made us. Genesis is much more than the how and when. There, God reveals the history of the human spirit—from beginning to end.

God created our first parents in His image. Because He is spirit, being in His image means Adam and Eve each had a spirit, as well as soul and body. With spirits, they could function in the unseen world. He commanded them to multiply, to reproduce others like themselves, and to dominate earth. The descendants of Adam and Eve would be spirits in natural bodies—a global population ruling Earth in both the seen and the unseen.

Being a spirit is necessary to relate to Him, a Spirit. Without our spirits, relationship with God is broken. Natural life is a shadow and a hollow husk of what God intended.

Sadly, our first parents disobeyed Him. Just as He warned them, they died instantly. Their bodies or souls continued, dead in spirit. Their exile from Eden was first in a series, culminating in separation from their Creator. In His place: the kingdom of darkness.

Their bodies and souls continued. Their sexual reproduction continued, and they were fruitful. But God's intended multiplication did not happen. The desired population of people in His full spirit image did not result. Adam and Eve bore descendants dead in spirit like themselves, down to the present day.

Creation continued also. When God reshaped Earth over the six days, He installed—in the animals, in the winds and waves, in Earth's very fabric—a desire to serve living spirits. Now suddenly, Creation missed the human spirits it yearned to serve. It would remain frustrated, its full capability dormant.

God, our Creator, sent Jesus. Although He was the Son of God, Jesus chose the title Son of Man—the representative Son of this dead humankind. What seems like underselling reflected His purpose: the recapture of people's original spirit identity. He defended His choice of rough, unqualified followers with this purpose. It's in the third New Testament book, Luke's Gospel, chapter 19:10.

The Son of Man came to seek and to save that which was lost.

Jesus came to save a situation that was lost—the spirit nature of man. He came to enable our birth as living spirits—God's original plan, long frustrated. God created our first parents as living spirits. Jesus was born a living spirit, divinely conceived in His mother, Mary. Likewise, any person who believes and follows Him is born anew as a living spirit.

In both His three-year ministry and His death, Jesus traded places with people. The Gospels (the first four books of the New Testament) relate the many ways He took on people's sorrows and gave them His joys. He obeyed Father God without fail. His death by crucifixion was Jesus' greatest achievement of trading places with people.

God raised Him from the dead; hundreds saw Him. Finally, Father God seated Jesus as the King of the Unseen World.

From there, at Jesus' request, God offers the Holy Spirit of God to everyone on earth who follows Him as Lord and Savior. When we do so, we are born as spirits. Only that birth permits us citizenship in His unseen kingdom—not natural birth.

This Holy Spirit also causes us to recognize Jesus as the Son of God. After these events occur, we relate to this three-in-one God with intimacy. We relate to Him as spirits—just as He, a Spirit, originally intended.

Jesus wants people to be rulers with Him in the unseeable world. The third book of the New Testament is Luke's gospel. The night before His enemies crucified Him, in verse 22:29, Jesus made this desire very plain.

> As the Father conferred upon Me a kingdom, so also I confer a kingdom upon you.

ACTORS OF THE UNSEEN

What is unseen to us is not inactive. God revealed in the Bible a large, very active, and invisible population of spirits. They outnumber mortal people. When we are born as spirits by faith in Jesus, we may perceive this population. Among us are spirits of several kinds.

The Holy Inhabitants

One type of spirit is familiar through TV shows and testimonies: angels. People accept the existence of angels and believe angels are good. Angels are present throughout the Bible and are far more than good. The spirits we call angels are holy—they serve God exclusively and unerringly. Because God loves people, serving Him makes them appear good to us.

In shape and appearance, angels resemble people. Their activities include things we also do: stand on the ground, prepare meals, light fires. Angels can interact with physical reality just like we do, but are not bound to it. In the popular mind, angels have wings and fly—because, as spirits by nature, they are unbound to our physical reality. Angels do not have unneeded wings.

Angels have the characteristics of spirit listed on page 33. They organize into ranks. They confer and coordinate. Angel spirits can sing, move, and act in synchronized unison. They also wage unseen war in unison.

They are verbal and speak frequently in the Bible. Usually they announce a decree of God, even without understanding it—especially as it pertains to people.

They serve people only because they are loyal to God. He favors mankind; they see it, so they favor us. But angels are vexed at the unholiness of people. The lasting word for our unholiness is sin; we do not serve God exclusively and unerringly. Were it not for God's favor on mankind, holy angels could well adopt an enemy stance toward people, who all sin.

In *Nobody Sees These Friends: Partners in the Unseen*, the eighth book of the *Unseen* series, we'll explore their cooperation with our human spirits.

The Bible reveals a second type of spirits: seraphim. God reveals them only in Isaiah 6, where they express the gravity of God. What Isaiah called seraphim might be the four holy cherubim (the plural of cherub.) Our popular fiction calls Cupid a cherub; he is anything but.

Unlike angels, cherubim are seen only twice in the Bible. At the beginning of his journal of visions, Ezekiel recorded what he saw in 595 BC (Ezekiel 1). The other is the fourth chapter of Apostle John's vision in 90 AD, named Revelation—the last book of the Bible. Other Bible places refer to them without description.

God revealed only four holy cherubim, versus angels, which are many. Angels have frequent interactions with people and each other. In contrast, no cherub exhibits any interaction with anyone in the Bible.

Physically, cherubim have heads and feet, but otherwise do not resemble angels or people. Cherubim have three sets of wings; their beating is louder than armies and sounds like many gurgling rivers. The head of each cherub has four faces—a lion face, an eagle face, a bovine face, and a human face. Each face points in a fixed direction. The cherubim have eyes all over their bodies.

To Ezekiel, the cherubim's bodies looked like burning coals. He saw fire full of lightning passing back and forth between them. In Revelation, John saw them fixed at God's throne. Ezekiel saw God's throne moving from Jerusalem, yet from that throne, the cherubim were rigidly unturning.

In John's vision, their continual chorus announces God's holiness and timelessness. When cherubim speak, they declare reality.

One task, and one only, occupies each cherub's mighty capabilities. They behold and respond to God's qualities. Their many eyes, their four faces, their broadcasting voices, and their multiple wings all serve that purpose only.

These two groups, angels and cherubim, are God's allies in the unseen. But not all unseen spirits honor the Spirit who made them and their world.

The Enemy Inhabitants

The Bible reveals invisible enemies of God throughout its entire time span.

We easily believe one type in our society: the demons. We understand they are not good, but evil and intent on harm—whatever the form.

Demons' focus is on individual people. Everything revealed about them is slavish: bound to evil, commanded by superiors, without liberty to deviate. They are not strategists or tacticians. Instead, they are the cannon fodder of darkness, the door-to-door invaders imposing darkness upon people.

The bulk of God's revelation about demons centers on their effect on people. Their nature and origin are hidden in the Bible. We explore these questions in the third book of the *Unseen* series, *Nobody Sees This Creation: The Origin of the Devil and His Replacements*.

The Bible reveals a second type of invisible enemies, angelic in their created nature and aligned with one unholy cherub. They are united in their effort to dishonor God. If they could unseat God, they would—they certainly tried.

The Bible describes these fallen angels and their leader. There are three primary sources. The twelfth chapter of Revelation in the New Testament reveals a war in the unseen. Around 720 BC, the prophet Isaiah saw the ultimate judgment of these enemies, described in his fourteenth chapter and expanded in Revelation chapter 20. And Ezekiel around 593 BC learned about the initial clash between God and the head of His cherubim.

The Non-Personal Entities

The Bible reveals that the unseen world includes non-personal participants. The previous types of beings discussed can all relate personally. In contrast, physical Creation and Sin respond to our choices without being engaged with us individually. They respond to agreement with us as iron responds to magnets.

Creation itself is a participant in the unseen.

God made us in His image and breathed His breath of life into us, giving us a unique connection with Him. But breath is not all we are. He formed our first father's body from dirt, giving us mankind a unique connection with Earth.

Jesus was the first man ever to be born as God originally intended: both flesh and spirit. He called Himself the Son of Man, a title from Old Testament prophecies. By using this phrase, Jesus identified Himself as the ideal offspring of Adam and Eve—like God originally intended. All that Jesus did fulfilled our Creator's mandate to rule the Earth. And what do we find Him doing?

By His mere word, storms calmed, winds stilled, and waves settled. At His will, water held up the weight of His body. Two fishes and five loaves of bread fed over five thousand people. Unfruitful trees withered overnight at His rebuke.

Once, people demanded taxes from Jesus. He told Peter to catch one fish and pay the tax with the coins inside it. Multiple times, dead bodies came to life at His verbal command. People's maimed limbs grew back. The deaf heard and the mute spoke. In place of every physical ailment, He transferred vigor, vitality, and newness.

Jesus did these things out of compassion. They were also testimonies to His identity. He was the Son of the Mankind we were meant to be. That's why Jesus elicited Creation's readiness to serve people alive in spirit. In the Son of Man, Earth recognized the first of its rightful rulers: a man made in God's image, alive in spirit and natural alike.

Creation yearns to respond to people when we agree with God and become living spirits. Until that occurs, physical creation exists as a hostage of darkness.

The Bible reveals a second force, most unwelcome: Sin. It also responds to our agreements. In the fourth chapter of Genesis, God Himself warned Cain about Sin as an entity with desires. The warning preceded Cain's decision to murder his brother Abel.

> If you do well, will you not be accepted? And if you do not do well, sin lies at the door. And its desire is for you, but you should rule over it.

Apostle Paul describes Sin in his own autobiographical testimony about trying to do good, and failing. Many are comforted by it, found in the seventh chapter of his letter to the Roman church, in the New Testament. There also, God reveals that Sin is an active entity.

In the only letter written by James, a leader of the early church, he warns us to recognize sin as temptation's baby.

> But each one is tempted when he is drawn away by his own desires and enticed. Then, when desire has conceived, it gives birth to sin; and sin, when it is full-grown, brings forth death. (James 1:14–15)

The Bible reveals that Sin is a being in its own right. Sin responds to our choices, which are sin's only door to active expression. If we do not choose agreement with God, then Sin gains an open door and brings death into our daily life and into our person. Sin responds to our unholy agreements, our arguments against our holy Maker.

The High Status of Human Spirits

Of all the races God created, the most elevated is the reborn human spirit. Despite the age-old fascination with angels, demons, and other unseen beings, only the living human spirit receives the highest honors in God's unseen kingdom. Mankind has eight distinguishing honors in the unseen.

First: Only people were created in God's image—not angels and not cherubim. He made no other spirit race as we were:

> Let us make man in our image. (Genesis 1:26)

Second: We reproduce. Unlike the angels and cherubim, mankind reproduces. If He made our first parents in His image, then the billions who have lived since then have been in God's image—absent their spirits. In a world designed to multiply agreement, all living things reproduce. But only one being reproduces God's image: the human being.

Third: God became human. Our first parents' disobedience looked like the death knell of our race. By rights, our Creator could have rejected us. But no: God Himself became a human being. The virgin birth of Jesus was with both natures, as our first parents had. He was born both a living spirit and a natural person.

Only our race was honored by the incarnation of God. He did not become an angel or a cherub.

Fourth: Unlike the unseen enemies, the rebellious human race did not lose His favor. Every human life is a potential spirit, the full image of God. After natural birth, all that is lacking is birth as a spirit. So God provided the means for that spirit to be born: faith in Jesus as Savior and Lord.

Other beings lost His favor forever by becoming His enemies. Angels may have wondered that people did not (1 Peter 1:12). The shepherds saw angels singing their amazement on the first Christmas: *"Glory to God in the highest [heaven], and on earth peace among men with whom He is well-pleased"* (Luke 2:14, AMP).

Fifth: Every human being can tell God, "I'm sorry. Will You forgive me?" We can repent from previous choices. In fact, we can even repent the choices of our forebears and first parents. No other race God created receives the opportunity to change back to His kingdom—only people. No other spirit type can be restored—only us.

Sixth: After His resurrection from physical death, God seated Jesus as King over all God has made. A human being occupies the throne of the universe—Jesus, the Son of God and Son of Man. No angelic creature, no cherubim, no other creature of God is on that throne, but a man.

Seventh: Only living human spirits are home to God's Spirit. Only we can know His thoughts and hear His voice within. The Holy Spirit fills no other inhabitants of the unseen—only human beings.

Eighth and last: Only living human spirits are royalty in God's kingdom. Rulership is only for human spirits alive through Christ Jesus. Every other spirit type was made a servant. The apostle Paul wrote this to the Ephesian church in the second chapter of his letter there, verse 6 (NIV).

> God raised us up with Christ and seated us with him in the heavenly realms in Christ Jesus.

As greatly as God honors us, not every person becomes a living spirit. Each person must choose which kingdom to agree with. Whichever choice it is, we repeat it multiple times daily.

All of us unwittingly choose the kingdom of darkness because we are born dead in spirit. The honors listed above create accountability for people, who will be judged for disdaining God and His honors upon our race.

The good news is this: everyone has opportunity to choose God's kingdom until they die. As we honor our Creator, all the honors above work to our benefit rather than our judgment.

WHAT MAKES IT ALL GO?

A spouse wants to go out for dinner. If the other agrees, off they go. But if the other wants to stay home, the two may argue. Agreement and argument are opposites. The urge to agree is latent in everything that exists. This urge came from God, who imagined and created all that is. The primary society in the unseen world is to agree.

Agreement

What is God like? We might think of His power, perfection, or timelessness. Theology lists His attributes: omniscience, omnipresence, and omnipotence. These outlines help our understanding.

God chose not to use outlines. Instead, He orchestrated the Bible as a compilation of reports from actual living people in specific circumstances.

These Bible records are the room-facing side of the tapestry. The backing of that tapestry is agreement between spirits.

God is one Spirit in three Persons, a three-fold Spirit: Father, Son and Holy Spirit. This triune nature is multi-personal. He is agreement personified. His internal agreement gives rise to more spirits, such as Adam and Eve: *"Let us make man in our image, according to Our likeness"* (Genesis 1:26). He created them in His image—each having a spirit, as well as a soul and body. With the male and female genders, they also could have multi-personal unity.

Apostle John saw another example of more spirits, in Revelation 5:6—although the how is not explained. *"…having seven horns and seven eyes, which are the seven Spirits of God sent out into all the earth."*

The imprint of His agreeing Spirit is throughout all Creation. God spoke everything into being in Genesis 1. The agreement within this Trinity was the only active force. Each utterance begins "Let," a social expression. When He created us in His image, His exact words were *Let Us*.

Let Us make man in our image, according to our likeness.

He stamped agreement upon reality like a seal on hot wax. Many words express this among people. Two Bible synonyms for it are *covenant* and *testament*. Agreement is in all our words today, from fandom to contract, from company to team to partnership. Appointments, fashions, markets—all activities presume alignment and agreement.

Even our creation as male and female was to reveal His agreement. He is multi-personal; we are in His image; therefore, we are multi-personal. Our sexual intercourse images Him and expresses His divine unity. He only honors sex within marriage of a man and woman, because marriage projects His multi-personal oneness. He made us in His image for showing His own faithful and loyal agreement; therefore He judges all other sexual activity, because it prostitutes us and obscures His multi-personal image.

Physical reality itself bears God's imprint of agreement. The Triune, agreeing God made it. Alignment among spirits is the tapestry backing of all Creation.

The molecules that comprise substances bond with one another. Atoms were the indivisible building blocks of all matter—until we learned they have parts too. Every atom has electrons circling nuclei. If the nucleus of an atom was as big as our sun, the orbit of its electron would be one hundred thousand times farther out than Jupiter is.

Within the nuclei are protons and neutrons with a bond so tight that splitting it releases nuclear destruction. When we split an atom, the energy released destroys hundreds of thousands of people and buildings.

Common at every level are bonds, *a.k.a.* agreement. From atoms to planets to people, everything bears the imprint of agreement. Its Maker is a Triune Spirit, agreement in Person. His drive to agreement permeates everything He imagines and creates.

A System to Multiply Agreement

The drive to align is also true of chaos, change, and reshaping. God imagined them and made them to multiply agreement. Reality is always bubbling into new arrangements and alignments. Every change requires a new alignment of intentions, will, and power from people.

The second law of thermodynamics expresses the observable process that energy disrupts order. The theory may be accurate, but in reality, the fruits of disruption are new alignments and multiplied agreement. The "change force" is the partner of the "agreement force." God implanted them both to reproduce the bonds of a common will. That is God's purpose for the tremendous variety of families, education, wealth status, politics, geography.

Nothing produces change as effectively as the free will of people made in His image. As we reproduce, the generations multiply free will, alignments, and agreements.

The result of change is always more agreement. Examples are everywhere. Cells divide in mitosis, and expand common purpose and agreement exponentially. Societies change and allow the emergence of new societies of greater agreement. Parents have children, raise them, and enlarge the agreed family identity.

Wouldn't you expect the multiplication of agreement from Someone who described Himself this way, in 1 John 4:8?

God is love.

Blessing

The God of agreement chooses to love. His enemies live in His agreement system of reality, but they choose to steal, kill, and destroy. God exhibits His love with divine blessing. All of us are under the blessing He put on our first parents. Although their disobedience brought severe consequences on us all, God never canceled out His blessing on His image-creature.

Then God blessed them. (Genesis 1:28)

God put the original blessing on the first man and woman. It's true that He reserved specific blessings for those who follow Christ Jesus and mature as spirits. These differ from God's general blessing on our race.

Every human being ever to live is under that blessing. Alongside all the wars, sorrows, and depravities of mankind, God's blessing on our race runs without impairment.

Entertainment fiction exhibits this as well. How many apocalyptic dramas depict the final exhaustion of God's favor on our race? None. We keep coming back. No other species keeps coming back.

With the traditional doxology we sing, "Praise God from whom all blessings flow." The testimony of the ages is that His blessing is a flow. He is not stingy or miserly with His blessing.

Human life can be tragic, but the origin is never His blessing. Our own divergence from agreement with our Creator undergirds every human sorrow and frustration. But thankfully, the Almighty God uses even the raw material of depravity that we supply Him. Even our sin feeds the fire of His heart to bless humankind.

Enemy Agreement

God even built agreement into His enemies. Hebrews 1:3 says that Jesus holds all things together by His word of power. "All things" includes the devil and his minions. They only exist at His will.

Hatred for God does not create an absence of agreement. To oppose

God is to hate freedom. Enmity with God induces slavishness and stifles the multiplication of agreements.

Natural people cannot see God's Spirit enemies by natural means, but we know they are there from the symptoms of their agreement-killing hatred. One symptom is rigidity. Darkness always imposes rigid order. As much as they hate God, its spirit inhabitants cannot remove His imprint of free alignment. The result is legalistic agreement.

A second symptom of darkness is their active opposition to free will. That is the only path of rebellion available to the fallen spirits of darkness. Detesting the constant rearranging produced by our free choices, the evil spirits surrendered their own freedom. From their fall long before the creation of man, these enemies are in slavery—their power of choice shriveled.

These evil spirits form the kingdom of darkness. They never want new arrangements. Rigidly hierarchical, prohibiting fruitfulness, the permanent condition of darkness is unrelenting imprisonment.

Darkness seduces its people-victims with illusory freedom from restraint. The inescapability of the imprisoning order is only reinforced. They hate beneficial change in situations, people, and groups. By resisting God's force of chaotic free will, they express their enemy status.

"WAR?" WHAT HAPPENED TO AGREEMENT?

The head cherubim envied God's position. We now know him as satan. His original name was Lucifer. The following books of the *Unseen* series expand this summary in more detail, with biblical references. The series includes a previous work, *The Rise and Fall of the Kingdom of Darkness*. We cover the full history of Lucifer in Book 3 of the series, *Nobody Sees This Creation: The Origin of the Devil and His Replacements*.

The Bible's few glimpses into that time can be summarized as follows.

A Brief History of Darkness

Lucifer secured the loyalty of a third of the angels. Together they attempted to unseat God and replace Him—a doomed effort resulting in their expulsion from God's presence.

God neither killed satan and his allied rebels, nor did He imprison them. They all kept their original spirit natures, and they continue to be active in the unseen world. God Himself remains the source of their existence.

The Bible reveals four forms of their punishment. First, God expelled them from His presence. He also transformed their physical nature to be on fire, without escape. He then exiled them to a restrictive place—to them, a prison. Whatever freedom the rebellious angels and cherub once had in God's presence, the opponents' exile has restricted.

The place of their exile is Earth.

It was after God exiled the rebels here that He created our race. He instructed us to dominate Earth—the one place His spirit enemies had any freedom. Although we fell also, the gospel about Jesus restores us to even greater intimacy with God. The status that the rebels had lost, God gives to mortal men.

Their fourth punishment: the humiliation of being conquered and replaced by mortal human beings. Thus, His enemies became the enemies of mankind.

Such an understanding of the hidden backing of the visible tapestry equips us to cooperate with the holy inhabitants. Together, we advance God's kingdom with all its joys.

Spirit Kingdoms at War

There are two kingdoms now. The word *kingdom* is a contraction of the long-ago phrase, "king's dominion." By definition, the king's word dominates his kingdom, and his subjects obey him.

The kingdom of darkness comprises the enemies of God, who follow Lucifer. The kingdom of God are the people and angels who follow Jesus Christ. Knowingly or unknowingly, every person chooses one of those two kingdoms.

God is King of the one, and satan is king of the other. In the Bible, God revealed satan is the ruler of this world. The society of mankind at large has chosen the kingdom of darkness.

The warfare of the two kingdoms is constant. This warfare is, in fact, permitted by God for the present. He uses the kingdom of darkness to test and confirm us as spirits who love Him only. Try as darkness might to upend God's plans for mortal beings, they always end up serving His purpose. He repeatedly tricks the kingdom of darkness with feints and ambushes.

A time is coming when He will end it. His enemies, both spirits and people, will be isolated forever into the order they so prize. Thus desolate of the God who is Love, they will never escape the eternal fire of His justifiable wrath.

Opposition to the kingdom of God identifies the entire kingdom of darkness. Slavishly obsessed, there is nothing constructive in the kingdom of darkness. Defense is their fundamental posture. They fixate their attention on hating God, everyone He loves, and all He does.

In contrast, productive goodness characterizes God's kingdom. Our fixation is on loving our King, agreeing with Him, and taking part in His work as He asks. The entire work is characterized on one hand by His love to bless mankind. On the other hand, we also express His nature of holiness to judge. We only give attention to the kingdom of darkness as part of that work.

God is driving darkness out before us. We play one role: His partners. Matthew 16:18 and Revelation 19:11–16 reveal the outcome of our partnership. Under the leadership of the resurrected Jesus Christ, we, His Church, are herding the rebel spirits into the fire of everlasting judgment.

> I will build My church, and the gates of Hades shall not prevail against it.

> Now I saw heaven opened, and behold, a white horse. And He who sat on him was called Faithful and True, and in righteousness He judges and makes war. His eyes were like a flame of fire, and on His head were many crowns. He had a name written that no one knew except Himself. He was clothed with a robe dipped in blood, and His name is called The Word of God. And the armies in heaven, clothed in fine linen, white and clean, followed Him on white horses. Now out of His mouth goes a sharp sword, that with it He should strike the nations. And He Himself will rule them with a rod of iron. He Himself treads the winepress of the fierceness and wrath of Almighty God. And He has on His robe and on His thigh a name written:
> KING OF KINGS AND LORD OF LORDS.

THREATS IN THE UNSEEN

The unseen world is very active. The popular desire of our day wants peace and love, tolerance and compassion. In reality, the unseen is a world constantly at war. The invisible is also full of threats.

The Threat of the Devil

People fear demons and the devil. The lurking presence of unseen evil beings is creepy. Their efforts to trouble people have led to legends and myths that terrify us. People have techniques to control the influence of these invisible enemies.

Each technique is an agreement with satan and the kingdom of darkness.

The fiction of the ages warns: do not make deals with the devil. He always includes fine print. Yet people unwittingly bargain with the devil anyway—in exchange for some safety from unseen terrors. Demons oppress people and torment them. Left to ourselves, we have no recourse. We are poor in spirit and cannot compete with ancient, eternal spirits who hate us.

The Threat of Jesus

Jesus posed a threat to the enemies of God. They had orchestrated the death of the human spirit in Eden. This evil kingdom knew that Jesus would awaken human spirits and foil their plan. They were right. Once human spirits in God's full image were reborn, God's enemies felt their defeat might be certain. They were right. The multiplication of living spirits adopted by God as their Father, filled with His Spirit—a mortal threat to the spirits of darkness.

Since our first parents died spiritually, the enemies of God had been the only living spirits on Earth. In Jesus, darkness only saw the threat of competing spirits. God's mandate at our creation, "Be fruitful and multiply," with the Son of God now on Earth to give people birth as spirits, would mean many human spirits in agreement with God, a new competition for the spirits of darkness.

A new army of people reborn as spirits would contest the enemies of God. Darkness knew we would attack the kingdom of darkness. Hell would always be in a defensive posture, always withdrawing its gates before our advance—and they knew it.

More spirits filled with God would challenge and end the dominion of Earth by darkness.

That is why the kingdom of darkness orchestrated the crucifixion of Jesus. Jesus would provide salvation for you by dying as your substitute, but God's enemies did not know it. In Paul's first letter to the Corinthian church, chapter 2:8, God specifically reveals His enemies' ignorance of the rationale for Jesus' death. God ambushed them, luring them to do what He wanted.

> "None of the rulers of this age [satan and his cohorts] knew; for had they known, they would not have crucified the Lord of glory."

Astonishingly, satan and his invisible cohorts would have preferred for Jesus to remain physically on Earth forever, rather than send the Holy Spirit and awaken an army of living spirits.

The Threat of the Church

Jesus gave a name to this new army of living spirits agreeing with God: "My Church," possessive. When Jesus had only twelve disciples, He told them that this group of living spirits would contest the very gates of hell. You can find the context for these statements in Matthew 16:18 and John 14:30, 12:31, and 16:8–11.

The gates of hell shall not prevail against it [the Church]. (KJV)

For the ruler of this world [satan] is coming, and he has nothing in Me.

Now is the judgment of this world; now the ruler of this world will be cast out.

And when He [the Holy Spirit of God] has come, He will convict the world of sin, and of righteousness, and of judgment.... of judgment, because the ruler of this world is judged.

No wonder the unseen enemies felt the necessity to kill Him before He created more spirits like Him—people born of the Spirit, full of rivers of living water, multiplying life in abundance. When people listened to Him, His very words were spirit and life. John's gospel describes these qualities in chapters 3:6–8, 7:38–39, 10:10, and 6:63.

The Threat of You and Us

When people are reborn as spirits, then we become capable for a successful rebuttal of our enemies' destructive efforts. One major reason the demons infested and tormented people so thoroughly during Jesus' three years' ministry on Earth is this: they saw in Him a living human spirit who would awaken other human spirits. They were not used to competition in the spirit world.

What a threat Jesus must have represented to the kingdom of darkness! For all human history, they held virtually uncontested sway for centuries as the only kingdom of spirits on Earth.

When God gives you spirit birth, because you believe and follow Jesus, you and God are in agreement. Your agreements were once with darkness, but now your agreements with God Himself are multiplying and displacing your former ones.

Jesus died as the substitute who traded places with you. He took your place, and you get His place: a spirit now alive, in agreement with God, recipient of His blessing and favor, adopted as son to a heavenly Father.

Granted, you are poor in spirit. The more you know God, the more evident your poverty is. Strangely to us, that is exactly how He likes it. God, who is Spirit and love, likes to bless out of love. We try to manipulate, cajole, and obligate Him to bless—He does not like it. By our pre-spirit nature, we try to earn and deserve; we bargain and jockey for the position of being owed. But God resists all IOU systems of trading and bargaining—a key subject in future books of the *Unseen* series.

You, Christian, are a spirit. Your spirit was born through faith in Jesus and agreement with Him. You are now a threat to the enemies of God—the kingdom of darkness.

God's enemies can only hope that Christians continue to avoid the Bible truths about our elevated status and authority in the unseen world. In Book Seven of the *Unseen* series, *Nobody Sees This Church: Resisting Darkness*, we will see eleven separate techniques used to disarm us as a threat.

Against us, evil spirits are now the ones with no recourse.

BUT GOD

The ferocity of the evil unseen to tempt Jesus, distract Him, and kill Him came from their fear of competition—living spirits agreeing with God, in a kingdom headed by Jesus Himself.

God's Trick on His Unseen Enemies

Satan's kingdom of darkness would never conceive of a plan to sacrifice themselves for anyone else. The logic of God was "deeper magic" than they knew. Jesus was our substitutionary atoner on His cross. Such action was foreign to their thinking.

To the unholy unseen, Jesus' primary threat was more living spirits like Himself. And they were right. By their reckoning, Jesus would dispense spirit birth to anyone who believed in Him. That is what happened. John 1:12–13 tells about its distinctiveness:

But as many as received Him, to them He gave the right to become children of God, to those who believe in His name.... born of God.

Jesus would restore Edenic multiplication of humans alive in spirit—but darkness did not know how. They simply knew they had to kill Him before He could. Nip it in the bud, before He could establish a kingdom. Actually dying to start His kingdom was an unfathomable concept.

Multitudes followed Jesus. Everyone—from darkness, to His disciples, to the religious leaders, to the Romans—identified Jesus' popularity as a threat. Yet Jesus resisted being crowned a king by the crowds in John's sixth chapter. He knew that to replicate Himself in you and me, He had to die as our substitute.

That's why the cup could not pass from Him in Gethsemane. Jesus' petition was not granted. He braved the torment and ended His monumental resolve with three simple words: *"It is finished."* The job was done.

If darkness had failed to kill Him, then no person would become a living spirit. Only thus could people be spirit-born.

Why Was Substitutionary Atonement Necessary?

God is holy love. Perfection and agreement in a Person, He is the Creator of all. Adam was the first whom He created in His own image.

Despite this advantage and honor, our first parents turned from their Creator. The one offended, not the offender, is the measure of the severity. Rejecting their perfect, infinite Creator was an offense beyond all measure.

As if jilting God wasn't enough offense, now nearly 7 billion of us repeat it constantly. Our first parents reproduced, not living human spirits in agreement with God, but people dead in spirit, all rejecting God without even knowing it.

All that God intended for Earth and His image-creature was lost after that original sin. And right at hand were enemies to gloat about God's dishonor. The kingdom of darkness savored a triumph over the plan of God.

Thieves should repay double to make things right with their victims. God Himself made this law in Exodus 22:7. What thief should atone for God's losses? Well, *man* should, of course.

But no person can do so. Each of us repeats the misdeeds from an early age. Not one of us makes up for our own offense. Our sin, measured by the One whom we reject, is immeasurable.

Everything lost to God's plan since our first parents' sin adds up to an infinite, immeasurable, and grave cost. Nothing in our spiritually dead condition can repay God. To atone and pay for this infinite consequence requires a person of *infinite being and merit.*

Thus the Son of God incarnated as Jesus—fully man because only man *should* pay, and fully God because only God *could* pay. As real as Jesus was, He never sinned. Even Jesus' enemies could not accuse Him of a sin. He was an acceptable sacrifice, both by His nature as God, and His sinless identification with mankind—the Son of Man.

God accepted His death as the full atonement for my sin, your sin, and the sin of every person who would turn to God at His call. I didn't die for my sin—a substitute named Jesus did. Therefore, only following Him in faith can bring about our rebirth as living spirits.

God forces no one to accept His substitutionary atonement. He made us in His image with the power of choice, therefore, God honors the choices we make. People are dead already in spirit and can choose to reject rebirth as living spirits. To do so, one need only disdain to believe and follow Jesus Christ.

The Scale of God

Our existence as spirits offends the kingdom of darkness.

After all, satan and his follower-angels had fought, and lost, a previous war. Their opponent then was a spirit army composed of angels, described sparingly in Revelation 12. Instead of waging His war against darkness with angels, God introduced a lesser race of beings as His next champion against darkness. Combat with an army of living human spirits—the same humans whom darkness has tricked for centuries—might be survivable for darkness.

The irksome thing for the kingdom of darkness is God's scale. How did God decide who should reign in His kingdom with Him? Easy—He picked the least qualified, most offensive race He had made. Here was the cherub created in perfection, and one little sin got him thrown out. Now here is humankind—a race that sinned at the forbidden tree even before they ate from the tree of life—and God chooses them?!

Perhaps this is why satan detests God. Jesus' mother Mary described God's habit this way, in the first chapter of Luke's gospel (third book in the New Testament), verses 52–53.

> He has brought down rulers from their thrones but has lifted up the humble. He has filled the hungry with good things but has sent the rich away empty. (NIV)

Chapter One: The Backing

Humankind was the least of all the races God made, having mortal bodies that needed the tree of life. Even worse, people were also the most costly to God. God planned an entire race in His image, with whom to enjoy intimate fellowship. When our first parents sinned, all their descendants were born alienated from Him.

The ultimate cost to God was His journey from heaven. The Second Person of the Trinity incarnated as a natural human with a living spirit, with one primary purpose: to qualify and to be killed as the substitute for God's wrath against our sin.

Why would God put Himself at the mercy of such a weak, habitual offender as mankind? Because God is love. By loving the least, He reveals His nature as love. It is His nature to bless out of love.

To investigate the origin of Israel and darkness' part in their exile is the purpose of the fifth book of the *Unseen* series, *Nobody Sees This Israel: God's Vanguard Against Darkness*. After Babel's division of humanity, the kingdom of darkness claimed nations to rule with their unseen principalities. God chose one also—the family line through Abraham, Isaac, and Jacob.

How He picked them is revealed in Deuteronomy 7:7–8a.

> The LORD did not set His love on you nor choose you because you were more in number than any other people, for you were the least of all peoples; but because the LORD loves you.

For His own love's sake, God loved Israel. Likewise, He chose you and me for His own love's satisfaction. God is giving the highest status in the unseen to reborn human spirits, to show His love. The loss caused when Adam and Eve forsook their living spirits, His love wanted back. He wanted you and me to have spirits, so we could be seated with Him.

> God ... raised us up together, and made us sit together in the heavenly places in Christ Jesus, that in the ages to come He might show the exceeding riches of His grace in His kindness toward us in Christ Jesus. (Ephesians 2:6–7)

The less deserving the love, the greater love it is. The love nature of God is thus revealed.

Reflection and discussion questions for this chapter are in the back of the book

---

CHAPTER TWO

Getting to Know Your Spirit

HELLO THERE

So you believed Jesus! God has accepted Jesus' sacrifice as the full atonement price for your sins and your poverty of spirit. His Holy Spirit has come into you and unleashed His cleansing force for sin and waywardness within you. You have verbalized resolutely to others: "I am following Jesus."

You have just been born as a living spirit. What is it like to be a spirit?

Time to Learn Spirit

What is spirit? Jesus made emphatic statements about it, so we must explore this so we can agree with Him. What was His understanding? The Old Testament was the only Bible compiled in His day—where did He find spirit there? Listen to His statements below. Imagine yourself a first century person hearing Him.

> Most assuredly, I say to you, unless one is born again, he cannot see the kingdom of God. (John 3:3)

> Most assuredly, I say to you, unless one is born of water and the Spirit, he cannot enter the kingdom of God. (3:5)

> That which is born of the flesh is flesh, and that which is born of the Spirit is spirit. (3:6)

He who comes from above is above all; he who is of the earth is earthly and speaks of the earth. He who comes from heaven is above all. (3:31)

He who has received His testimony has certified that God is true. (3:33)

The hour is coming, and now is, when the true worshipers will worship the Father in spirit and truth; for the Father is seeking such to worship Him. (4:23)

God is Spirit, and those who worship Him must worship in spirit and truth. (4:24)

He who believes in Me, as the Scripture has said, out of his heart will flow rivers of living water. (7:38)

Is the word "spirit" only a synonym for being saved, or a metaphor for believing in Him? Without excluding that meaning, can we identify more? Did He mean more than simply being saved?

I believe Jesus did—as this book will amply show. His *"most assuredly"* is very emphatic. He expected we would live as spirits after salvation. But how? What does it mean? How did He demonstrate it?

These questions are especially important in our time. We live in times that have a prominent place in God's overall schedule. And that's why you bought this book: to learn about your spirit, and to help others likewise. The line between the seen and the unseen is less distinct now.

An Order of Activation

For God, a Spirit who is I AM THAT I AM, all characteristics exist simultaneously, with no beginning.

The Bible described three young men as growing strong in spirit. Samuel, John the Baptist, and Jesus each impressed those around them. Some evidence of spirit was compelling enough that their lasting reputation in their childhood was strong in spirit.

Scripture does not explain what that evidence was. It does not give a sequence of development for our spirit's characteristics. However, there is a parable from common human experience: growing into adulthood.

The infant has only *perception* to begin with. No other self-knowledge exists. The first thing perceived is discomfort, both bodily and emotionally. Crying after birth is its *expression*. The next layer of recognition is *community*: "I am not alone. Others respond to my expression." This tacitly affirms both the perception and the expression of the baby.

Soon a human child becomes self-aware—*identity*. The youngster discovers mirrors and learns that he (or she) exists separately from others, as a unique *presence*. With only a few years of growth, its own unique *attributes* fuel the child's preferences and responses. In teenage years, *identity* formulation percolates within. *Community* becomes a critical element of that identity. Next a person understands having a *will and power of choice*. Finally we grow the ability to *commit* to our principles and to others: marriage, work, sport, and church.

Deeper into the Bible

God has revealed everything needed for truth in the Bible. The Word of God tells all we need about being saved spirits. But very little is in outline form. Most of the Bible's revelation is between the lines. Book Two of the *Unseen* series is *Nobody Sees This Unseen Realm: How to Unlock Bible Mysteries*. There, you'll find advanced techniques to unlock the unseen world in the Bible.

We begin the nine-book series with this list of characteristics of a spirit. The following applies to any spirit: evil or holy, angelic, or human. It may not be accurate or exhaustive. As you mature, you will sharpen your understanding of God's Word. If you go further in the *Unseen* series, the foundation you gain will propel you higher up and further in.

I expect you to exceed the biblical discoveries in the *Unseen* series. You are welcome to render it outdated. We want everything that God gave us in His Word—no holds barred.

The Characteristics of Spirit

Identity—spirit has its own identity. My spirit's identity is not dependent on any external reference. I am not a spirit because some person or institution says I am. I am a spirit—period. Whether anyone else knows it, or agrees, is irrelevant.

Will—spirit can determine, prefer, desire, think, and act. Spirit exercises its will of its own volition. A spirit needs no external power in order to choose. Spirits have the power of choice. Wherever the power to choose is present, there is a will to exercise. Note: choices may be available, yet the power to choose one over the other may be missing.

Attributes—a spirit has personhood. Your spirit has unique expressions, distinct from other spirits. Spirits don't combine, merge, or meld. Each of our spirits is an individual person whom God created when He saved us. Each spirit will be an individual, distinct person for eternity.

Presence—a spirit is a definite being. It is not an indefinite force. It can be present with other spirits.

Expression—a spirit can communicate. Its expression influences other spirits, unsaved people, and Creation itself. The Bible shows us that spirits communicate with words, pictures, and sensations.

Perception—a spirit can perceive other created beings. As a result, spirits can communicate with, and can receive from, other spirits.

Community—spirits prefer relationship. They relate to one another both in pairs and in groups.

Commitment—spirits commit themselves. They commit to their own identity and to other spirits. Without a commitment, a spirit does not thrive. A spirit's will and commitment dance together. A spirit cannot be lackadaisical, but instead exercises its will to commit and to uphold commitment.

Spirit and Self-Recognition

The veiled truths of Scripture about our spirits are not low-hanging fruit. At some point a born-again person would properly recognize, "Hey—I'm a spirit!" There is a dawning upon realizing: "I am not only *filled with* the Holy Spirit—I *am* a spirit as well."

Some never awaken to their spirit identity. A variety of factors leave their spirits inactive or impotent. One factor is the current maturity state of the Church—which is advancing, thankfully.

Our own spiritual maturing requires us to develop in each of these spirit characteristics. But what happens when we do? What is our life like as we grow in spirit?

SPIRIT IDENTITY

The Identity of God

When Jesus said God is spirit, He was not introducing anything new. God identified Himself as a spirit fourteen hundred years earlier, to Moses at the burning bush. God had just given Moses a task far beyond his capability: liberate the enslaved Hebrews from the Egyptian Pharaoh.

Moses asked what name he should use for God, who replied in Exodus 3:14,

I AM WHO I AM.

Those five uppercase English words translate one four-consonant word of the Hebrew language in which Moses wrote Exodus. Those four consonants are YHWH. Why did God identify Himself to Moses with them?

God used His identity as a Spirit to serve as His name. YHWH means that He depends on no other spirit for His existence. He uses that name to say His identity is unaffected by time or by circumstance. YHWH also separates Him; no creature can assess or package His identity.

This is the nature of spirit identity. Our usual forms of personal identity are much different: our actions, appearance, job, family, and possessions. Those all vary with time and circumstance—but not our spirit.

He imparts this spirit identity to everyone who follows Jesus Christ. Jesus described your spirit birth in the fourth New Testament book, John's gospel chapter 3:6–8.

> That which is born of the flesh is flesh, and that which is born of the Spirit is spirit. Do not marvel that I said to you, 'You must be born again.' The wind blows where it wishes, and you hear the sound of it, but cannot tell where it comes from and where it goes. So is everyone who is born of the Spirit.

Spirit, Soul, Body

Christians can live as if the awakening of our spirit added to what we already were before our salvation. We wrongly think that our spirit's birth merely augmented our fleshly capacities.

This is not accurate. Jesus purposely chose the words "born again," to signify an entirely new level of existence for people.

All our lives before salvation, we had only our soul and body, bequeathed to us by our first parents whose sin killed their spirits and ours. Even after being saved, we can continue to identify ourselves by that limited existence.

It's easy to accept that limit. Soul and body are sufficient for this seen world. With our soul, we have emotions, mind, and will. With our body, we have a means of growth and of participation, controlled by our soul. This combo of soul and body bereft of a living spirit, the Bible calls *the flesh*.

The birth of your living spirit is no mere addition to your flesh. It is the birth of a competing identity that must either rule your flesh or be ruled by it.

> Do not offer any part of yourself to sin as an instrument of wickedness, but rather offer yourselves to God as those who have been brought from death to life; and offer every part of yourself to him as an instrument of righteousness. (Romans 6:13 NIV)

WHO SAYS?

Who am I? Who gets to decide? Who governs my identity? These questions are not often asked because the assumed answer throughout mankind is, "I do."

> All we like sheep have gone astray; We have turned, every one, to his own way. (Isaiah 53:6)

Spirit and Personality

We think of our personality possessively. It is ours, built into our very person. Whether we consider our intelligence, talents, or anything unique to us, "it's mine."

This self-possessed identity is the very mistake Lucifer made. Isaiah 14, Ezekiel 28, and Revelation 12 describe it. Lucifer walked on the fiery stones which surrounded the throne of God, guarding it before anything else was made. His prominence was second only to the Triune God Himself. He was the most exalted of God's creatures.

But Lucifer wrongly thought that his qualities were his possession. They were his to keep, dependent on no one else. If he could replace God, Lucifer would still be himself.

Jealous of God, proud of himself, Lucifer sought to replace God. He failed. God took Lucifer's perfect qualities and stripped him. The fiery stones he once walked upon, God put within him, an inescapable nature of constant inner burning. Lucifer has all that fire in his person. He has become satan.

God has the power to make us whom He decides. We too have such a power of choice: who am I?

Human personality results from several influences. The first is our genetic nature; the second our upbringing and life experiences, including demonic oppression; and third is our choice with that raw material.

Our genetic nature is born with Adam's seed of death (Romans 5). Alive only as soul and body, we are born dead in spirit.

Our upbringing and experiences bear the weight of innumerable other people with their choices, both good and sinful.

These two together set us up with situations and relationships, the raw material for our individual choices. Genetics and environment draw the boundary lines of our playing field. Our choices within those boundaries are the third builder of personality.

Whether that field of play is well drawn or poorly, based on truth or on lies, built by love or by lovelessness, we each have choices available—toward God or away. Isaiah 53:6 is plain about those choices: *"All we like sheep have gone astray."*

These three influences set my personality. Is it rigidly cemented? Our world and culture say yes. Psychology and academic sciences say yes.

Suddenly, I'm born as a spirit, and I'm filled with God's Holy Spirit. In an instant, God Himself lives in me and is my constant Father. There is a new, dominating influence to reform me. Now who gets to say what my personality is? My Father and I, in agreement—we determine it.

Is it too late? After all, my personality is partially the result of past sin and sinful choices, both knowing and unknowing. Will my personality always be the fruit of a poison tree? No, because my personality can improve. It happens when I agree with who God says I am. God made everything by speaking it. He also speaks who I am. My unique personal nature is His creation.

When I become a living spirit, for the first time I can learn what He says I am. I now can be liberated from the curse of my former choices. I can receive healing from generational curses. My soul and body can be delivered from demonic oppression.

Whatever personality originated with those influences, my Creator can improve with my agreement. The King of who I am decrees anew who I am.

Lord God, I repent of the decisions and choices that defined my personality by disobedience, independence, and self-provision. Please cleanse me of those, and make me who You decree me to be.

Spirit and Relationship

Spirit is for relationship. A solitary spirit is not the natural condition of a spirit. Community and commitment are characteristics of spirit, and they require relationship. So central is relationship to a spirit, we could say spirit is relationship. Thus, God Himself is a Trinity, three Spirits in one, and hell is the isolation of the spirits that rebelled against Him.

This does not mean spirit depends on relationship. The identity of a mature spirit is secure, fully formed, and without need of feedback. The spirit of the living Christian seeks relationship. The mature spirit delights in agreement, which presumes relationship. Agreement requires at least two.

Spirit and Encounter

Two Christians in relationship in the kingdom of light are two living spirits in the unseen. There, each is confident and secure about their own identity. When two or more spirits encounter one another, there is interaction as confident and self-accepting spirits. The love of God flows from each one, and each is satisfied.

Agreement Breakers

The love that flourishes when two born-again Christians relate is simple to understand. Why isn't it our constant situation? Because there are forces that break agreement.

One tactic is to handicap you. These influences may handicap your identity so you can't be an effective agree-er. For example, evil spirits that promote insecurity can oppress a Christian's life. When that Christian relates to other living spirits, he or she can't be independent. Insecurity uses others to fill a gap. There are innumerable such examples.

Your spirit is born by the Holy Spirit and fully alive. All capabilities available to any spirit are available to you immediately. Yet maturing to your full security and function as a spirit is a process. Until it is complete, the kingdom of darkness and its allies use your weaknesses against you. They want to impair your ability to function in agreement with other Christians.

The kingdom of darkness also seeks to distort and destroy existing agreements. Many will be clear in Book Seven of the *Unseen* series, *Nobody Sees This Church: Resisting Darkness*.

Examples of agreement breakers include personal immaturity, lack of understanding, measurements, and pressures to be right. The Christians coming together can have a polluted, twisted encounter, subject to deception. Even though they are living spirits, they have not completed maturing.

A maturing spirit can eventually relate to anyone with contentment.

The Christian who has sought maturity as a living spirit can be merciful and loving to any person. Such a Christian can discern and respect the identity of other Christians.

The letters of the New Testament, by Paul, Peter, John, James, and Jude, were written to churches having problems with such divisive forces. In each case, they admonished the recipients to love one another, to maintain fellowship (*a.k.a.* agreement), and to expose the kingdom of darkness.

One example is Apostle Paul's injunction to the church in Ephesus, an ancient metropolis on the western shore of modern-day Turkey—Ephesians 5:8–14.

> For you were once darkness, but now you are light in the Lord. Walk as children of light (for the fruit of the Spirit is in all goodness, righteousness, and truth), finding out what is acceptable to the Lord. And have no fellowship with the unfruitful works of darkness, but rather expose them. For it is shameful even to speak of those things which are done by them in secret. But all things that are exposed are made manifest by the light, for whatever makes manifest is light. Therefore He says:
>
> "Awake, you who sleep, Arise from the dead, And Christ will give you light."

In a Triune Image

I walked this morning and prayed. You initiated a conversation about a prayer promise You made to me a year ago. I continued on the general theme of what I want.

Suddenly I realized how selfish—all about what I want. I stopped and arrested my thoughts. I asked You, "What do You want?"

The answer was forthcoming: *I want the creature made in My image to reflect my Triune nature.*

Those words packaged an entire world of meaning. Those words contained all the ideals for human love, community, and shared endeavors. But all at once, the depravity, the shortfall, the hatred, the self-centeredness shoved those ideals out. So many qualities of fallen mankind make the ideal seem so unreachable and impossible.

You showed me Your desire for us to reflect Your Triune nature:

- to father, nurture and meet others' needs, as God the Father does:
- to enter others' lives with service and sacrifice, as the God the Son does; and

- to be partners and companions with others, and intimate with some, like God the Spirit.
- I agree with You, Lord God. May I represent Your Triune nature with all my contacts today.

> that they all may be one, as You, Father, are in Me, and I in You; that they also may be one in Us… that they may be one just as We are one: I in them, and You in Me; that they may be made perfect in one. (John 17:21–23)

THE GRID

Each moment of life, we have to interpret our existence—both ourselves and the environment we are in. Our interpretation always has a foundational belief, like a grid or a template. We have common sayings to capture this: to see the world through rose-colored glasses, the glass is half-empty or half-full, and see eye-to-eye, for three examples.

Our Foundation

Jesus expects His followers to use His foundational belief: the Word of God. We are to interpret the world on that foundation.

> Therefore, whoever hears these sayings of Mine, and does them, I will liken him to a wise man who built his house on the rock: and the rain descended, the floods came, and the winds blew and beat on that house; and it did not fall, for it was founded on the rock.
>
> But everyone who hears these sayings of Mine, and does not do them, will be like a foolish man who built his house on the sand: and the rain descended, the floods came, and the winds blew and beat on that house; and it fell. And great was its fall. (Matthew 7:24–27)

All people are born spiritually dead. As young children, our grid of interpretation was our family and parents. As teenagers, the grid was school and peers' opinions. As adults, our mates and our work influence became our grid. Common to all the spiritually dead, our foundation was self-preservation in a threatening world. We have interpreted everything on this foundation: *what threatens me, and how can I protect myself?*

To a spiritually dead person, God is the greatest threat. The enduring image of the fig leaf depicts this succinctly. *"I heard You, and I was afraid because I was naked, so I hid"* (Genesis 3:10 NIV). Feeling nakedness means shame, and helpless vulnerability prompts fear. To protect ourselves, we control. This shame/fear/control pattern is in every person.

Enter Jesus. Once we are reborn as living spirits, He offers us a new grid, a new interpretive foundation. He is blunt and merciless to our old foundation of self-preservation and fear of threats. In Matthew 6:31–32 and 16:24–25 are two examples.

> Therefore, do not worry, saying, "What shall we eat?" or "What shall we drink?" or "What shall we wear?" For after all these things the Gentiles seek. For your heavenly Father knows you need all these things.
>
> If anyone desires to come after Me, let him deny himself, and take up his cross, and follow Me. For whoever desires to save his life will lose it, but whoever loses his life for My sake will find it.

He described following Him as self-denial. He likened being a Christian to carrying an electric chair on our back—today's cross. Jesus forcefully challenges our old template for interpreting everything by self-preservation; to follow Him is death and self-denial.

Even when we become Christians, follow Jesus, and are reborn with living spirits, our old grid of identifying threats persists. To replace it with His foundational belief, we undergo the process called discipleship. Disciples learn from their teacher. Jesus is our Teacher and we are His disciples.

A New Grid of Father-Love

Jesus gives us birth as living spirits. That's our new foundation for interpreting our existence. We now have a love relationship with God the Father. This is the same way Jesus interpreted everything. Consider the following statements His apostles recorded in their gospels, because they understood: the template to interpret our existence is the Father's love for them, for me, and for you.

> Look at the birds of the air, for they neither sow nor reap nor gather into barns; yet your heavenly Father feeds them. Are you not of more value than they?... Now if God so clothes the grass of the field, which today is, and tomorrow is thrown into the oven, will He not much more clothe you, O you of little faith? (Matthew 6:26, 30)

At that time Jesus answered and said, "I thank You, Father, Lord of heaven and earth, that You have hidden these things from the wise and prudent and have revealed them to babes... All things have been delivered to Me by My Father, and no one knows the Son except the Father. Nor does anyone know the Father except the Son, and the one to whom the Son wills to reveal Him. (Matthew 11:25, 27)

Do not fear, little flock, for it is your Father's good pleasure to give you the kingdom. (Luke 12:32)

If anyone loves Me, he will keep My word; and My Father will love him, and We will come to him and make Our home with him. (John 14:23)

In that day you will ask in My name, and I do not say to you that I shall pray the Father for you; for the Father Himself loves you, because you have loved Me, and have believed that I came forth from God. (John 16:26–27)

He who did not spare His own Son, but delivered Him up for us all, how shall He not with Him also freely give us all things?... For I am persuaded that neither death nor life, nor angels nor principalities nor powers, nor things present nor things to come, nor height nor depth, nor any other created thing, shall be able to separate us from the love of God which is in Christ Jesus our Lord. (Romans 8:32, 38–39)

Faith: the Foundation of Love

This grid for understanding everything—yourself, the world around you and God—requires faith.

Our foundation of self-preservation in a threatening world is long-practiced. Everything in our world supports that interpretation. All that our mind, body, and soul experience reinforce the urge to protect ourselves against threats.

Only faith that an unseen Father loves us can overpower this urge. Only faith in Jesus' death in one corner of the world two thousand years ago can overpower the self-preservation interpretation. Our grid of faith is based on the love shown then, and on the love shown us daily by our Father. From Him, all blessings flow.

Our new interpretation is by faith: we are spirits made alive. An unseen Holy Spirit fills us. We are participants with authority in an unseen world. Our identity is unthreatened. Whether seen or unseen, the threats to mind, body, and soul are no threat to our spirits.

I am safe with my Father. I am safe with my Father. I am safe with my Father.

We are safe with the Father of our spirits.

Identifying the Source

When are we acting out of spirit, and when out of our flesh, our natural self? How can we know?

One clear mark of self's ascendancy is trust in our competencies. We overestimate what we can do, see, feel, think, and speak. Simultaneously, we underestimate our inability to control. Inversely, accepting our inadequacy is the mark that our living spirit is superior to our flesh. In my book *Inadequacy*, we thoroughly explore it, our new best friend.

The Friction Brings the Blessing

Perceiving what could be, and what actually is, produces friction. There are moments when our confidence in natural ability is disarmed, when our reliance upon the world's methods is exposed for its vanity. Our old grid of assessing threats is activated despite our efforts to control ourselves and our environment.

We see our poverty of spirit.

In His first recorded teaching, Matthew 5:3, Jesus said that is the key to God's blessing.

Blessed are the poor in spirit, for theirs is the kingdom of heaven.

Why is this blessed?! Because our spirit is activated by faith. Faith can flourish when we admit our poverty of spirit. When we think we are rich in spirit, faith is not needed. An overestimate of our adequacy hamstrings our faith. Overconfidence in the flesh stifles our faith.

Spirit and Harm

Where is my core identity? If it is in my flesh, that is my natural self, where many harms are available. Identifying threats becomes very challenging, constant, and complex.

When one of those harms occurs, it can consume the attention of my flesh. Body and soul commandeer our energies to resolve that harm and to satisfy our desire for safety. The harm and its wound spotlights our insecurity.

Our first parents felt this. They sinned, and instantly the spirit God had given them died. They tried to fix their sudden harm with the inadequate safety of fig leaves. Left to our natural selves, we repeat the futile pattern. We try successive fig leaves—hoping to find the safety for the naked insecurity.

This is no longer necessary for a Christian with a living spirit. If my identity is my spirit, made alive by You, there is only one harm that can befall me—Your forsaking.

You forsook someone, the One who least deserved it. *"My God, My God, why have You forsaken Me?"* (Mark 15:34) Therefore, Jesus' death is a substitute for the eternal death I deserve.

Jesus, because You endured my forsaking, I never will have to. Oh, thank You! Thank You, Jesus! You traded places with me. What I deserve, You got—separation from the Father and the combined robbery of my sin. What You deserve, I get—safety, security, and intimacy with the Father. I feel so loved by You, Lord Jesus.

How much safety did You have? How much security did You have with the Father? Is that really what I get? If I didn't believe it, I would call it unbelievable—it defies the imagination.

Now, I am like You. I, like You, have a living spirit. My spirit is born into a secure identity. I do not have to live in fear. None of the natural threats, not any of them, can harm my safe identity. My security is unaffected by the presence or absence of natural safety.

My spirit is eternal, unthreatened by any natural, temporary threat. My spirit has no identity in anything of its own, but rather derives its entire identity from one unassailable Source. I have a spirit identity that is independent of all circumstances but one: You, speaking me into existence.

> Do not fear them who can kill the body but cannot kill the soul. Rather, fear Him who is able to destroy both body and soul in hell. (Matthew 10:28)

Spirit and Strength

Because the nature of my spirit is measured solely and entirely by my agreement with God, then by definition, the more receptive and attentive I am to God, the stronger my spirit.

Reflection and discussion questions for this chapter are in the back of the book

---

CHAPTER THREE
SPIRIT DEFINED

LIFE AND DEATH

Who made up the idea of spirit? Who created spirit in the first place? Where do spirits come from?

When our parents couldn't answer such childhood questions, we may have learned not to ask. But questions and curiosity are part of our heredity. Puzzles are often our best leaders. They help us sniff out answers, like a good detective.

The allure of our questions is one way our Father encourages us to be kings who search out His mysteries (Proverbs 25:2). Puzzles form a prominent technique in Book Two of the *Unseen* series, *Nobody Sees This Unseen Realm: How to Unlock Bible Mysteries*.

Spirit and Philosophy/Reason

Using reason, philosophers have tried to identify spirit, though not in biblical terms. Rene Descartes in the early 1600s assumed that an evil, all-powerful genius was trying to fool him. He solved his puzzle with the famous phrase, "I think, therefore I am."

Immanuel Kant in the late 1700s wrote about the most indivisible components of knowable things, an unwitting attempt to isolate the components of spirit.

Friedrich Nietzsche in the late 1800s reduced personhood to one essential: power—as in "might makes right."

Sigmund Freud, in the early 1900s, theorized the id, ego, and superego to identify the indivisible elements of human personality.

As these examples show, reason can only take a person so far. Spirit is rational, but it is not subject to or known by reason. Predictably, philosophers reached no consensus. Instead, by publishing unique "discoveries," they thought themselves out of relevance.

Origin of the Spirit

God is spirit. There are angelic spirits—some holy, some evil, but all angelic. They all owe their origin to Him. The Bible does not reveal how He created them. One sentence contains it, *"In the beginning, God created the heavens and the earth"* (Genesis 1:1).

Iniquity originated in those spirits before God created the human race. It was first revealed in the covering archangel, Ezekiel 28 says. His iniquity was a desire to supplant God, Isaiah 14 reveals, which also names the archangel, Lucifer. From Revelation 12, we understand that war in heaven resulted and that a third of the angelic spirits followed Lucifer into evil.

Then there is our race. Us, He made in His image—unlike the angelic spirits. He imagines you and speaks you into being. Your creation then begins with conception. Even that event culminates a long chain of events arranging for your parents, early upbringing, and ancestry.

The human baby is born a potential spirit, but dead. When are they spiritually dead? At least when they awaken to the law (Romans 7:11) with individual responsibility. By being born at all, they inherit a legacy of deadness (Romans 5:12).

When saved and filled with the Holy Spirit, a new spirit is born and activated. By definition, a person's spirit is in relationship with God when born through salvation. This is the one and only defining identity of a human spirit made alive.

> And this is eternal life, that they may know You, the only true God, and Jesus Christ whom You have sent. (John 17:3)

Everything the Christian thinks to be biblically possible and desirable has its origin in his/her identity as a living spirit reborn as a child of God.

Eternal Life

Only by faith in Jesus can a spirit be born in a mortal person. The Christian who follows Jesus has eternal life. In Scripture this is far more than eternal existence after we die. It begins immediately, precisely because our spirit springs up, alive forever.

Soul and spirit are different. All mortal people have souls, and their souls will exist eternally. Without spirits, soulish eternity alone will be terrible, with punishing consequences. The Bible reveals hell to be the eternal existence of souls who were never born as spirits by following Jesus.

> Depart from Me, you cursed, into the everlasting fire prepared for the devil and his angels.... These will go away into everlasting punishment.... (Matthew 25:41, 46)

Only people with living spirits can have the abundant life Jesus offered to all men.

> ... but the righteous into eternal life. (Matthew 25:46)

> I have come that they may have life, and that they may have it more abundantly. (John 10:10)

Dead Spirit

Deadness means the potential spirit is not born. If mortal death occurs before the spirit is born, then the potential spirit is never realized.

Something dead may decompose or be preserved; the *condition* does not define the deadness. Rather, the *rigid and set finality* is the essence of deadness, because there is *no potential* for renewal, change or growth.

Deadness includes incapacity for self-perception. Someone dead in spirit is not even aware that they could have a spirit. Being dead in spirit prevents perception of spirit. Such a one cannot perceive or even define being alive or dead.

The person with no spirit cannot worship God, know Him, or love Him. Facts and practices and traditions and even power and gifts are possible. Yet the practitioner can still be dead in spirit, not worshipping Him in spirit and truth.

By definition, a dead person does not know God and is dead in spirit. Otherwise, he or she would be alive, and have a living spirit (John 17:3).

SPIRIT, SOUL, HEART

Soul and Spirit

For my first forty years as a Christian, I thought soul and spirit were synonymous. (Never mind the fact that God actually is skillful and discriminating in His choice of words.) Thinking thus, human beings comprised soul and body, and being born again with a spirit was only an augmentation of our soul.

But this misunderstanding, that spirit is just super-soul, has severe deficiencies and empowers religion to enslave the saved. First, it leaves much Christian experience unexplained. Second, a Christian is deprived of many resources in the Spirit. Third, sanctification remains soul-based and powerless—the treadmill Paul described in Romans 7.

In contrast, the distinct existence of soul and spirit has great explanatory power for the Old versus New covenants.

In the Old Testament, a few were born as spirits, but only for a part in God's plan for us. The invitation was neither widespread nor frequent. As Apostle Peter wrote, *"To them it was revealed that, not to themselves, but to us they were ministering"* (1 Peter 1:12). Abraham, Moses, David, Elijah, and Elisha are the primary examples. The New Testament recognizes some outside Israel as born in spirit, such as Melchizedek.

Jeremiah's isolation stemmed not merely from the treatment he received, but by the fire in his bones, his spiritual birth.

> Because you speak this word, behold, I will make My words in your mouth fire. (5:14)

> I did not sit in the assembly of the mockers, nor did I rejoice; I sat alone because of Your hand, for You have filled me with indignation. (15:17)

> His Word was in my heart like a burning fire shut up in my bones; I was weary of holding it back and I could not. (20:9)

The eleven disciples received the spiritual birth described in John 1:12, which Jesus confirmed in Matthew 26:41 (*"the spirit is willing"*), and John 13 (*"made clean, but not all of you"*).

In our timeline, the disciples' filling with the Holy Spirit followed their previous spiritual birth. Spiritual birth and the filling of the Holy Spirit may occur simultaneously, such as with Cornelius in Acts 10—but that is the exception. It also may not occur at the same time. For example, the three thousand new believers on Pentecost Day didn't receive tongues of flame or speaking in tongues.

Everyone is born with a soul, but only those given the right to become children of God have a spirit. Once born in spirit, the maturing process must begin.

Spirit and Heart in the Pentateuch

Are the words *heart* and *spirit* synonymous in the Bible? Or does it reveal distinctions? A review of the Bible's first five books unveils the premises that endure throughout its pages. Those books are Genesis, Exodus, Leviticus, Numbers, and Deuteronomy. We call these five the Pentateuch (pronounced "Penta-tuke"). In the Bible these books are referred to as the Law, although they contain much prophecy and history as well.

The New King James Version has spirit in twenty-eight instances in the Pentateuch, with differing applications. The Spirit of God is indicated directly or by implication ten times. Evil unseen spirits, *a.k.a.* familiar spirits, are intended in four uses. The balance refers to the spirit of life (1), the spirits of mankind of which the Lord is God (3), or the spirit of a man (5) or a certain spirit attribute such as troubled (1) wisdom (2), jealousy (3), anguish (1), willing (1), an ancestor (1), and different spirit (1). Insiders (Jacob, Moses, Caleb, Joshua) are described as having a spirit, and two outsiders (Pharaoh, Balaam).

God's Spirit hovers over the face of the deep. He works, and He rests from His work. God's Spirit can fill a person, imparting wisdom, understanding, knowledge, and craftsmanship. The Spirit of God can be distributed from person to person (Moses onto the seventy, onto Joshua). The Spirit of God can rest on people.

In contrast to "spirit" is the Pentateuch's use of "heart," a far more frequent 104 times in the New King James Version. The physical heart is used as a reference point for attire such as the high priest's ephod. But usually the Pentateuch speaks of our heart as a synonym for soul. When the Pentateuch (and the Bible as a whole) uses "heart," it refers not merely to emotions and affections, as we might, but to our soul with its mind, body and emotions.

What activities of heart does the Pentateuch describe? How do they contrast with the spirit?

The heart is far more active and variable than the spirit, and thus the greater frequency of mention. The heart is not either/or, as the spirit of a man is; instead, imagine the heart on a scale of -100 to 100. Resolve and resolute personal passions, policies, or plans occur in the heart; the spirit in contrast is more characteristic of a man's person. The heart can be faint as well as resolute. In contrast, the spirit is more stable and unchanging. Circumstance heavily influences the heart which becomes discouraged, but the spirit influences and even makes the circumstances.

Fluidity characterizes our heart in the Pentateuch, with qualities that ebb and flow. It thinks evil, grieves, commits, imagines, and laughs. It can be depleted and refreshed. Our hearts can fail us, can yearn for another, and with surprises can stand still stunned. Our heart can be glad. God can also harden the heart. The heart can suffer at a more sorrowful level than body. Sorrow can fill our heart. Our heart can turn and change its resolve. In the heart, we can empathize and relate to the experiences of others. The heart can be willing; it can be stirred.

We can experience desire in our heart. When there is abundance, the heart can become proud and deceived. The heart can tremble and feel terror; it can melt with fear. The heart can perceive—or not. From the heart, we can follow dictates.

The Pentateuch reveals the engagement of our heart with others, and with God. The heart and spirit of a person can synchronize with one united will. The heart of one person can influence the hearts of others. People's hearts can be united. In place of love and unity, our heart can harbor hate for another. We can incline our heart to disloyalty and betrayal, and can turn away from God and family. In our heart, God can strike us with confusion, madness, and blindness.

The heart can be loyal as well. In the heart is integrity and from it we speak things by which we bind ourselves. The heart can love God. It can love Him in full, implying in part as well. The heart can seek Him fully, implying also in part. The heart reflects on God and on His authority. In it, we can store up what He says. The heart can receive wisdom from God; it can also forget beneficial experiences and lessons.

The Pentateuch reveals that through troubles, blessings, and circumstances God is testing our hearts. Tests reveal the quality of our heart—to Him, to ourselves, and to others. The heart, like the body, can be circumcised and uncircumcised. Abraham's covenant of loyalty with God required the circumcision of male infants on the eighth day; the Pentateuch applies this covenant loyalty to our hearts.

Conclusion? The Bible's first five books speak of spirit and heart as two different things. Spirit stands in contrast to heart. Heart is the image of the tapestry; spirit is the backing. Spirit is personhood itself, apart from circumstances and changes. Spirit is unseen and enduring.

THE LANGUAGE OF SPIRIT

Language, by its very definition, refers to the *perceptible* expressions of reality, but what about the *im*perceptible elements? For those, God uses the words available to us, to package His truth for our discovery.

We press new words, and new uses of old words, into our language. By maturing as living spirits, our vocabulary about spirit will sharpen as well.

Our English words often do not capture the Bible languages' words for the original discovery. That's why preachers and teachers often highlight the meaning of the original word in Greek or Hebrew.

This applies to our rediscovery of our living spirit. The word for it in the original language of the New Testament is *pneuma*.

The Greek Word *Pneuma*

In 1885, a Greek-English Lexicon of the New Testament[1] was translated from Grimm and Wilke by Joseph Henry Thayer. It devotes four pages to one word: *pneuma*. That is the Greek word used by New Testament authors and speakers when they refer to spirit. As we shall see, it had a wide range of meanings, like our words *bar* or *set*, which has 430 distinct definitions. Air, wind, breath, and spirit are four of the meanings for the Greek word *pneuma*. (Our words pneumonia and *pneuma*tic come from it, signifying air or breath.) Usually, the context tells you which meaning the author intended.

Lexicographers are those who document, categorize and define the usage of each vocabulary word in the New Testament. They identified one hundred different uses of the one word, *pneuma*. Despite so many meanings, the native Greek speakers two thousand years ago would know the meaning intended. For us, it takes effort.

To illustrate, imagine the gospel was first written in English, and frequently used *set* (430 meanings), *run* (179 meanings) or *take* (127). How would our readers know which of the many definitions we intended?

The context often determines the intended meaning. We know Jesus meant the wind when He first used *pneuma* in talking with Nicodemus, because he then used the words *blow*, and *hear the sound*.

But just two sentences before, He used *pneuma* for something other than physical wind. *You must be born of the pneuma. That which is born of the pneuma is pneuma.* How did He expect Nicodemus to know the different uses?

The primary clue when *pneuma* refers to the Spirit of God is the adjective holy, *hagia* in Greek. Other clues are the use of a definite article, "the," in Greek *to pneuma*.

Pneuma means spirit—whether good or evil, divine or human, active or passive. Hebrews 4:12 describes the Scripture itself as *"piercing to the division of soul and spirit,"* using the word *pneuma*. What distinction is that? Only in Scripture can we find truth about the spirit. The verse in Hebrews describes how the Bible penetrates and describes unseen reality—to unique and unexcelled depths.

Spirit, *pneuma*, is unseen. After the work of our excellent lexicographers, what are you left with?

Number one: to describe Himself, God chose a language with a versatile, non-precise word for spirit. Why would He do this?

The only answer is that God wants to describe something beyond the limits of human language. By using such a versatile word, *pneuma*, He is painting a picture. Like the pointillist painters of the early twentieth century, He paints individual dots with each use of *pneuma*. And to appreciate such paintings, we must stand back, contemplate the entire image, and see the whole meaning.

Number two: God chose the Greek language and its *pneuma* to paint a very specific picture: the essence of true reality. Because *pneuma* is so versatile in its meanings, the sum total of its uses describes all existence. Thus the New Testament reveals that spirit is the reality, and all else serves as the dots to express spirit.

The analytical within us might see only the dots in God's pointillist portrayal. But if we want understanding, we will step back and take in the complete image. Once you let the dots recede into background, you can interact with the entire picture that results from its technical elements.

But our discoveries of the unseen world are immature. As a result, our languages are too immature for communication about it. The foundation of all reality is spirit: *pneuma*. Each hearer and reader's maturity will determine what they receive when the Bible uses the word. Jesus expressed this succinctly in His most repeated statement:

He who has ears, let him hear.

New Words

We create new words to express new understanding. This is true in any language. The more discoveries in society, the more words arise to name them and their implications. Two examples are *reboot* and *download*. Sometimes we give new meanings to existing words such as *text* or *cell*.

With time, its newness wears off and we can take it for granted. The words used for it remain—such as our word for making a phone call, *dial*. But with their original meaning in the distant past, we give new meanings to those words—meanings loosely tethered to the original discovery.

For instance, the Catholic church once designated November 1st as an annual holiday named All Saints' Day. Honoring the saints who had died gave a holy feeling to the preceding evening, which was named Hallowed Evening. The contraction is Halloween. The holiday is no longer celebrated, but the word remained, with a completely contradictory meaning.

Every language experiences these dynamics, including the three languages used to write the Bible: Hebrew, Greek, and Aramaic.

Vocabulary for Spirit

What words can we use to talk about our spirits? The first apostles understood Christians are living spirits. This forced them to develop a specific Bible vocabulary. We will review several of the words in the *Unseen* series.

The vocabulary they used in Greek is translated into the words of other languages. Bible translation is a gigantic field of study. Thousands of people have given their lives to it and deserve honor for their efforts.

Translators face a persistent challenge: choosing the words and phrases in English to convey the meaning of the original languages. As stated above, languages and vocabularies change.

The word choice of a translator is influenced by their understanding and maturity. A translator without understanding about living spirits may select their English words with a deficiency. When the intended meaning of *pneuma* is spirit, the translator has to decide: what spirit? The Holy Spirit or a Christian's spirit? An angelic or an evil spirit?

When the word for *holy* appears with *pneuma*, it is likely about the Holy Spirit. Therefore, *pneuma* comes into English with a capital S, and we read it to mean the Third Person of the Trinity, the Holy Spirit.

Yet often the Bible authors use *pneuma* without the Greek word for *holy*. Written Greek does not use upper and lowercase letters as English does. The English translator has to make a judgment call: a capital S Spirit, or a lowercase s? Without the presence of the word *holy* in the original language, the translator's experience and assumptions come into play more heavily.

When *pneuma* refers to our living spirit, the English should read lower case s spirit. However, an immaturity of understanding about our living spirit makes English translators inclined to identify *pneuma* to mean Spirit, uppercase.

In Acts 6, the apostles call for men to help with food distribution, and require two qualities outlined in verse 3 which in Greek are πλήρεις πνεύματος καὶ σοφίας. Neither the word holy nor the definite article precede πνεύματος so the translation suggested is "full of spirit and wisdom." Yet the bulk of English translators have "Holy Spirit" there or capitalize Spirit to indicate Him. This exemplifies the blind spot a translator can have if unaware of the tapestry backing, namely that saved people are born as spirits.

When the word *pneuma* stands by itself, the biblical authors may have intended to refer to our living spirit, and to the life and the world of spirit. They would then purposely leave off the word *holy* to avoid confusing our spirit with the Holy Spirit. This is particularly true if elsewhere in the same passage by the same author, a clear reference to the Holy Spirit is made. How else would they make the distinction?

The Bible text gives clues to distinguish between spirit and Spirit. One clue is contrast. If *pneuma* means our living spirit lowercase, then we would expect a nearby contrast to the flesh. If *pneuma* by itself refers to the Holy Spirit, then we would expect a nearby contrast with unholy spirits.

Another clue in the text is application. If *pneuma* without *holy* is used for the Holy Spirit, the application in the passage concerns what the Holy Spirit does and is. Otherwise, the suggestion would be to translate the word lowercase, referring to our living spirit, as I suggest for Acts 6:3.

The Bible authors developed the original Bible vocabulary to describe Christians' nature as spirits made alive. But over the centuries, the Church lost that understanding. Now our doctrines have undervalued it, and English translators don't see that meaning when *pneuma* stands by itself. This is true throughout the churches and denominations of Christianity.

Now, in our day, the unseen world is becoming impossible to ignore any longer. I believe that maturing as a Church will make our translators ever more accurate about *pneuma*. God's timetable is forcing our language to catch up.

The Indirect Teaching

The Bible does not directly state the truths about our living spirits. People have been Christians all their lives without seeing them. Why didn't the New Testament authors give us a plain theology of spirit?

Remember that God hides things for us to discover (Proverbs 25:2). When the Bible doesn't say what we expect or prefer, there are good reasons.

The first reason is the common knowledge dynamic. Consider: breathing is essential to live. You don't see it taught in the Bible, because it is common knowledge.

Likewise, our identity as living spirits was a common experience in the early church. The pouring out of the Holy Spirit was the confirmation of a Christian. A spirit identity was common among all their recipients.

Not all of us have that once-common experience. We would like an outline. Christians today have differing interpretations and expectations; a Bible outline would settle that, once and for all.

There is a second reason that our spirit identity is between the lines, not taught explicitly. The apostles' motivation in their writings was to solve problems. Their letters specifically addressed deviations in churches. Their gospels compiled specific incidents to support the churches, both in their outreach and in their shortcomings. The truths about our spirits undergird the solutions and prescriptions that they wrote, now comprising our New Testament.

A third reason that the truths about our spirits are not explicit in the Bible: the New Testament does not contain everything that Jesus or His apostles taught. In Apostle Paul's letters to churches and people, he sometimes refers to the teaching he gave them during his visit there. That teaching is not in the Bible.

One such place is Troas (which we know as Troy). Once, Paul taught the church there all day until midnight. Eutychus dozed off and fell out the window, dead. Paul raised him up. If they wrote the teaching or took notes, we don't have it.

And sometimes, Apostle Paul would exhibit incredulity at the deviations of his recipients, by saying, *"Do you not know?" "Have you not heard?"* These expressions refer to teaching he previously gave them, which they forgot, and which was not recorded in Scripture.

A final reason: the first leaders of the Church recognized that rebirth as living spirits created a new race. The great power with which the Holy Spirit filled these believers activated their spirits for full function. Besides the miracle *dunamis* power we know about, He also filled them with a Romans 8:11 power, like I have experienced since December 3, 2006. This kind of Spirit power makes our spirits and bodies as fully alive as Jesus was after resurrection.

This surge of life was a common experience and would have been frequently discussed among believers, just as we do today with common experiences. All the apostles' basic teaching to new churches would have included it.

It would have been beyond all conception for the New Testament writers that one day, the Church would forfeit this explosive truth. The apostles felt no need to repeat and codify the consistent, universal, and repeated experience of all new Christians. Certainly we can excuse them for assuming the best about us. Could they have expected that this splendid spirit life would one day be forgotten?

Peter may have felt this might happen. The Church knew the truth and was established in all that God had revealed to the present. Peter wanted to preserve that progress for future generations as well.

> For this reason I will not be negligent to remind you always of these things, though you know and are established in the present truth. Yes, I think it is right, as long as I am in this tent, to stir you up by reminding you, knowing that shortly I must put off my tent, just as our Lord Jesus Christ showed me. Moreover I will be careful to ensure that you always have a reminder of these things after my decease. (2 Peter 1:11–15)

Poverty of Spirit Mourned

When we awaken to how little attention a person has given their Creator Spirit, we see how poor we are in spirit. In Jesus' beatitude list, mourning follows this poverty of spirit—but what prompts the mourning?

At least this: how little of the deserved attention I am giving to my Creator and Sustainer.

> God is Spirit, and those who worship Him must worship in spirit and in truth. (John 4:24)

When you realize you have been continually biting the Hand that feeds you, there is a sickening feeling— "What have I done?!"

Then the fright sets in—recognizing the inescapable curse from God earned by biting that hand. "I could have died and gone to hell! I didn't even know! What have I done to myself?!"

Next comes a dawning of the contrary evidence. "I've set myself on a path to hell—yet here I am—on Earth?! Why haven't I been destroyed, called to judgment, exiled forever? Why am I not in hell right now?"

This is when you realize how gracious and magnanimous that Hand has been despite your biting it. Seeing that love, you can only contrast it with the hate you have given back to Him. And you mourn.

This was the persuasive logic of Jonathan Edwards' well-known sermon, *Sinners in the Hand of an Angry God*, by which God sparked the Great Awakening in the early 1700s.

Spirit Undefinable

Despite this chapter's title, *Spirit Defined*, we've only defined more mysteries about it.

The unseen inhabitants would not experience this limit, because they would be describing their common experience. If we sought to describe our bodies, we would have no such limit, because we are quite used to them. Our limits in defining spirit are one symptom that we are poor in spirit.

Throughout this Book One, we are forced to describe our living spirit indirectly. After all, it is not subject to mental identification. Spirit is not emotional. It is independent of circumstances. Without those reference points, it's difficult to identify spirit directly.

Doubtless, this is one reason the Church has been slow to understand our living spirits.

The limits of human language also limited God in revealing His Spirit identity. To overcome this, He became one of us—a man born of a woman.

Apostle John described God's elegant solution in chapter 1, verses 14 and 18 of his gospel.

> And the Word became flesh and dwelt among us, and we beheld His glory, the glory as of the only begotten of the Father, full of grace and truth.... No one has seen God at any time. The only begotten Son, who is in the bosom of the Father, He has declared Him.

Reflection and discussion questions for this chapter are in the back of the book

---

CHAPTER FOUR
TOWARD GOD

WORSHIP IN SPIRIT AND TRUTH

Jesus spoke often about spirit. He expected us to understand Him as we mature. Two thousand years have passed since He rose from the dead—and we are still learning about spirit.

In John 4:24 Jesus spoke with a woman at a Samaritan well. He told her that *"God is Spirit and those who worship Him must worship Him in spirit and in truth."*

God is spirit—so full of spirit energy in fact that He is Trinity, three in one. In fact, Revelation repeatedly refers also to the seven spirits of God (1:4, 3:1, 4:5, 5:6.)

Since God is spirit, we understand why His worshippers must worship Him in spirit—but why the pairing of spirit with truth? Other pairs might be more to our way of understanding the Bible: love and truth, faith and love, faith and prayer, justice and servanthood—some preferred Christian virtues of our time.

The woman had asked about the proper place of worship, a religious truth question. In effect, Jesus' answer says that place no longer matters. While it did, salvation was from the Jews. Theirs was the revelation from God. In Jerusalem was the authorized priesthood for regulating worship.

But worshipping in spirit and truth now supersedes the place of worship. We have Jesus to thank for this freeing development. Our salvation requires no pilgrimage. No priestly approval hangs over our heads or blackmails us into compliance. Every other religion uses these means of controlling people, but not ours. Now God has replaced the place-bound, priest-regulated religion. People can be born as spirits and relate directly to God—without intermediaries.

The severance of true worship from place individualizes it and removes it from priestly regulation. Therefore, to worship the true and jealous God, one may not merely worship in spirit, but must worship in truth as well. Each worshipper is accountable to worship God in truth—but what does this mean?

Our Western point of view sees that word *truth* and thinks, "accurately, with proper doctrine, factually correct," and the like. Jesus' statement includes those; He does talk with her about truthful beliefs with authoritative sources: *"salvation is of the Jews"* (John 4:22). But accuracy is not the standard He speaks of.

In His conversation with the Samaritan woman at a well, Jesus is not teaching but evangelizing. When He brings up her serial marriages, it's plain He intends personal truthfulness with oneself and with God. His pointed inquiry about her husband fingers her failure. He does so not to gloat cruelly as religion does, but to restore her to the candid self-honesty required to worship God as spirit. Thus her report to the townspeople is comprehensive of all her untruthful life: *"Come, see a man who told me all things that I ever did."*

Jesus emphasizes the truth necessary to be the worshipper God seeks. Each worshiper is accountable to subordinate his own ideas and preferences about worship to the truths which God has revealed. This truthfulness is far more than accuracy—it is agreement with God's assessment of you.

THE PROBLEM TOWARD GOD

God seeks such worshippers—the very kind we are least able to become. Being dead in spirit, no one can give Him the worship He wants. If He is seeking worshippers in spirit, what hope is there for people?

Poverty of Spirit

Jesus said, *"Blessed are the poor in spirit"* (Matthew 5:3).

For poverty of spirit to be blessed—rather than rich in spirit—is unexpected. God is eager to make new royalty in the kingdom of heaven, and for Him to make you one, you must be poor in spirit. This is backward to our thinking. But it meets the first condition of spiritual birth: self-perception as poor in this essential identity.

The subsequent Beatitudes reveal the qualities that can result from this initial recognition of one's spiritual deadness. Each of them describes successive layers of character that follow the awakening to our spiritual poverty.

Spirit and Curse

The Bible reveals that God's wrath is constant (Psalm 7:11) and generates a global curse which is now a self-operating force of nature (Zechariah 5). Someone dead in spirit cannot define, identify, or avoid the curse of His wrath against our sin. They only know it from its effects and expression.

From this curse no spiritually dead person can escape. Only God can initiate escape. Charles Wesley captured this is the fourth stanza of his hymn, "And Can it Be?"

> Long my imprisoned spirit lay Fast bound in sin and nature's night; Thine eye diffused a quick'ning ray, I woke, the dungeon flamed with light; My chains fell off, my heart was free, I rose, went forth, and followed Thee.

God's curse destroys the dead person who refuses the simple step of coming to Him for spiritual birth. To provide escape from the self-operating curse, God continually woos a person but we can shun that wooing. When someone refuses God's advances, they forfeit the only way to escape the curse of His wrath. Our repeated refusal of His wooing cements the deadness of those who do it.

The Searching Spirit

> God has revealed them to us through His Spirit. For the Spirit searches all things, yes, the deep things of God. (1 Corinthians 2:10)

The spirits of God are six times described in Revelation and Zechariah as searching—specifically searching throughout the earth. It's reflected in the thirsts of our own spirits.

> Blessed are those who hunger and thirst for righteousness, for they shall be filled. (Matthew 5:6)

God describes His searching Spirit to the prophet Jeremiah.

> I, the LORD, search the heart, I test the mind, Even to give every man according to his ways, According to the fruit of his doings. (17:10)

The Spirit of God is not a static force, nor even a power force. He is not an It. He is a Person who delights in throughput. The Holy Spirit functions as a conduit—from God to other spirits. What does He search for? In the verse above Paul wrote, *"the deep things of God."* The Holy Spirit then seeks people with whom to share those things.

He hovered over *"the face of the deep"* (Genesis 1:2) because there was no one and nothing for interaction. One result when God re-formed Earth in six days was to provide the Spirit with recipients, both place and people.

> For the eyes of the LORD run to and fro throughout the whole earth, to show Himself strong on behalf of those whose heart is loyal to Him. (2 Chronicles 16:9)

Apostle Paul also writes why God filled us with His Spirit: *"that we might know the things that have been freely given to us by God"* (1 Corinthians 2:12).

Inside me, inside everyone saved, lives this searching Spirit of God, who wants us to know what He finds. Like He said in John 16:11–13 and 1 John 2:20–27, we know all things—from Him. He wants to reveal His findings to our spirits. *"He will take of what is Mine and declare it to you"* (John 16:13).

Our rebirth as spirits isn't merely to be filled with Him. Like the gospel, His filling is a means to an end. Peter understood this. The first chapter of his second letter says this:

> His divine power has given to us all things that pertain to life and godliness, through the knowledge of Him who called us by glory and virtue, by which have been given to us exceedingly great and precious promises, that through these you may be partakers of the divine nature. (2 Peter 1:3–4)

The gospel and the pouring out of the Holy Spirit had a purpose: that you may be partakers of the divine nature. Apostle Paul agreed in Romans 8:29, in different words.

> He also predestined [us] to be conformed to the image of His Son.

The good can be the enemy of the best. Likewise, being enamored of the Spirit's filling slows our maturity. It's like always dating and never marrying. He called us to be like Jesus. The Holy Spirit will not tolerate or honor our fixation on His filling; He fills us for a purpose.

Of course, He will leave us where we prefer to be.

Angel Fiction

I watched two movies last night, *Interstellar* and *Arrival*. Angels and the unseen are obviously on people's minds, but in the Hollywood ungodliness they can only imagine aliens.

Movies are made within the boundaries allowed by a man-centric universe. "It's all about me!" Their fictional presences fall in line accordingly.

When true angels visit, serve, and otherwise honor men, it is not for the merits of our nature but for our un-desserts! They see only the glory of the one they serve, and they serve the weakest whom He favors most.

Thine be the glory.

The true, holy angels are not interacting with us primarily. They are interacting with God Almighty—and with us for His sake. The only angels promoting man's me-first outlook are the unholy ones, seducing us by our own self-directed sin.

THE SALVATION OF THE DEAD

The searching spirits of God reveal the love of God. He is the original Spirit, with spirit characteristics. We are made in His image. Our spirit characteristics after we are born again enable a love relationship between us who were once dead, and Him who is Life itself.

Spirit Population

God is populating the new heavens and new Earth by the continuing birth of new potential spirits. In John 5:20 (NIV), Jesus says, *"My Father is always at His work, to this very day."*

Think of the fruitfulness of God. He imagines and speaks you into conception—every single person. Think how many billions and billions of potential spirits that He has caused to be born in mortal bodies!

He is creating new royalty in the kingdom of heaven (Matthew 5:3). He wants the harvest to be large (Luke 10:2). Only living spirits in relationship with Him comprise that harvest. But the gate is narrow. For there to be living spirits requires many, many billions of potential spirits to be born of mankind, because the vast majority of people choose death and identify their Creator who loves them as a threat.

The Purpose of Salvation

When the dove descended upon Jesus, everything in existence changed. It wasn't only an endorsement, an addition, a rite of passage, a *sine qua non* ("without which, nothing") for His salvation ministry. The dove's descent included them, but they were not the purpose of Jesus' filling by the Holy Spirit.

Jesus was filled with the Spirit of God because that was the *purpose* of His salvation ministry. He was the Son of Man—a representative of our inheritable authority. Our first parents forfeited their spirits, which died. With them died their dominion over everything on Earth. Each one of us still gives it away unwittingly. Jesus reintroduced what God originally intended.

> The Son of Man has come... to save that which was lost. (Luke 19:10)

> ... that He might be the firstborn among many brethren. (Romans 8:29)

When the Holy Spirit drove Jesus into the wilderness to be tempted, this was not a mere test. It was not a preening end-zone dance. It was the fire into which the newly forged sword was plunged for tempering.

Salvation is not the last stop in the Christian life—it is the first.

The Beatitudes and Salvation

Jesus' first teaching in the New Testament lists nine personal conditions that are blessed. He calls them *blessed* because each condition has a blessed result. As we have discussed, the nine conditions are backward to our thinking.

Jesus did not give the Beatitudes as a separate path of salvation. Salvation is by faith in His death for sin and receptivity to His teaching. So how do the Beatitudes dovetail with salvation by faith? This way: His death for sin presumes the dead spirit of every person. All who would come to Him for salvation are dead in spirit until they do so.

God is continually creating new spirits when a dead person is saved, born again, a living spirit. His raw material is the spiritually dead who see their poverty of spirit. His supply of spirit attracted us and attracts everyone who sees their spiritual poverty.

What opens the sluicegate for new spiritual birth? The recognition and apprehension of one's spiritual poverty before Him. That recognition is a precondition of salvation by faith.

Layered on to that: Blessed are those who mourn in repentance and confession, for they will be comforted as I forgive them and mature their spirit.

Layered onto that: Blessed are those who see their standing before the Judge and meekly surrender to his righteous judgment of them, for I can trust them to inherit the entire earth.

Layered onto that: Blessed are such people who crave the righteousness they lack, for I will satisfy them. And the subsequent layers follow as we mature.

The Birth of a Spirit

When is our spirit born? Is it when we believe in Jesus? Or does the Spirit's filling birth our spirit? If we are born into a Christian family, is our spirit born then?

Jesus spoke to the disciples as if they had spirits, in Matthew 26:41, when He said their spirits were willing. He had not completed His saving work. They had spirits born before its completion—when? Jesus didn't say *when*, but He did say *how*: they believed Him and acted accordingly.

When Jesus washed the disciples' feet in John 13:10 and 17:8, He spoke of their spirits. They had living spirits because they had been with Him, because He gave them God's words and because they accepted it. He vouched for them to the Father in John 17:8.

> For I have given to them the words which You have given Me; and they have received them, and have known surely that I came forth from You; and they have believed that You sent Me.

Many believed Him. He did not trust them because they only believed. They did not receive Him or accept His word. He did not speak or relate to them as if they had spirits; in fact, quite the opposite, as if they did not. John records it in his gospel, chapters 2:23–24. 6:26 and 8:37.

> Now when He was in Jerusalem at the Passover, during the feast, many believed in His name when they saw the signs which He did. But Jesus did not commit Himself to them, because He knew all men.

> Most assuredly, I say to you, you seek Me, not because you saw the signs, but because you ate of the loaves and were filled.

> You seek to kill Me, because My word has no place in you.

The parable of the four soils in Mark 4 describes two that receive the Word of God and believe it—yet neither persist nor bear fruit.

A person's spirit is born when one believes Jesus' message and receives Him as Savior and Lord into his or her life. John began his gospel with a succinct statement about that spirit birth, in 1:12.

> As many as received Him, to them He gave the right to become children of God, to those who believe in His name.

Spirit and the Gospel

Therefore, the gospel is a means to an end. It is not the end itself. Evangelicalism presents the gospel as the end. This limited understanding leaves the Church as a permanently immature infant, almost a collection of stillborn spirits.

Jesus died to produce a result: to populate the kingdom of heaven with proven human spirits. This is the "why" behind much of the Bible. The long centuries of Israel's covenant are explained by that result, to be covered in Book Five of the *Unseen* series, *Nobody Sees This Israel: God's Vanguard Against Darkness*. It explains why the outpouring of the Holy Spirit accompanies salvation, and why speaking in tongues was the Spirit's selected gift to the Church.

Populating Earth with proven human spirits is why He is building His *ekklesia*.

Spirit and Faith

"Abraham believed God." That's what caused the credit of righteousness (Genesis 15:6).

A human spirit derives its life entirely from relationship with God. However, God is unseen by any sense of the natural self. He is spirit.

He is an unseen Spirit without whom no spirit has life and must remain dead.

How is our spirit to derive life from unseen Spirit? It is by faith.

THE GRANT, THE FILLINGS, AND THE REWARD

When a person is born as a living spirit, an immediate change occurs from their natural life. In addition to evidencing the birth of their spirit, it is a confirmation of God's favor.

The Grant of Righteousness

The spirit and the flesh are contrary to each other, Scripture says. Fleshly will or fleshly capabilities can learn, produce, and enhance natural qualities—but not righteousness. It is a mistake to think that righteousness and our nature can cooperate; they are contrary to one another.

Despite this conflict, Christians often identify righteousness using patterns of the natural self. They are on a treadmill doomed to fail, because our flesh and our spirit are at odds. Apostle Paul is very plain in Galatians 5:17.

> For the flesh lusts against the Spirit, and the Spirit against the flesh; and these are contrary to one another, so that you do not do the things that you wish.

Righteousness is a grant to faith (Genesis 15:6, Romans 4:3–4). Righteousness is of the spirit (Romans 14:17). The flesh, and its components mind, body, and soul, cannot transact in righteousness. By definition, righteousness belongs to the unseen world of spirit. It is only evidenced in the visible world of the flesh.

When we live as a spirit, we experience righteousness as our nature. That's how David could say in Psalm 18:23, *I was also blameless before Him, and I kept myself from my iniquity.* This will relieve many frustrated Christians. Apostle Paul did not write about a treasure we have yet to earn, but a treasure already given us. That treasure is the knowledge of God through faith in Jesus Christ.

> For it is the God who commanded light to shine out of darkness, who has shone in our hearts to give the light of the knowledge of the glory of God in the face of Jesus Christ. We have this treasure in earthen

vessels, that the excellence of the power may be of God and not of us. (2 Corinthians 4:6–7)

Yes, the flesh continues to beset the living spirit. Yes, the flesh continues with its weaknesses and frailty. Yet the light of God in our hearts, and our vital life as a living spirit, is undiminished.

So we have a continual effort of warfare. Our living spirit has a constant challenge: asserting the superiority of spirit over flesh. Therefore, the Christian is constantly dying, daily crucifying themselves, and being given over to death daily (2 Corinthians 4:11–12, Luke 9:23).

The First Filling

The filling of the Spirit occurred in Acts chapter 2, after the disciples were already reborn as spirits when they submitted to Jesus.

The drama of Pentecost Day marked a clearer demarcation for them. The filling of the Spirit was a maturing event for them. They sprang suddenly from the maturity of children in the spirit to the maturity of fully functioning adult spirits.

In the natural, becoming an adult does not mean we mature no further. Likewise, the filling of the Spirit does not eliminate the need for spirit maturing. The evidence is throughout the New Testament.

For example, Apostle Peter made a severe mistake in Antioch, which Apostle Paul described in Galatians 2. There, Peter even backed off his three-time vision from God in Acts 10, and treated Gentile Christians as lower class. That occurred many years after the Holy Spirit filled Peter. The need to mature as a living spirit persists our entire life in flesh.

The entire leadership of the Jerusalem church provides a second example. Acts chapters 15 and 21–22 reveal their need for maturity. The Jerusalem church leaders continued to regard the Jewish leaders too highly; they placated the Sanhedrin in a detente (Acts 21:20–24). The church leaders in Jerusalem actually feared the Jews more than they respected Apostle Paul their brother. Thus, they asked Paul to join in the placating when he brought the offering of the Gentile churches. The political exigencies of placating Jewish leadership made them blind to love and loyalty. Even worse: when Paul's defense opportunity arose, not one of the Jerusalem leaders appeared on his behalf.

Apostle Peter in his later life recognized that our effort to mature as a spirit must be continual. He himself exhorts Christians to *"make every effort with all diligence"* to mature as spirits (2 Peter 1:5). These efforts are the subject of Chapter 10, *The Discipleship of Our Spirits*.

Apostle John also recognized the danger of failure to mature, explicitly stating that some fell away from the Church for lack of attentiveness to true spirit maturing (1 John 2:19).

Maturing must follow the birth of our spirit, as Hebrews 5:13–14 presumes.

> For everyone who partakes only of milk is unskilled in the word of righteousness, for he is a babe. But solid food belongs to those who are of full age, that is, those who by reason of use have their senses exercised to discern both good and evil.

The Continual Fillings

The immaturity of the apostles and leaders, even after their filling by the Holy Spirit, may surprise you—until you look around you. The ones you know personally still exhibit immaturity. Filling of the Spirit does not make us perfect.

Three incidents in the New Testament show the apostles' expectation that we are filled by the Holy Spirit continually, over and over, more and more.

First is Acts 4. After their first taste of persecution, the Christians all prayed together with resolute determination. They stood on the Word of God from Psalm 2. Next, in 4:31, everyone who was filled on Pentecost Day was filled again!

> And when they had prayed, the place where they were assembled together was shaken; and they were all filled with the Holy Spirit, and they spoke the word of God with boldness.

Later, in a second incident, they selected deacons to relieve the teaching apostles of body management duties. One qualification was *"full of the spirit and wisdom"* (Acts 6:3). The apostles recognized that, although the Holy Spirit was indeed poured out on all flesh, not all sought His filling equally, or matured with equal resolve.

The deacons were not men whose voice vibrated, whose hair stood on end, because the Holy Spirit was heavier on them. The Holy Spirit is not a force, as in the Star Wars ideology, where some have more midochlorians than others. These deacons were men who sought to be filled with the Holy Spirit continually and whose spirits were recognized to be strong.

Our third example is Paul's command to Christians, included in his letter to the Ephesian church, 5:18. If the filling of the Holy Spirit was a onetime thing, Paul would not command us to be filled with Him. To be filled with the Spirit is something we can do repeatedly and continually:

> Do not be drunk with wine, in which is dissipation; but be filled with the Spirit.

God the Rewarder

For clarity: there is no rank among spirits. Like our forebears, we fight for the truth of salvation by faith, rather than works. We reject false doctrines of hierarchical merit.

But these truths do not obscure God's nature: He is a rewarder. Our emphasis on salvation by faith makes this teaching rarer, but He is unchanged. Scripture repeatedly reveals His pleasure in rewarding. God desires to reward our spirits. That's why Apostle Paul talked about the prize.

God describes Himself to Abram as *"your exceedingly great reward"* (Genesis 15:1). The same truth is in 1 Samuel 26:23, Psalm 62:12 and Jeremiah 17:10.

> The LORD rewards everyone for their righteousness and faithfulness.

> You reward everyone according to what they have done. (NIV)

> I the LORD search the heart and examine the mind, to reward each according to their conduct, according to what their deeds deserve.

As part of this, He keeps books as seen in Daniel 7:9-10 and Revelation 20:11-12.

> The Ancient of Days took His seat... the court was seated, and the books were opened.

> I saw a great white throne and Him who sat upon it. [John next saw] the dead, great and small, standing before the throne, and books were opened. After that, the dead were judged according to what they had done as recorded in the books.

By His confident knowledge of heavenly book-keeping, Jesus taught often about rewards, such as Matthew 5:12, 6:2, 4, and 10:42.

Chapter Four: Toward God

Great is your reward in heaven... They have their reward.

Your Father, who sees what is done in secret, will reward you.

That person will by no means lose their reward.

You give credit of righteousness to faith, plain in Genesis 15:6 and Romans 4:22–23.

Abram believed God, and it was credited to Him as righteousness.

Now it was written not for his sake alone that it was imputed to him, but also for us. It shall be imputed to us who believe in Jesus.

Lest I appear to surrender salvation by faith, let's be clear. No rewards we could earn ever offset the condemnation of God's wrath against our offenses. Only one infinitely large righteousness can reconcile us to God, and there is one: Jesus. God's wrath can only be satisfied in that one way: faith in the atoning self-sacrifice of the one Righteous Man.

By opening a righteousness treasury for us, Jesus credits His righteousness to us, who receive His substitutionary atonement and follow His Lordship.

Jesus' one giant credit of righteousness is our only way to be reconciled to God. But importantly, Jesus did not deactivate God's rewarder nature. In fact, because faith in Jesus establishes us as righteous, He records in His books each incident of our trust and obedience. He rewards us every time that we believe Him over the competition. God credits these to us as righteousness. That's one reason He promised us a very great reward (Matthew 5:13).

The Bible warns Christians not to forsake our rewards. It's good to cherish our salvation by faith! But without diligence to receive credits of righteousness, our offense to the rewarding God is even more severe. As Hebrews says, *"How shall we escape if we neglect so great a salvation?...See that you do not refuse Him who speaks."* (2:3, 12:25)

Peter exhorts high-level diligence to prepare for judgment by Christ Jesus in 2 Peter 2:21, 3:17.

For it would have been better for them not to have known the way of righteousness, than having known it, to turn from the holy commandment delivered to them.

You therefore, beloved, since you know this beforehand, beware lest you also fall from your own steadfastness, being led away with the error of the wicked.

Hebrews 6 and 10 further emphasize this diligence, *"do not cast away your confidence, which has great reward"* (10:35).

JESUS IS THE JUDGE

The apostles preached a gospel featuring Jesus as the Judge of all men. Jesus Himself told the disciples,

The Son of Man ... will reward each according to his works. (Matthew 16:27)

The Father Himself judges no one, but has committed all judgment to the Son. (John 5:22)

In our time, we have minimized the preaching of Judgment Day. This disobeys the book of Acts. The apostles preached salvation by faith in Jesus and the filling by the promise of the Father. But that's not all: they also preached Jesus as the Judge. Paul preached this as an essential gospel fact in Acts 17:30–31.

Truly, these times of ignorance God overlooked, but now commands all men everywhere to repent, because He has appointed a day on which He will judge the world in righteousness by the Man whom He has ordained.

Paul speaks again in Romans 2:16 of *"the day when God will judge the secrets of men by Jesus Christ, according to my gospel."*

We must be very diligent. Paul exhorted us, *"Let us not grow weary while doing good, for in due season we shall reap if we do not lose heart"* (Galatians 6:9). Each of us faces continual choices. Even as we age, when aches and pains cool our inner fires, we are not to grow weary.

King Solomon described life *under the sun* in Ecclesiastes—meaning a fleshly life, devoid of a living spirit. This life can be vain and tiresome; our past good deeds can look like a bed of rest. God warns us not to grow weary, because we can so easily do it. Forgetting our poverty of spirit, we can act rich in spirit and think we have done enough.

As he neared his execution, Paul wrote this in 2 Timothy 4:7–8:

I have fought the good fight; I have finished the race; I have kept the faith. Finally, there is laid up for me the crown of righteousness, which the Lord, the righteous Judge, will give to me on that Day.

Our living spirits have their existence and identity by one reality only: God giving us birth. There is no rank among human spirits. But there are rewards that differ among us because that's God's nature as a rewarder.

DEFENSELESS

My spirit is alive—but defenseless. It has no arms to fight, no legs to flee. And against my living spirit, the kingdom of darkness deploys its minions to oppress me, to stifle my spiritual vitality, to retard my spirit's maturity, and to deceive me into cooperating with its purposes.

I'm just like a baby, who is defenseless. A helpless baby is at the mercy of adults. Yet, considering Who loves me, and gave me spirit birth, could I possibly be any safer?

If He lets me be tested by these unseen opponents, I trust Him.

If He permits me to cooperate with them until I learn how not to, I trust Him; He is a good Father.

If my loving Father sends me into the wilderness to be tempted by them, I trust Him.

If He is willing for things to take forever, I trust Him. He is a good Father.

If He says that I am safe, then I am indeed safe. No matter what I perceive, I am safe.

The unseen makes my poverty of spirit inescapably noticeable. How am I, a human living spirit, to have any standing in this society of spirit beings?

Throughout history, people have been aware of angelic beings, both good and bad. So impressive are they that people call them sons of the gods, at least semi-divine. These angelic spirits have bodies, but different—moving in more dimensions than our five: up, down, sideways, time and thought. Compared to them, I'm just little bitty me.

Well—not quite, because Someone lives in me.

If anyone loves Me, he will keep My word; and My Father will love him, and We will come to him and make Our home with him. (John 14:23)

Jesus said that to the twelve on their most defenseless night. Jesus told them He was leaving—and they could do nothing about it.

Jesus went *"like a lamb to the slaughter"* (Isaiah 53:7). But He was not defenseless.

> Do you think I cannot now pray to My Father, and He will provide Me with over twelve legions of angels? (Matthew 26:53)

I see what His defense was: ask the Father. That indeed is my defense. True—my spirit has no arms or legs, but it can communicate. I will ask the Father like Jesus did. With God on my side, who can be against me?

> If God is for us, who can be against us? ... Who shall separate us from the love of Christ? ... In all these things we are more than conquerors through Him who loved us. (Romans 8:31, 35, 37)

Reflection and discussion questions for this chapter are in the back of the book

---

Your spirit can only live if God gives it life. He has revealed the pathway: when you mourn your poverty of spirit and surrender all pretense that you deserve to be a spirit. The abject despair of this recognition makes God's provision for you clearer than ever: the work of Jesus on His cross. Throw yourself on the merit of Jesus Christ because His death eliminates the barriers hindering your intimacy with the Father—barriers of your agreements with Sin and darkness.

John the Baptist said that repentance was the qualification for the Kingdom of God. Here's such a prayer that may help if you are new to this understanding.

Almighty God, can You ever forgive me and accept me? I admit that You owe me nothing but rejection, because I have disdained to pursue Your intimacy—offered to me at such a great cost. To make matters even worse, I've actually treated You as if You owe me something, when in fact I owe You all—my Creator whom I have spurned.

In honor of Jesus' sacrifice, I relinquish all pretense that I can please You and earn blessings from You. I admit my fault, so proudly supposing that You owe me. Please accept Jesus' perfection on my behalf, and count my offense against His death for my sin.

I beg Your help to pursue the relationship that You have offered me, and to follow Jesus as His disciple. I'll do what He asks, listen for His leadership, and welcome Your Holy Spirit to live in me and help me.

The above prayer is not only the qualification to be born as a spirit. It expresses the only attitude that permits intimacy with God moment-by-moment. Any other attitude poisons us with the pride and jealousy that Lucifer first demonstrated.

CHAPTER FIVE

The Capabilities of Spirits

A VIEW AND A WILL

Spirit and Point of View

POV is an acronym used in gaming. The controls allow the player to see a scene from different points of view, abbreviated POV.

We all have one strongly dominant POV: from behind our eyeballs, from within our feelings, behind the grid of our thoughts and beliefs. What if, like a game player, we could flip a switch and glide between multiple points of view?

Jesus exemplified this POV fluidity. He customized his replies to people by perceiving their POVs. His answers illuminated the limits of their existing POVs. Each person's question became a shoehorn by which He squeezed them into a new POV.

One famous example is the man who asked Jesus, *"Who is my neighbor?"* Jesus' reply was the parable of the good Samaritan ending with a question: *"Who was a neighbor to the wounded man?"* Jesus thus exposed the self-centeredness of His questioner's point of view.

He still does that with us, exposing our point of view—if we will have ears to hear.

Jesus' miracles are one evidence of His radical POV. If His miracle method was the same each time, we could identify a formula; we could fit His miracles within our existing POV. But His methods varied widely.

Not even faith was required every time! The only common factor was Him and His authority.

What would your POV be if you were Him? He was unbound by time, sequence, proximity, and observable cause and effect in the seen world.

And He expected us to believe that about our spirits. Nothing illustrates it better than Matthew 14:28–30. when both Jesus and Peter walked on the water.

> And Peter answered Him and said, "Lord, if it is You, command me to come to You on the water." So He said, "Come." And when Peter had come down out of the boat, he walked on the water to go to Jesus. But when he saw that the wind was boisterous, he was afraid; and beginning to sink he cried out, saying, "Lord, save me!" And immediately Jesus stretched out His hand and caught him, and said to him, "O you of little faith, why did you doubt?"

No one has rebuked me for little faith, but I haven't walked on any water yet. I haven't withered a fig tree. Compared to Jesus' POV, I am very poor in spirit. How about you?

We Christians are living spirits, and Jesus considers us to be like Him—unbound by time, sequence, proximity, and observable cause-and-effect in the seen world.

Isn't this what we believe when we pray? When we lay hands on someone for healing? When we love the strangers we meet?

Our praying alone shows we accept a portion of our unseen authority. We actually believe prayer is effective—which requires us to believe that the unseen and indirect actions of speaking and willing can cause things to occur.

Jesus' POV can be ours, and we will do even greater things than He did. He Himself said so, recorded in John's gospel.

> He who believes in Me, the works that I do he will do also; and greater works than these he will do. (14:12)

We all welcome the greater things, but He uses the everyday obstacles of life to develop our POV to be like His.

There are troublesome people in my life. What if, instead of despair, my spirit can perceive the world from their POV? Can I see God's POV also? Then I could see the unseeable fears provoking unwelcome behaviors. Can

I see the demons oppressing the person, and the stronghold organizations of those demons? Yes, I can and do. So can you.

Mercy for them activates in us. Lovingly responding to their genuine fears overrides our despair or vexation. Jesus did this. So can we.

We grow up thinking ourselves limited to our physical identities and religious behaviors. But what if we can see with angels' POV? In fact, can we be present with unseen angels, and they with us? Can we possibly confer with angels about the assignments God has given us each? After all, isn't this cooperation within the petition *Thy kingdom come*? (More is to come on this in Book Eight of the *Unseen* Series, *Nobody Sees These Friends: Partners in the Unseen.*)

What if, instead of being a victim of circumstance, my spirit can see God's POV? Then, like Him, I can watch the undesired event as a disinterested, unaffected person. I can see that it serves His purpose. I can see the interlocking influences from His POV.

Understanding that you are a living spirit unlocks such a liberty of POV.

POV Alerts

Signals and alerts help me, though. The day's activities and concerns so quickly consume my mortal attention!

One valuable signal is agitation. We easily attribute vexation, agitation, and irritation to our flesh and its mind, body, and emotions. When agitation arises, we can default to it like a helpless leaf floating along and tossed by river currents of life. The POV of our flesh imposes its potent emotions, definite opinions, and energetic activity.

But I can instead perceive the agitation in my spirit if I pause and still myself before Him. That's the way to push my POV button. Seeing what God sees subordinates my earthbound POV to my spirit POV.

Rapidly, the agitating concern becomes apparent to me. I see it at arm's length. The agitation is then stripped of its hiding place. Its secret influence is disarmed. I behold it from a kingdom POV. Its power to agitate me becomes minuscule. My living, perceptive spirit receives what God and His angels see.

The tapestry backing to many Bible exhortations is this: our spirit's liberty to determine our point of view.

One such exhortation is in Apostle Paul's letter to the Philippians, chapter 4. The text suggests that two leading women were at odds, and within the church, people were taking sides. Paul's admonition is to mind their POV.

Whatever things are true, whatever things are noble, whatever things are just, whatever things are pure, whatever things are lovely, whatever things are of good report, if there is any virtue and if there is anything praiseworthy—meditate on these things. (v 8)

Spirit and Will

In our natural selves, we muster up willpower. We say people with assertive personalities have much willpower.

In the spirit, this is not true. The evidence of will in the spirit is simple: agreement with the Spirit who created us. The life of our spirit exists entirely because of our faith relationship with Him. It is pass/fail, and we pass if we agree with Him.

It is either/or. There are no shades. Either we agree with Him, or we do not. Every circumstance asks us to make this basic choice, the only question that our spirit-will must respond to.

Everything He permits into our lives is to test our agreement with Him. Maturing as a living spirit is a process: we increase our agreements with Him into more and more corners of our being.

But not every Christian chooses to expand agreement with God. Those who do can still have blind spots. We can neglect our spirits. When we willfully blind ourselves to our unseen *arguments* with God, it strengthens our *agreements* with darkness.

Maturing in spirit unveils those areas. We continually discover where we have unwittingly argued with our precious Father and Savior.

That's one reason we are increasingly poor in spirit and mourning—even after we are born again. When we endure this gauntlet of His inspection, our mournful poverty of spirit grows. The result is that we mature as spirits. It's backward to our intuition, which associates maturity with self-confidence.

Different Christians can grow differently as spirits. That would make sense if our spirits have will, and therefore freedom.

The apostle's letters to people and churches demonstrate that our spirits mature in different ways. They wrote their letters to churches and Christians who were clearly following Jesus and were living spirits. Yet simultaneously, the maturity of the people addressed varied widely.

People described by the apostles had differing levels of intensity and growth as living spirits. Paul can say of Timothy, *"I have no one like him."* In contrast, Paul says of the Christians in Jerusalem, *"At my first defense no one stood with me, but all forsook me. May it not be charged against them"* (Philippians 2:20, 2 Timothy 4:16).

But the common ground for every spirit, non-elective, is to agree with our Creator God and our Savior. This is on or off, pass or fail, up or down. There is no gray about this, according to the Bible.

THE SENSES OF YOUR SPIRIT

The spirit perceives, but how? I want to mature in my spirit. That means intimacy with the Spirit who made me—perceiving His voice, actions, and will.

How do I see, hear, learn? In the natural, I know that answer; people have taught me. In the spirit, there is one teacher—the One described by John in his first letter.

> The anointing which you have received from Him abides in you, and you do not need that anyone teach you. (2:27)

The Sense for God

Is the spirit limited to the flesh's five senses?

No, the spirit has at least one sensory pathway of its own. Your spirit's unique sense is perceiving what God perceives and expresses. Jesus exemplified this sense in many places; one is chapter five of John's gospel, using the words *see* and *show*.

> Most assuredly, I say to you, the Son can do nothing of Himself, but what He sees the Father do; for whatever He does, the Son also does in like manner. For the Father loves the Son and shows Him all things that He Himself does. (John 5:19–20)

The Holy Spirit Himself exemplifies this. Jesus described the Holy Spirit's sensory ability this way, using the words *hear* and *take*.

> He will not speak on His own authority, but whatever He hears, He will speak; and He will tell you things to come. He will glorify Me, for He will take of what is Mine and declare it to you. (John 16:12–13)

These describe the sense of a living human spirit for God's voice. Jesus, with His spirit, saw what the Father, a Spirit, showed Him. The Holy Spirit—also a spirit of course—hears and takes what belongs to Jesus, and declares it to us because we also are living spirits, with the ears to hear Him.

The dead in spirit have only the five senses of flesh; they cannot perceive what God perceives and expresses. When we are born again as living spirits, we gain a unique sense: perceiving God's senses, responses, and expressions.

God has always desired to give people this sense for Him. In the prophetic rebuke to the high priest Eli in Shiloh, God said, *"I will raise up for Myself a faithful priest who will do according to what is on My heart and mind"* (1 Samuel 2:35). This presumes that He wants us to know it. He wants to share His heart and mind with us—just like we share ours with one another.

Dietrich Bonhoeffer wrote in *The Cost of Discipleship*[2] that we Christians have only one direct relationship—with Jesus Christ. By necessity therefore, our spirit made alive by Him, for Him, must perceive Him. As Jesus Himself said,

> My sheep hear My voice, and I know them, and they follow Me. (John 10:27)

A spirit made alive by God is a holy spirit in relationship with Him. A spirit He has made alive is filled with His Holy Spirit. Therefore, in our spirit, we can perceive what He perceives. We can express what He expresses, at His direction.

Our spirit's sense perceives the unseen world and its qualities. What we perceive with our spirit is not perceptible to any of the five mortal senses.

Sorcery over the centuries has sought this sense, this perceptive capability. They seek it apart from God, the Spirit who created all. Sorcerers and witches seek an "independent" means of control. Darkness seduces them to replicate satan's own prideful independence. Thus, practitioners of witchcraft and other sorcery seek to perceive the spirit world while avoiding God. Their "independence" from God leaves them as loveless slaves of all else.

In contrast, a communion exists among our saved and holy spirits that is not possible through any natural senses. The community of living spirits is the only one on Earth where God Himself is the center.

> The natural man does not receive the things of the Spirit of God, for they are foolishness to him; nor can he know them, because they are spiritually discerned. But he who is spiritual judges all things, yet he himself is rightly judged by no one. For "who has known the mind of the Lord that he may instruct Him?" But we have the mind of Christ. (1 Corinthians 2:14–16)

The Sense for the Bible

The mind of Christ means we have a sense for His voice in the Bible. The Bible is His Word. Because the human race is dead in spirit, we cannot know a God who is spirit. We can perceive His qualities and influence, but no intimacy is possible. Paul described our despairing condition in Ephesians 2:12.

> At that time, you were without Christ, being aliens from the commonwealth of Israel and strangers from the covenants of promise, having no hope and without God in the world.

God took action in His love for His image-creatures: He revealed Himself. The Bible is that revelation. To learn more about the Bible's miraculous composition and preservation, see my wife's book, *The Bible: the Life of a Book*[3] by Diane Renfroe. Seeing God's methods for assembling and protecting the Bible renders your faith in its divine authority unassailable.

The fulcrum of the entire Bible is Jesus Christ. In Him, God made the ultimate revelation of Himself. Apostle John reflected on his three-year discipleship with Jesus with these words in John 1:18.

> No one has seen God at any time. The only begotten Son, who is in the bosom of the Father, He has declared Him.

We could not reconcile our dead spirits with God, and He wanted to solve it. So God the Son was incarnated as Jesus of Nazareth, a human being—fully God and fully man. The entire Bible, both before and after Jesus, points to Him.

God does not reveal everything we wish He would. In the Bible, He reveals Himself. Could we truly wish for anything greater?

We are filled with the Holy Spirit—yet He still does not reveal very much outside the Bible. Without reliance upon His written Word to know Him, we have no basis for discerning His unwritten words to us.

Because He is Spirit and His kingdom is not of this world, He gave us a means to identify Him. That means is His Bible. By knowing His Word well, we can embrace what is from Him and reject what is not.

He withholds Himself from people who try to skip the Bible. In fact, He permits them to make up gods—but not without penalty. The danger we all face is to make Him in our image. Instead of submitting our conception of Him to what He revealed about Himself, we prefer a God who fits inside what we know and like already—our comfort zone. This is why A. W. Tozer's opening sentence in *The Knowledge of the Holy*[4] says "The most important thing about a man are his thoughts about God."

Identifying His voice can be influenced by our personal preferences and wishes. His enemies in darkness vigorously try to trick us into worshipping distortions of the true God. Any distortion will do! Worship in spirit must also be worship in truth (John 4:24).

Truly, we need the Bible. Anyone who professes to know God without reliance on His Word is at monumental risk—or a purposeful deceiver.

Christians do not read the Bible as the dead in spirit read it. Large numbers of people read the Bible, yet receive no intimacy with God. But to us living spirits, it is our Father's Word, our Lord's voice, and our Counselor's guidance.

Even after our eyes leave its pages for other matters, the words of the Bible ricochet within us. As water drips through coffee, the living water of Scripture filters into us through our daily cares and activities. The words of the Bible infiltrate us at every level when we seek Him, our life.

The course of the day brings intersections of Bible and life. We gain a new understanding of a Scripture when an incident in our lives mirrors it.

The Word of God is the primary subject of the Book Two in the *Unseen* series—*Nobody Sees This Unseen Realm: How to Unlock Bible Mysteries*. To mature as a spirit, you must yield to your sense for the Bible. It is God revealing Himself to us.

The Sense for Other Spirits

The spirit characteristics of community and commitment show that our spirits also have a sense of each other. When you know without words that someone is filled with the Holy Spirit, your spirit sense is active.

Apostle John wrote in 1:3 of his first letter, *"This we proclaim, that you may have fellowship with us, and our fellowship is with God and His Son Jesus Christ."*

The fellowship he's describing is not a physical one requiring proximity. After all, he is writing a letter from a distance. This is a fellowship of spirits. John can write confidently about their anointing to know all things, even being distant, because their fellowship comprises the same spirit characteristics. Chief among them: God is at the center of the spirit network.

Jesus said to me in 2020, "To function as a living spirit, with the authorities and responsibilities I've outlined in Scripture, you need the ability to perceive spirits. I give you that. It is included in being a maturing living spirit, and especially necessary for fulfilling your calling."

Lord, I am not equal to this. "Right—you are not. But I live in you and I am. We will do it together."

Is it what You want for every follower of Jesus? "Paul, what is that to you? Follow Me!"

STRIVING

Striving is an intense degree of will. There are differing degrees of will. We will to eat for instance. But one degree is needed to eat a snack, another to eat a meal, and another to break a long fast.

Our spirit has a will. The will of our spirit is our core power; all other abilities and attributes stem from it. But can our spirit strive?

Spirit Striving

Our spirit has identity. It is born by relationship with God through faith in Jesus Christ, and through the indwelling Holy Spirit of God. Our spirit is born into a unique, unseen person.

Then what? We exert our will with intensity; we will to advance with Him. Paul gives us his own example in two of his letters, the first one to Corinth and his only one to Philippi.

> Do you not know that those who run in a race all run, but one receives the prize? Run in such a way that you may obtain it. (1 Corinthians 9:24)

> Forgetting those things which are behind and reaching forward to those things which are ahead, I press toward the goal for the prize of the upward call of God in Christ Jesus. (Philippians 3:13–14)

Judging from Paul's example, our spirits can press on, strain forward, have goals and desire prizes.

Paul's example affirms the many Bible statements that God is, in fact, a rewarder. To desire a prize and to win a race imply rewards. The eleventh chapter of the letter to the Hebrews says we must believe that God is a rewarder. Jesus also said it in Mark's gospel.

> But without faith, it is impossible to please Him, for he who comes to God must believe that He is, and that He is a rewarder of those who diligently seek Him. (Hebrews 11:6)

> For whoever gives you a cup of water to drink in My name, because you belong to Christ, assuredly, I say to you, he will by no means lose his reward. (Mark 9:41)

Like Paul, we want His highest and best rewards. We strive to attain them.

The Striving of the Natural

The conduct of our natural selves includes striving. We can bend the will of our natural selves to subdue our natural impulses. But this is not spirit.

When I was born again after a school assembly in 1972, I became a living spirit. I did not know it. No one told me what I should do. I was only conscious of God's displeasure for certain behaviors—which I (mostly) respected. Like most people, I picked what to comply with, and felt excused for what I ignored, since my good deeds put God in my debt—so I thought.

After two years of hit-or-miss Christian living, I went backpacking into the Grand Canyon in 1974. There, God activated my spirit. The majesty of creation and its Creator opened me like a can opener. My natural self was shocked by my damning disregard for the love of God.

I knew little then, either, but I couldn't *do* nothing—so I strove. I intently listened at church to do what they said. I constantly read the Bible so I could do what it said. Work, friends, reading, family—in all my actions and relationships, I strove to be godly.

These forty-six years of striving—what have they produced? I know the Bible. I can pray. People respect me. God honors me. But my spirit is the same spirit. None of the striving added to my identity. From the moment I believed, I was a child of God.

> But as many as received Him, to them He gave the right to become children of God, to those who believe in His name. (John 1:12)

My striving has enabled maturity, with fuller perception and expression, and I am glad. But outer, natural evidence are not the same as my spirit, nor are they evidence of a living spirit.

We can strive and succeed in the flesh without maturing in spirit. Jesus described this in the miracle workers of Matthew 7:22–23.

Many will say to Me in that day, "Lord, Lord, have we not prophesied in Your name, cast out demons in Your name, and done many wonders in Your name?" And then I will declare to them, "I never knew you; depart from Me."

Apostle Paul's name was Saul before his faith in Christ, and he strived to be the best Jew. In Philippians 3:4–8, Paul uses those years to illustrate the fruitlessness of striving. He contrasts that natural striving to being a living spirit who strives to know God intimately.

If anyone else thinks he may have confidence in the flesh, I more so: circumcised the eighth day, of the stock of Israel, of the tribe of Benjamin, a Hebrew of the Hebrews; concerning the law, a Pharisee; concerning zeal, persecuting the church; concerning the righteousness which is in the law, blameless.
But what things were gain to me, these I have counted loss for Christ. Yet indeed I also count all things loss for the excellence of the knowledge of Christ Jesus my Lord, for whom I have suffered the loss of all things, and count them as rubbish, that I may gain Christ and be found in Him.

All natural striving seeks to put God into our debt. As commendable as the behaviors may be, we try to create an IOU for God. We the creatures want to obligate the Creator of everything. Our plan is to get what we want, by giving Him what He wants.

Obligating God is what Job attempted. His story is the last book before the Psalms, in the Old Testament. God prized Job but would not give Job an IOU. The book tells the story of how God's heavenward call stripped Job of every evidence that his striving had obligated God.

This is our state of immaturity, and when we mature, we mourn it. We hunger and thirst for righteousness, and our hearts' desires for Him are purified of IOU-based striving.

POWER AND WEAKNESS

Our society sometimes equates spiritual identity with supernatural power. Take, for example, the Star Wars movies. Neither gadgets nor technology nor skill won victory in that fictional universe. Instead, the victors won by using "the force," a quasi-spiritual unseeable reality, as in, "I'll know it when I see it."

But the living Christian spirit is personal—not fictional at all.

Spirit and Weakness

Apostle Paul used his second letter to Corinthian Christians to correct their undiscerning preference for corrupt visiting ministers. Paul distinguished between the Matthew 7:21–23 type of IOU works that obligate God, and the works of reborn spirits. Corrupt ministers trade upon their success at lassoing God—but a true minister is poor in spirit.

> But we have this treasure in earthen vessels, that the excellence of the power may be of God and not of us. (2 Corinthians 4:7)

There is no natural, internal, or innate power of spirit in us. The Christian's poverty of spirit is a permanent condition. We are born in spirit, yes—by the will and power of Another. But for being a spirit, you and I have nothing that is required.

We mature into Jesus' Beatitude results, the second half of each one. Yet the more we do, the poorer and meeker we become.

> for theirs is the kingdom of God
> for they shall be comforted
> for they shall inherit the earth
> for they shall receive mercy
> for they shall be satisfied
> for they shall see God
> for they shall be called sons of God
> for theirs in the kingdom of heaven
> for great is your reward in heaven

No wonder Paul wrote the Corinthian church, *"And who is sufficient for these things?"* (2 Corinthians 2:16)

Just like us, Apostle Paul wrestled with this condition. It seems backward: God has a plan for us, and we do not have any resources to contribute to it. In fact, Paul complained to the Lord three times when God gave him a messenger from satan to pester him. Surely that is at odds with God's plan—?

Contrary to expectation, He told Paul to stop asking. God explained to Paul what His purpose was: *"My grace is sufficient for you, for My strength is made perfect in weakness"* (2 Corinthians 12:9).

In His plan, our inadequacy strengthens our connection to the Father. Our inadequacy does not hamper Him. God's vision, ambitions, and plans fit *His* resources—not *ours*. Thus, our inadequacy drives us to His adequacy, and His alone. That is how He wants it—permanently.

What hinders His plans is our pride to think we can contribute with our capabilities. God says He created Lucifer in perfection. But with pride in that perfection, Lucifer concluded he could replace God, and started the rebellion in heaven.

It is never God's plan for us to contribute with pride. The Lord Jesus ascended to the throne through weakness, and so do we. We are weak and inadequate, and comprehensively so. It is not just our flesh, nor is it only our isolation within the world. Our weakness is more than our vulnerability to darkness and its temptations. Rather, our weakness is a permanent poverty of spirit and always produces meekness in us. "*Who is equal to these things?*"

Even Jesus said, *"I am meek and lowly in spirit.* He described the result as a yoke, turning us into burden bearers: *"Take My yoke upon you."* A yoke sounds like work and slavery, but His is *"an easy yoke"*—not a heavy burden, for *"My burden is light."* In fact, *"you will find rest for your souls"* (Matthew 11:28–29 KJV).

How backward and glorious is the kingdom of God!

Spirit and Its Power

All Christians are poor in spirit. There are none who are not.

Yet, as poor as we are, Father God still gives us the honor of choosing. God awaits our choices because this life is for our testing and proving. The experiences in this natural world present constant choices for our spirit. Our power, despite our poverty, is to choose.

It is in this seen world that our early choices center: who our friends are, what our moral behaviors are, the steps we take to grow as Christian spirits. Following Christ Jesus wholeheartedly gradually pushes our choices into the unseen realm: whether we trust Him or our own abilities, wisdom, and quality.

The highest and best use of our power as living spirits is to pursue God. Our highest and best choice is Him.

What churches often identify as spiritual power is, in fact, the outgrowth of a persistent, consistent choice to love and yield to our Father. That choice has one cry:

Thy will be done on earth as it is in heaven. (Matthew 6:10)

With that cry in our hearts, we yield. We do not crave to do miracles, to amaze with testimonies, or to draw crowds. At His direction, those happen. These manifestations followed Jesus and His apostles, and also follow us. He chooses the times and places for those manifestations; we do not. We listen for His choices and cooperate with Him—because it is Jesus whom we crave.

A person can choose away from the Lord Jesus. Judas did. Peter did. Numerous people in the New Testament are named who chose not to continue. When we make such a choice, our spirit gradually withers by distance from its source of life—like a coal removed from a fire. This withering is not the weakness of the poor in spirit, which grows by seeking God. It is the weakness of not mourning it.

That withering spirit becomes a liability to the Body of Christ and a tool of the enemy. Often, they leave our fellowship and can even disprove all evidence that their spirit ever lived.

> They went out from us, but they were not of us; for if they had been of us, they would have continued with us; but they went out that they might be made manifest, that none of them were of us. (1 John 2:19)

In contrast, the maturing spirit chooses the Lord and feeds upon the success of doing so.

> And everyone who has this hope in Him purifies himself, just as He is pure. (1 John 3:3)

WHERE IS MY SPIRIT?

Naturally, in becoming living spirits, we might ask, where can my spirit be? Where can it go?

The Bible holds some tantalizing hints. Apostle Paul wrote a strange statement in his first letter to the Corinthian church when he advised they hold a disciplinary meeting. He prefaced his advice with this:

> In the name of our Lord Jesus Christ, when you are gathered together, along with my spirit, with the power of our Lord Jesus Christ. (1 Corinthians 5:4)

Spirit Unbound

Our spirits are unseen. Your spirit lives in the world of spirit. In the Bible, God reveals that spirits are not time-bound, not place-bound, and not even sequence-bound. If dreams are any indication, plots can shift, and time can telescope or zoom.

The book of Revelation exhibits a fluid sequence of time. Old Testament prophecies reveal both near- and far-time, all mixed together. This time trombone will help to understand the entire *Unseen* series. A further introduction is in Book Two, *Nobody Sees This Unseen Realm: How to Unlock Bible Mysteries*.

One characteristic of spirit is to be present. In the natural, we identify our presence—by surroundings, by time, by who we are. But in the spirit, according to the Bible, these identifiers are unneeded. Prophetic dreams hint at this. In them, every natural clue to where, when, and who we are is disarmed.

God wants me to be a spirit who sees what He shows, agrees with Him, and intends what He intends. For this to happen, I cannot limit myself to who or what I think I am. I am who *He* says I am—end of story. He is my Lord. He alone gets to say who I am.

Plausibly, that's the sort of training Jesus received those forty days in the wilderness. This explains how we need so much effort to understand Him. He spoke as the first human spirit, with a spirit's point of view—a brand new frame of reference. No one around Him had the POV of a living spirit. They did not know it even existed, except John the Baptist.

No wonder Creation itself recognized Him.

Spirit Unbound 2

Dream: Another train, destination unknown. Other than that, I can't remember the details. But when I awoke and asked You about it, You said, "you are unbound." His *you* was plural. Even in my sleep-fog, the Scriptures began coming together, like the pieces of reality taking shape.

> To you I give the keys of the kingdom: whatever you bind on earth will be bound in heaven, and whatever you loose on earth will be loosed in heaven. (Matthew 16:19)

That binding and loosing also pertains to us. We ourselves are unbound in heaven—and therefore unbound on earth. Jesus introduced His ministry as one of unbinding and of freeing, in Luke 4:18.

Jesus said, *"In the world, you will have trouble"* (John 16:33). He knew others can torment us and trouble us in the natural—but that is not the most binding reality. We are unbound from the natural. We are bound to the reality of heaven.

What forms can this unbinding take? In our spirit, we perceive it.

As I checked this out with You, You reminded me: "unbound by time, by the law of nature, and by linear sequentiality."

Later: "unbound by proportionality. All your life you have been bound to one-to-one fruitfulness and now everything is released for disproportionate results. Don't be surprised when results far exceed the effort spent!! It is the way things will be from now on."

No wonder we have a saying, "out of all proportion." It describes the mismatch of just desserts and actual events.

This raises questions about the relationship of our spirit and our body, and physical objects.

Reflection and discussion questions for this chapter are in the back of the book

---

CHAPTER SIX

THE SPIRIT, THE SOUL, AND THE BODY

EACH IN THEIR PLACE

When God made us, He did not create ghosts. We were not a subclass of angels. He created us tripartite: spirit, soul, and body. The sin of our first parents caused the death of every person's spirit. Our souls and bodies remained. The Bible word is "the flesh" and refers to a person's soul and body in combination. These are sufficient for life in the natural. When we are born again as spirits through faith in Jesus Christ, we are restored to Adam and Eve's original nature: spirit, soul, and body. Our flesh does not happily submit to our spirits.

The Body is not Bad

Throughout Church history, ascetics have believed our bodies were evil. They believed it more spiritual to have no physical needs—as if spirit is good and body is bad. This dualistic belief persists with telltale symptoms: Pure love good, emotions bad. Altruism good, self-interest bad. Personal maturity good, physical aging bad.

Examples include the original heresy of the Gnostics. They regarded the physical creation (including our bodies) as the source of all evil. Although the Gnostics died out, the belief manifested again in the monastic vow to be poor and celibate, disdaining the faith of all who did not take the vow. Early medieval hermits disavowed all association with worldly people. The practice of self-flagellation arises from this mistaken belief.

The unbiblical dualism persists. Some Christian traditions today still construe the flesh to mean only our body. Thus, believers believe wrongly that restraining the body is the job of their soul. This is the fox watching the henhouse, a venture doomed from the beginning—as any poor in spirit person recognizes and mourns.

Apostle Paul summarily dismisses these views in 1 Timothy 4:1-5. Everything God created is good, including our bodies. He said so Himself in Genesis 1:31. *"Then God saw everything that He had made, and indeed it was very good."*

The Place of Our Spirit

When we believe and follow Jesus Christ as our Lord and Savior, our birth as living spirits occurs. But Christians have lived as if that birth was extra—as if salvation only added to what we already were. Most Christians I know have never understood their birth as a spirit. They believe that salvation only augmented the natural capacities they had before salvation. The Holy Spirit merely increases their morality, love and holiness, in this view. This thinking sees the image of God in only our soul and body—which the Bible calls our flesh.

The flesh is not body only, or even primarily. The flesh is our soul and body in concert, with which we willingly choose sin. Our spirit must master our flesh; not vice versa. Apostle Paul relied heavily on this distinction in Romans about Christians' sins, such as 6:13 and 7:18.

> Do not present your members as instruments of unrighteousness to sin, but present yourselves to God as being alive from the dead, and your members as instruments of righteousness to God.

> For I know that in me (that is, in my flesh) nothing good dwells; for to will is present with me, but how to perform what is good I do not find.

These last few years I've been reflecting on the Scripture and listening to God about our spirits. I now see another reason that the Church has been slow to mature. Churches differ in which truths about our spirits they welcome. Not all churches treat believers as living spirits.

Churches of every denomination subordinate our spirit identities and prioritize the fleshly identity. Thus, the flesh is preeminent and our spirit was born simply to make our soul and body happy. The Corinthian church demonstrated this priority structure when they abused communion (1 Corinthians 11:20-28). We see this today in the need-based marketing described in Chapter Ten, *Church of Spirits*.

Jesus purposely chose the birth statements He used with Nicodemus in John 3:3, 5–6. He chose them to communicate that an entirely new being, an entirely new level of existence, was at hand.

> Most assuredly, I say to you, unless one is ***born again***, he cannot see the kingdom of God... Most assuredly, I say to you, unless one is born of water and the Spirit, he cannot enter the kingdom of God. That which is born of the flesh is flesh, and that which is born of the Spirit is spirit.

My flesh is my soul and body in agreement to do things my own way. My living spirit is no mere addition to that flesh. My spirit is now a competing identity given birth by God, and my spirit wants to please Him. Either my spirit rules my flesh or is ruled by it.

> And do not present your members as instruments of unrighteousness to sin, but present yourselves to God as being alive from the dead, and your members as instruments of righteousness to God. (Romans 6:13)

The Place of the Body

> But if the Spirit of Him who raised Jesus from the dead dwells in you, He who raised Christ from the dead will also give life to your mortal bodies through His Spirit who dwells in you. (Romans 8:11)

I now have a living spirit, and the Spirit of the God who raised Jesus is in my spirit. He Himself renews my mortal body; He is God Almighty living inside my skin.

God spoke my spirit into existence when I was saved. Ever since, I've been growing in spirit. My body prospers because it is filled with His Holy Spirit, who raised Jesus.

I lived many years as though my spirit was an add-on. With the teaching I had, I thought my spirit was simply an additional resource to satisfy my natural self. But now my soul and body serve my spirit more and more.

> For the flesh lusts against the Spirit, and the Spirit against the flesh; and these are contrary to one another. (Galatians 5:17)

Our Body

Lucifer fell with his jealous pride. God's punishment drastically affected his body.

Both before and after, he had a body that manifested his spirit. In that body, he suffered consequences for rebellion. It is that body which the mighty angel will chain in the Abyss for one thousand years. After that time, God will release satan to test all the nations of the earth. At the completion of that test, God will throw satan, with his body, into the eternal lake of fire.

Revelation chapter 20 describes these events. They all require that satan has a body.

God gave us bodies as well. Everything He does with us involves our bodies. Our tests and blessings alike all affect them. At Judgment Day, every person must stand and give account to Jesus, who said He is the Judge (John 5:22-23). When He makes His judgment, it is in our bodies that He will cast us into hell or welcome us into heaven.

> Fear Him who is able to destroy both soul and body in hell. (Matthew 10:28)

> If our earthly house, this tent, is destroyed, we have a building from God, a house not made with hands, eternal in the heavens. (2 Corinthians 5:1)

The principle is this: our mortal bodies are not a mere carrier for our spirits. We are born again as living spirits, yes—and our bodies are part and parcel of our entire spirit existence.

Apostle Paul writes in Scripture, 1 Corinthians 15:42, 52, that God raises our bodies in an immortal and eternally healthy condition.

> The body is sown in corruption; it is raised in incorruption.

> It is sown in dishonor; it is raised in glory.

> It is sown in weakness; it is raised in power.

> It is sown a natural body; it is raised a spiritual body....

> As was the man of dust, so also are those who are made of dust; and as is the heavenly Man, so also are those who are heavenly....

> We shall all be changed, in a moment, in the twinkling of an eye.

BODY MEETS SPIRIT

What happens when our spirit wakes up inside our body? Do we feel something? Does our body gain extra powers?

Disabled by Spirit

I will never see a disabled person the same way. As I've been growing in spirit, I've had many days of disabled stamina, disabled motivation, fatigued body, and other symptoms. All these are with no physical impairment to explain them.

You explained it to me: "This is the physical traumatization caused by participation in the spirit world." Jeremiah is one who describes it, in Jeremiah 10:19 and 23:9.

> Woe is me for my hurt! My wound is severe. But I say, Truly this is an infirmity, And I must bear it.

> My heart within me is broken Because of the prophets; All my bones shake. I am like a drunken man, And like a man whom wine has overcome, Because of the LORD, And because of His holy words.

Jesus slept while water was splashing into his boat and onto his body (Mark 4:38). Mere peace of heart doesn't explain His depth of sleep. It was also His physical disabling. Jesus constantly ministered to thousands of clamoring people—an unrelenting throughput of spirit. It's well-portrayed in Season 2 of the highly influential, crowd-funded series, *The Chosen*.

It's easy to see this disabling in pastors as well. In my observation, they underestimate the effect of their spiritual throughput. Pastors' defense against temptations weakens. They can turn to excesses or even sins for palliative relief. This explains why gluttony and adultery so easily beset pastors. We must deal rightly yet have mercy as well. Like our pastors, we need mercy.

Life through Death

What about Romans 8:11? The Holy Spirit gives life to our mortal bodies, Paul says. The spirit-disabling influence described above seems opposite. How does this fit with our experience?

God's Holy Spirit lives in our skin. The will and perception of our spirit activate and enable increasing intimacy with God. Our intimacy with Him replaces our reliance upon youthful resilience. His Holy Spirit supplies resurrection vitality to us, affecting even our physical body.

Youthful sufficiency eventually subsides, and one of two things occurs. On one hand, decaying forces beset those who are dead in spirit. The rate and method of decay vary widely. Although delay and mitigation are possible, the dead in spirit have no resource for restoring the lost youthfulness.

But us? We are filled with the Spirit that raised Jesus from the dead. He revitalizes us continually. He replaces our diminishing youthfulness with the stamina of heaven. Like an unseen heart, He pumps that same resurrection life-power through our bodies. Our very blood courses with the same Spirit who raised Jesus' dead body.

We still age. Jesus raised many from the dead, who aged and died again—even Lazarus. But we are filled with the Spirit that raised Jesus; therefore, we have greater expectations for our aging. We are relieved from the inevitability of decrepitude.

The Spirit Gives Life

How will the Holy Spirit give life to our mortal bodies? There is a counter-intuitive answer given by Jesus in Luke 9:24 and by Apostle Paul in 2 Corinthians 4:11.

> Whoever desires to save his life will lose it, but whoever loses his life for My sake will save it.

> For we who live are always delivered to death for Jesus' sake, that the life of Jesus also may be manifested in our mortal flesh.

Our physical bodies can manifest the vitality of the Holy Spirit in a dance of two forces, a partnership. Our daily disabling occurs as the unseen world engages our spirit. This engagement occurs on many horizons in our lives: social interactions, church participation, character growth, and work habits, to name a few.

An example common to all is the daily choice between relying on God, or upon ourselves. This choice is daily, minute by minute and second by second. When we pursue God, the tests multiply and can overwhelm our physical resources.

Those who hunger and thirst for righteousness choose death for fleshly self-reliance. The middle verse of the Protestant Bible, Psalm 118:8, describes it well.

It is better to trust in the LORD Than to put confidence in man.

Our spirits are alive. If we resolve to mature in spirit, our resolve affects every moment. He promises success to those seeking to mature. Our spirits become dominant over our flesh and over all of our lives. Our fellowship with God's Spirit inside us activates His physical resources. He then imparts His Holy Spirit vitality to our souls and bodies.

> For though He was crucified in weakness, yet He lives by the power of God. For we also are weak in Him, but we shall live with Him by the power of God toward you. (2 Corinthians 13:4)

The Body, Proving Ground for Spirit

The body and the natural self have a heavenly purpose: to provide a place for a human spirit to be born, and then provide a means of its testing, maturing, and proving.

Why wouldn't God provide a better body? Longer lasting? More capable? Superpowers? One reason: passing the test isn't a guaranteed result even if our bodies were perfect. Lucifer was created in perfection, yet rebelled. Perfection doesn't make sin unavoidable, because archangels Michael and Gabriel did not rebel. Adam and Eve were created in perfection, yet they sinned.

Another reason: the natural self, whether body, mind, or soul, is weak, and that is beneficial. Jesus said it this way: *"The spirit is willing, but the flesh is weak"* (Matthew 26:41). It's beneficial because the weakness of the natural is a necessary component of being a spirit.

Our spirit must be humbled and brought to meekness. It is not automatic. The body and the natural self provide the place for God to knead our spirits like dough. If we accept that, then we will become proven in the meekness necessary to be an exalted spirit in the kingdom of heaven.

Spirit and Resurrection

Jesus was born with both a natural body and a living spirit. After He died from crucifixion, His natural body rested in a tomb. Meanwhile, 1 Peter 3:19 says that His living spirit went to satan's prison. Jesus preached to the half-breeds with angelic paternity from before the flood (Genesis 6:1-6). Then Jesus rose from the dead, and His living spirit and body were reunited—plus, plus, plus.

He could walk through walls. People saw Him appear and disappear. Yet

Jesus also ate and showed His wounds to others. He could hide Himself from recognition. Jesus could breathe on people, He could build fires, and He could still produce miraculous catches of fish.

Our natural birth differs from Jesus who was never dead in spirit. But when we are saved as Christians, our spirit birth is just like His. Jesus first said this in John 3:3 to the famous teacher, Nicodemus. He asked Jesus if we had to reinsert ourselves into our mother's womb. This type of argumentation uses a nonsense picture, but Jesus persisted to explain we must be born of spirit—just like He was. Now, as Christians just like Him, we have both a natural body and a living spirit.

That's one reason He said things like John 14:12, *"Most assuredly, I say to you, he who believes in Me, the works that I do he will do also."*

Now His body is not among us—but His Holy Spirit is. He is among us, with us, and inside our skin. Jesus' natural body and spirit are reunited in the unseen realms to which He ascended.

So what about you? Like Jesus, a time will come that death separates your spirit and your natural body. Then they will be reunited in resurrection. And then will you be able to walk through walls, appear and disappear, like He did? Do you have to die before it happens? It doesn't sound like you do, from Jesus' statement: Whatever He did, the one who believes in Him will do better.

Who knows what lies ahead for our spirits as we mature?! Apostle Paul said that Creation itself eagerly awaits its freedom when the sons of God are revealed. Well, we are here now. Our bodies are part of physical creation, and they are eager to respond to the Holy Spirit living in us.

Eternal life permeated twentieth century evangelism because it addressed people's fear of death. This fear is less prominent in the twenty-first century, and eternal life is not motivating as it once was.

But there is a new desire awakening everywhere. It is the desire for a living spirit, so people can make sense of reality. Unlike eternal life in heaven, waiting until death is not required.

The powers of the coming age are here to taste already.

MIND MEETS SPIRIT

Technological advance in our times puts more demands on our minds. Otherwise, we would have called it techno-emotional or techno-physical. In a dance of the proverbial chicken and egg, more tech demands more mind, creates more tech, demands more mind, *ad nauseam*.

Such forces cause us to identify ourselves by our minds. One symptom: the aliens of modern fiction always have gigantic heads, and not big hearts or gigantic bodies.

Observation and Perception

We Christians are living spirits. Jesus welcomes us at an equal level to Himself. What else could He intend when the Bible says we are seated with Him in heaven? Or when He says we will do greater things because we believe in Him?

Our spirits interact with a world that is not known logically. We have no standard to impose upon it. No power of mind identifies or even perceives the world of unseen spirits. Mind is powerless to judge spirit and the unseen world.

Instead, the spirit world is internally logical to itself, not to us. To live where our spirits function fully, we must subordinate our natural logic to the internal logic of the unseeable world. To manifest Him truly, we believe that His full completeness dwells in us. *"For in Him dwells all the fullness of the Godhead bodily; and you are complete in Him, who is the head of all principality and power"* (Colossians 2:9–10).

For this to occur, our minds must submit to our spirits. This is difficult for us. Our Western civilization is so bankrupt in spirit that we have only the barest language and words even to express the idea.

Your spirit was born into an unseen world that you can observe and perceive. Your spirit, God's Spirit, and angelic spirits can be authoritatively, definitely, and accurately known. But none are known by your mind.

Our minds serve our spirits; there are at least two ways. The first is mentally observing what God says in the Bible. The second is assessing the godly consistency of spirit's perceptions. Our mind assesses the plausibility of our perceptions and matches them up with the Bible's revelation.

Spirit over Mind

In our day and society, we rely on our minds for control. I am glad we have such a means of control. Yet, if we impose our mind's limits on our spirit, we stunt our spirit's maturity.

The Bible's word *flesh* is our soul and body in combination, which encompasses our mind. Mind, like our flesh, must be tamed by spirit. The flesh and its mind are antagonistic to the spirit within us.

> I thank You, Father, Lord of heaven and earth, that You have hidden these things from the wise and prudent and have revealed them to babes. (Matthew 11:25)

> For the flesh lusts against the Spirit, and the Spirit against the flesh; and these are contrary to one another. (Galatians 5:17)

> That which is born of the flesh is flesh, and that which is born of the Spirit is spirit. (John 3:6)

> Beware lest anyone cheat you through philosophy and empty deceit, according to the tradition of men, according to the basic principles of the world, and not according to Christ. (Colossians 2:8)

The highest and best use of your mind is yielding it to your spirit. Your spirit made alive is where you fellowship with God—not in your mind. Your mind is part of God's image. Its purpose is to serve your spirit as you walk with God through life.

Denominations

God distributed His Church into many denominations over the last five hundred years. Each tells its members what they must believe and must not. Boundaries include not only beliefs but also acceptable behaviors, both moral and organizational.

Boundaries are important. Even the Garden of Eden had boundaries. Our reading of God's Word must fall within God's boundaries.

Each denomination has preapproved interpretations of the Bible. With these, it distinguishes itself and protects its members. These interpretations often originated from true Christian experience or in scriptural theology. Martyrs forged them in blood. Gifted minds formulated these interpretations and limits. Whatever your Christian group, don't lightly regard these hard-won and long-tested protocols.

These same preapproved interpretations are often misused—for control.

Many Christians use their mind only within the framework of their group's preapproved beliefs. One motive for such self-limitation is lack of confidence in themselves. Another is the desire to fit into their group.

And leaders in the name of guarding the flock will sometimes prohibit even the asking of unapproved questions. These are some reasons that church participation is not the same as being born again. Many are the testimonies of people being saved after years in church.

I Want It All

We become a living spirit because we follow and yield to Jesus Christ. This event of spiritual birth does not require us to disavow our group's boundaries. Within its lines, we can use our minds to explore. We can devote our mental powers to justifying the boundaries themselves.

We living spirits have the same potential that Adam had in Eden—and the same power of choice. Jesus constantly presents a choice question to each of us: "How much do you want?" He honors our power of choice by letting us have what we choose.

I choose to follow Jesus no holds barred, wherever He leads. My choice requires me to subordinate my former boundaries and protocols. This includes my old limits and habits of thought. Each of these Scriptures expresses the necessity of leaving old ideas, limits, and comfort zones.

> When I was a child, I spoke as a child, I understood as a child, I thought as a child; but when I became a man, I put away childish things. (1 Corinthians 13:11)

> So Elisha turned back from him, and took his yoke of oxen and slaughtered them and boiled their flesh, using the oxen's equipment, and gave it to the people, and they ate. Then he arose and followed Elijah and became his servant. (1 Kings 19:21)

> Then Jesus said to them, "Follow Me, and I will make you become fishers of men." They immediately left their nets and followed Him... And immediately He called them, and they left their father Zebedee in the boat with the hired servants, and went after Him. (Mark 1:17–18,21)

> Then He said to another, "Follow Me." But he said, "Lord, let me first go and bury my father." Jesus said to him, "Let the dead bury their own dead, but you go and preach the kingdom of God." (Luke 9:59–60)

We outgrow former limits, protocols, and obligations—even good ones—by maturing in the spirit. My wife and I identify ourselves as MethoBapTerIcAliaCostals for this reason. In each of those groups, we have grown. We received lasting benefit from them. And from each we left. Growing in spirit, we outgrew the limits imposed.

When you want it all, you leave things you like, to pursue Him. This puts you in abject dependency on what He says. It's a good thing.

Man shall not live by bread alone, but by every word of God. (Luke 4:4)

As newborn babes, desire the pure milk of the word, that you may grow thereby, if indeed you have tasted that the Lord is gracious. (1 Peter 2:2–3)

Simon Peter answered Him, "Lord, to whom shall we go? You have the words of eternal life." (John 6:68)

How Do You Know?

This dependent hunger for Him and His words fully unleashes our minds. Old blindfolds upon our thinking fall away. We read the Bible, and it explodes in our spirits. What we have heard and read for years is new. Truths we thought we knew yield incomprehensible depths. This engagement with God in the Bible is the sign that your spirit is receiving its nourishment.

One milestone of maturity is the fifth Beatitude, *"Blessed are those who hunger and thirst for righteousness, for they shall be filled"* (Matthew 5:6). In simple terms: you always want more of the Word of God. You are never satisfied; you never feel you need no more.

Observation

The Bible is easily the most influential book in human history. People of every nation, tribe, and tongue hold their Bibles dearer than life itself. This is because God has "electrified" His Word with His intimacy.

Our minds serve our spirits by studying it. While our levels of interest can vary, many are those who study its original languages, who spend hours daily in its pages, who paste Scriptures wherever the eyes may land.

Each of us is accountable to use our minds, especially observing what God says in His Word. Among people are unique abilities, aptitudes, and opportunities. He judges each by the ones He gave to us—not what He gave to someone else.

What all are accountable for is to observe what's in the Bible. Everyone's mind can do it, at some level. Observation is submission. It's possible to come to the Bible with predetermined ideas, and the only things we will see in it reinforce our predetermined conclusions. This is deductive reasoning, and not true observation.

Deductive reasoning is like the prosecution and defense in a trial. Each has predetermined their conclusions. All facts they choose to present support their preconceived notions. But not everyone in the trial may use deductive reasoning. The jury must use inductive reasoning, holding off the temptation to prejudge the case. They must listen to all the facts from both prosecution and defense. The jury can't exclude any but must weigh all the facts presented. Inductive reasoning only reaches a conclusion based on all the observable facts.

We must come to Scripture with inductive reasoning. Laying aside the things we want it to say, we observe what it actually says.

God gave us powerful minds. They can expose and conquer our preconceived notions. Book Two of the *Unseen* series is *Nobody Sees This Unseen Realm: How to Unlock Bible Mysteries*. Using our minds for observation will be a significant topic there.

Perception and Plausibility

Our mind's second area of service to our spirits is to test what they perceive. Mental logic cannot know the unseen world of spirit, but with our minds, we can compare our perceptions to the Word of God and test them.

God is very reliable. He has honored His Word. Nothing God does will go against His Word. By our observations of what the Bible says, we get the boundary lines for what our spirits perceive.

After your unseen spirit activates, you can see the unseen world—good and bad alike. You are a ruler in the kingdom of God. Lest you overestimate your competency for this position, remember that your primary qualification is that you are poor in spirit.

Blessed are the poor in spirit, for theirs is the kingdom of heaven. (Matthew 5:3)

To function effectively in the unseen kingdom is impossible for our spirits without God's instruction, the Bible. We study and memorize the Bible with our minds. Every moment of the day, our minds can apply what we have learned in the Bible. Meanwhile, our living spirits continually perceive unseen reality. Our minds help test that perception by matching it with the Word of God.

The match may not be one-for-one, or direct, or cause and effect, or testable. Logic in the spirit world is foreign to your mind. The mind is the servant, and your spirit is the judge. The match is made with your mind; the judgment is made in your spirit. Often, the mind can only test plausibility; it cannot test reality. The events, persons, encounters, and dimensions of the unseen world defy the limits our minds require.

Suppose this example. An angel makes himself perceptible to you. How do you recognize the perception? Not mentally, but in your spirit. Your first impression is, he wants to assist you because he sees God's favor on you. How do you test if your perception is accurate? The mind can't do it; no element of the encounter is measurable mentally.

But your mind can match what your spirit perceives with what the Word of God says, such as Hebrews 1:14, *"Are they* [angels] *not all ministering spirits sent forth to minister for those who will inherit salvation?"*

Take the example a different direction. Suppose that the angel you perceive instructs you to rebuke satan. Your mind can supply the appropriate Scripture, Jude 8–9, *"Likewise also these dreamers defile the flesh, reject authority, and speak evil of dignitaries. Yet Michael the archangel, in contending with the devil, when he disputed about the body of Moses, dared not bring against him a reviling accusation, but said, "The Lord rebuke you!"*

Your mind sees a mismatch between the Scripture (the *Lord* rebukes satan) and the angel's instruction (*you* rebuke satan). Your mind helps your spirit to make the judgment, "This is not a holy angel my spirit perceives, but a deceiving one." This is exactly the type of mental recognition Jesus required when satan quoted Scripture to Him in the desert temptations.

For your mind to serve your spirit, read and study the Word of God habitually. Whatever your past shortfall, you can start afresh.

Mental Health

Using the full power of mind available to us, our society funds a huge health care system. Risk-capital investment enables all the research, studies, and facilities. Such investment predisposes all medical training to prescribe the treatments the system needs to continue. This is not bad; we need our medical technology and systems.

But if all we have is a hammer, then all we see is nails. Likewise, if all we have is medical or psychological resources, then we will see such causation in every condition. Our tech-heavy world mentalizes and medicalizes human problems. Sin, spiritual oppression, and spiritual confusion are diagnoses of last resort, if considered at all. The unseen world's influence on mental health is completely ignored by many.

This willful blindness to the unseen world obscures its potent contribution to mental disturbance and upset. What better place to hide an evil, unseen influence than in mental confusion or instability? But health practitioners will medicalize and psychoanalyze even demonic oppression. The very word *psyche* comes from the Greek word in the Bible used for our soul.

The unseen world affects our minds in another way. Spiritual perception can mess with a person's mind. In the Bible, those who receive revelation are sometimes unable to respond. As a side effect, it can be much harder to respect or meet mainstream behavioral expectations. Society shoves aside such people, and even institutionalizes them when this happens.

Correct diagnosis of mental health ignores no causation—even when the unseen world is its cause. Nor does demonic oppression in mental health problems disqualify medical treatments. No potential cause or treatment is out of bounds for consideration.

Of this principle there is no better exemplar known to me than Dr. Paul Tournier, the Christian Swiss psychologist whose works are still readily available, such as *The Healing of Persons*[5].

Not Cheap

Do you want to mature as a spirit? Then a free observation of the Word of God is absolutely indispensable. Responding to the invitation of God in the Bible requires work and sacrifice.

My wife and I have left home and family to grow as spirits and to plumb God's Word. We have paid a personal cost in relationships, churches, business, friendships, financial security, and family peace. Jesus' disciples and early Christians all did the same. Jesus put it in stark terms in Luke 9:26 and 14:26.

> No one, having put his hand to the plow, and looking back, is fit for the kingdom of God.

> If anyone comes to Me and does not hate his father and mother, wife and children, brothers and sisters, yes, and his own life also, he cannot be My disciple.

We want to be fit for the kingdom of God. Economic production is still a necessity, as is medical care, family love, and other responsible actions. Yet all are subordinate for someone who has put their hand to the plow.

Jesus has rewarded my wife and me. He will reward your choice to go higher up and further in.

CREATION MEETS SPIRIT

Creation, all of physical reality, responds to me as a living spirit. Creation doesn't respond to someone who is dead in spirit. Such a person would interact with created physical reality like my shoes interact with a sidewalk—using it, but not engaged with it.

Physical Reality

> It is the Spirit who gives life; the flesh profits nothing. The words that I speak to you are spirit, and they are life. (John 6:63)

We read this metaphorically—as though Jesus is using an analogy. This is a habit we use often, to dismiss what the Bible says. In fact, He is describing reality.

God, a Spirit, created all physical reality. Physical creation is the fruit of spirit reality. God's unseen world is the original, superior, determinative, and binding reality. Jesus presumed these truths in Matthew 16:19.

> Whatever you bind on earth will be bound in heaven, and whatever you loose on earth will be loosed in heaven.

With this understanding, the Scripture is much more easily explained. Jesus said the flesh counts for nothing. He knew that nothing in the physical world is primary, contrary to our thinking. The unseen world is primary.

God made Adam and Eve from Earth's dust, and told them to dominate all of it in Genesis 1:27–32. His command had a universal scope and authority. Adam and Eve were entire beings in God's image: body, soul, and spirit. They were not cavemen who would forage, hunt mammoth, and make babies.

Jesus had Jewish admirers after He fed the five thousand. He told them they could not live without the food that was His body and His blood. Besides offending them, Jesus also expressed the reality that physical is subject to spirit: *"It is the Spirit who gives life; the flesh profits nothing"* (John 6:63).

Look at our hidden beliefs about prayer. Our petitions about a problem make it sound like physical reality is more binding, harder to change, and superior in influence versus spirit reality. Thus, from the outset, our prayer is out of bounds. Our hidden beliefs about physical reality are out of sync with God. They are out of sync with Creation, who recognizes our authority as the sons of God.

When we ask for spiritual intervention by God, it reveals that hidden belief that physical reality has authority over our living spirits. The Hebrews did this as well. When Pharaoh's army had the Hebrews cornered, the people cried out to the Lord as if He had abandoned them to die. He replied to Moses in Exodus 14:15–16, *"Why do you cry to Me? Tell the children of Israel to go forward. But lift up your rod, and stretch out your hand over the sea and divide it."*

God didn't do anything. He told Moses to do it. Physical Creation was subordinate to the authority of Moses and mankind. We don't trust this, and it is one reason our prayers and miracles aren't manifesting at the rate expected.

God answers some prayers, with patience for our immaturity. Suppose a child has a demanding attitude. His or her parents want the child to ask politely, but recognize that time and consequences are needed. If the child asks a little more politely each time, the parent rewards him. "Well, he has momentum, and he's trying. We'll keep training him." The parents agree to the child's request, even though he didn't ask perfectly.

God would prefer to answer all our prayers, and waits for us to grow into mature faith that He and His will are superior to every roadblock. Jesus put it emphatically and unmistakably in John 14:12–14:

> Most assuredly, I say to you, he who believes in Me, the works that I do he will do also; and greater works than these he will do, because I go to My Father. And whatever you ask in My name, that I will do, that the Father may be glorified in the Son. If you ask anything in My name, I will do it.

The Jealousy of God

James 4:2–3 says, *"When you ask, you ask wrongly, out of friendship with the world. Do you not know how jealous God is?"* At the moment that a disappointment or need presses in, we can make it even worse by activating God's jealousy. We do this when we can least afford it. How?

Friendship with the world includes treasuring it more than Him. We are friends with the world when we identify the physical world as most binding, most determinative, and most impossible.

Our God is jealous in response. He feels we are asking Him and the world of spirit to become subordinate to the physical where we feel the need.

The Magnetism of Creation

Jesus' three-year ministry proved the supremacy of His Spirit over every element of Creation. The apostles likewise raised the dead, healed the lame, and spoke words of life and of death. The Bible shows Creation repeatedly responding to them.

The apostles' kingdom purposes activated a magnetism in Creation. Paul described us Christians as the sons of God in Romans 8:19–22. The advent of living spirits on Earth activates physical Creation. Paul's words *until now* signify that Creation was released as soon as people became living spirits through the gospel. The Bible says that Creation itself rejoices to partner with us.

> For the earnest expectation of the creation eagerly waits for the revealing of the sons of God. For the creation was subjected to futility, not willingly, but because of Him who subjected it in hope; because the creation itself also will be delivered from the bondage of corruption into the glorious liberty of the children of God. For we know that the whole creation groans and labors with birth pangs together until now.

Creation has a delight in you as a living spirit. Wherever you touch it, there is an effect. It wants to respond. The Christian fiction of C. S. Lewis, J. R. R. Tolkien, George MacDonald, and Charles Williams all depicts this magnetism. Serving you befits Creation's purpose—the kingdom of God manifested in His image-creatures.

Creation delights to serve living spirits who are intimate with God its Creator. Serving us releases Creation from its long sleep of frustration.

The Authority of the Christian Spirit

Jesus gave us authority to bind and loose on Earth. He also gave us the mirror authority in heaven. This authority presumes that our spirits are authoritative over our bodies and all physical reality. What we bind in heaven is bound on Earth precisely because the spirit is where all binding and loosing originates.

The kingdom of darkness dreads us for that reason. If we awaken to our level of authority, they have no refuge from us. We are the big dogs in their unseen world. After all, it isn't the gates of the world that retreat before us, but the gates of hell—the dominion of darkness. The authority in the unseen which we have as living spirits is unexcelled.

So they deceive us to be ignorant and afraid of that reality. Darkness cannot contest our authority in the world they consider their own. *"I will build My church, and the gates of Hades shall not prevail against it"* (Matthew 16:18).

God welcomes us into the unseen and gives us spirit birth. Yet after becoming spirits, we continue undervaluing spirit in favor of the physical. When we fixate on physical reality and surrender as if it's primary, we agree with darkness—not with God.

The thousand-year reign of Christ in Revelation 20 shows the supremacy of spiritual reality over physical reality (and social as well). Life on Earth is so prosperous for that entire time—how?

Christians and the Church face three opposing forces: the world, the flesh, and the devil. The devil and the demonic powers are exiled during that one-thousand-year reign, but the world and the flesh remain. Despite their presence, the global reign of Christ is secure for the entire millennium.

This shows the dominant reality is the spiritual. Jesus, with His Church, is the only contestant in the spirit world. The world and the flesh are subdued by the spirit. Their influence cannot override the authority of our spirits in concert with Jesus.

Not everyone is saved during that period. Only with the release of the second contestant—satan—do people suddenly contest the reign of Christ. When the millennium ends, the vast bulk of humanity aligns with the devil in his last-gasp effort. But until satan's release, even the wickedness of the unsaved is subdued.

Because of our earth-centered thinking, we consider spirit to be an overlay upon the natural. We are like the medieval world before Copernicus, thinking everything revolves around what we see before us. In fact, the spirit is primary, original, and superseding. Physical reality is a fitting and desirable expression of it.

When Jesus fasted forty days, He was stripped of the old way. He returned in the power of the Spirit—so described by people who thought of the physical as most real and of the spirit as an addendum, a power, a force.

In fact, He had spent those forty days in close contact with the unseen: conversations and interaction with satan and supply by angels and even by wild animals given favor for Him. After that, He saw the true basis of all that is: *"Man shall not live by bread alone but by every word that proceeds from the mouth of God"* (Matthew 4:4).

Apostle John came to understand this. He used the available words and concepts to describe to his hearers and readers what we are saying above, namely: everything originated and had its being in the works of spirit, and what we experience as reality is a consistent expression of it.

With this in mind, reread the prologue to John's gospel:

In the beginning was the Word, and the Word was with God, and the Word was God. He was in the beginning with God.

All things were made through Him, and without Him nothing was made that was made.

In Him was life, and the life was the light of men. And the light shines in the darkness, and the darkness did not comprehend it.

He was in the world, and the world was made through Him, and the world did not know Him.

But as many as received Him, to them He gave the right to become children of God, to those who believe in His name: who were born, not of blood, nor of the will of the flesh, nor of the will of man, but of God. (John 1:1–5, 10, 12–13)

***Reflection and discussion questions for this chapter
are in the back of the book***

CHAPTER SEVEN

LIVING AMONG SPIRITS

OBLIGATIONS

In the unseen world, the host of heaven is attentive to obligations. Spirit beings operate according to obligations—a first principle of their being. Relationship and commitment are core characteristics of spirit.

The continual worship in heaven is revealed in Revelation chapters 4 and 5. The songs of the cherubim, the angels, and the saints all begin with one statement that God commands obligation: *"You are worthy."*

The kingdom of darkness is equally concerned about obligations. It consists of formerly holy angels, and a cherub who was created perfect but fell. By their created nature, they work by obligations. But in contrast to our kingdom, the structure of darkness is a rigid command structure with hierarchical inflexibility and a penal code that never varies. Begun by a rebel, the kingdom of darkness is hyper-vigilant against rebellion, and none has ever been revealed within its ranks.

Isaiah describes satan's ultimate demise in chapter 14, where his former subordinates taunt him about his humiliation. References to satan's former greatness include these excerpts from Isaiah 14:5–17. Each statement presumes the oppressive and unrelenting authority that satan exercised while roaming the earth.

> The LORD has broken the staff of the wicked, The scepter of the rulers; He who struck the people in wrath with a continual stroke, He who ruled the nations in anger, is persecuted and no one hinders. The whole earth is at rest and quiet; They break forth into singing.

"Have you also become as weak as we? Have you become like us? Is this the man who made the earth tremble, Who shook kingdoms, Who made the world as a wilderness And destroyed its cities, Who did not open the house of his prisoners?"

Jesus drove many demons into pigs in Mark 5. Even they expressed fear about returning to the prison system of darkness. For those demons, oppressing human beings must have felt like shore leave feels to a sailor who serves in the boiler room.

Whether holy or evil, the host of heavenly spirits can be recognized by their obligations.

IDENTIFICATION

To be active as a living, ruling spirit in the unseen world calls for discernment. How do we identify our spirit, the unseen, and the beings of the spirit world? If the Bible assumes spirit, then how do we navigate socially among them?

Identifying Spirit

If Apostle John wanted to write a letter to help Christians identify and know unseen reality, then his first letter would be the exact result. Repeated phrases include *"by this we know"* and *"if someone says but."* Frequent words include *know, darkness, world*, and *love*.

What are the signs we expect when the unseen kingdom of heaven is manifesting? Miracles, angels, prophecies, deliverance, church success, emotions, crowds, feeling God's presence, authority, excellent preaching, authority, and followers.

Jesus tells us to expect the miraculous: *"these signs will follow those who believe."* He said also, *"by their fruits you will know them"* (Mark 16:17–18, Matthew 7:20). Paul said such works were the marks of an apostle also (2 Corinthians 12:12).

Miracles and fruit can be signs of unseen reality—but their presence is not a sufficient indicator of God's kingdom. Miracles may not signify the desired unseen reality! *"Many will say to Me on that day, Lord, Lord, have we not prophesied in Your name, cast out demons in Your name, and done many wonders in Your name? Then I will declare to them, 'I never knew you; depart from Me, you evildoers'"* (Matthew 7:22–23).

John's signs of the spirit provide a deeper window. He does not mention the miraculous signs. It is a fellowship (1 John 1:3) in which God's testimony is uppermost (1:1–4, 5:6–11). In relationship with Him, there is communication that is intimate. A relationship with the Father is effective in the natural (1:2-2:2, 2: 27, 3:18–23, 5:11–16). God has put within us as an anointing to know all things (2:20–27). As a result, the biblical consistency of our beliefs about Jesus and His commandments is also a sign of the spirit (2:3–8, 18–27, 3:18–4:6, 5:3–5).

The fellowship is not only internal for you and God. It is also external, toward others—both within and without the fellowship of the saved. Signs of the unseen spirit include an ever-increasing purity of life (1:5–2:8, 3:28–9, 5:17–21) and perfected, reciprocated love that is free of fear between Him and us (2:9–14, 3:10–17, 4:7–5:2). Even the world sees our differentiation (3:10–15).

The divine analogy undergirds all that John writes in his first letter. This analogy says, as Jesus is to the Father, so are we to Jesus. One such verse is 4:17, *"As He is, so are we in this world."*

Just as miracles do not signify God's kingdom, neither does trouble say we are outside His kingdom. We all want the comforts of a tranquil life and work to get them. But their presence or absence is not an evidence of a living spirit.

Consider Apostle Paul. His life contained all the miraculous signs, yet none of the comfort and ease we expect. He had to fend off influential people who wowed the Corinthians (2 Corinthians 10:7–12:13), and Jewish Christians who perverted the gospel among the Galatians (6:12–13). He had to plead for his life in Roman courts and suffered all his life (2 Corinthians 11:23–29). Clearly, Apostle Paul had a living spirit! But the evidence of a living spirit did not include comfort and ease—not for Jesus, nor for His apostles, and not for us.

Senses for Identification

The Lord's guidance to me about identification and discernment was cited earlier. "To function as a living spirit, with the authorities and responsibilities I've outlined in Scripture, you need the ability to perceive spirits. I give you that. It is included in being a maturing living spirit, and especially necessary for fulfilling your calling."

This is a fact of life for Christians. The *Unseen* series is motivated to impart this confidence to all Christians.

Dead Spirits

In the world of spirit exists one razor-sharp principle: either we respond to God as He deserves, or we do not. Doing so makes us worshippers; otherwise not. People can't survive as spirits without His word of life. God told our first parents, *"In the day you eat of it, you shall surely die"* (Genesis 2:17). Adam and Eve lived nine hundred years more. Yet they were dead in spirit, from the moment they went their own way.

Wait a minute. Adam and Eve were created as living spirits, and then they died as spirits. Can that happen to me? Can I put my faith in Jesus, be saved, be born as a living spirit, and yet die in spirit like Adam and Eve?

A related question: was Judas alive in spirit? Judas did miracles and cast out demons (Luke 10:1–20).

Jesus did not talk in outlines, and did not give a direct answer to this puzzle. But the Scripture reveals guidance about it.

In the parable of the talents in Matthew 25:30, Jesus included a servant given one talent who did not meet his master's expectations. *"Cast the unprofitable servant into the outer darkness. There will be weeping and gnashing of teeth."*

Another Scripture is Hebrews 6:4–6 which says, yes, people born as spirits can die.

> For it is impossible for those who were once enlightened, and have tasted the heavenly gift, and have become partakers of the Holy Spirit and have tasted the good word of God and the powers of the age to come, if they fall away, to renew them again to repentance, since they crucify again for themselves the Son of God, and put Him to an open shame.

Jesus was clear, as was Paul, that when we are unfaithful to Him, it is not without consequence. *"But whoever denies Me before men, him I will also deny before My Father who is in heaven"* (Matthew 10:33). And 2 Timothy 2:12 says, *"If we deny Him, He also will deny us."*

On the other side, Scripture gives ample assurance: if we are faithful to Him, He is faithful to us.

> Therefore whoever confesses Me before men, him I will also confess before My Father who is in heaven. (Matthew 10:32)

> He who has begun a good work in you will complete it until the day of Jesus Christ. (Philippians 1:6)

> Work out your own salvation with fear and trembling; for it is God who works in you both to will and to do for His good pleasure. (Philippians 2:12–13)

Therefore, it is appropriate to fear God, even as Christians. *"And do not fear those who kill the body but cannot kill the soul. But rather fear Him who is able to destroy both soul and body in hell"* (Matthew 10:28).

We know we are poor in spirit and meek, not equal to His truth. We mourn we cannot give Him what He deserves, and repent.

I do not want to find out if my spirit can die. I want to finish as a living spirit.

YOUR SPIRIT AND EVIL ONES

The approach of a holy angel is terrible if unveiled. In their presence, our poverty of spirit is acutely palpable. Holy angels in the Bible gravely intimidated everyone who met with them.

The evil angels are still angelic; they too are intimidating. But they are twisted to deceit. Their purpose is eternal spiritual death for you.

Darkness has failed to keep you dead, away from Jesus, and unborn as a living spirit. But its evil spirits continue their efforts to trick you back if they can.

God's Use for Darkness

God has delayed the imprisonment of satan and evil spirits—but why?

That's not even the hardest question. First Kings 22, Job 1–3 and other passages show satan having access to God's presence. How can this be? Take it further, to actual cooperation between God and evil spirits, so that they afflict Saul and Ahab with God's authorization. Apostle Paul describes more such cooperation in 2 Thessalonians 2:7–11.

> For the mystery of lawlessness is already at work; only He who now restrains will do so until He is taken out of the way.... And for this reason [refusal to love the truth] God will send them strong delusion, that they should believe the lie.

Apostle Paul actually experienced God's cooperation with darkness. He wrote of a messenger of satan that God sent, when he described his thorn in the flesh.

> And lest I should be exalted above measure by the abundance of the revelations, a thorn in the flesh was given to me, a messenger of Satan to buffet me, lest I be exalted above measure. Concerning this thing I pleaded with the Lord three times that it might depart from me. And He said to me, "My grace is sufficient for you, for My strength is made perfect in weakness" (2 Corinthians 12:7–9).

And really the hardest question of all is how the Holy Spirit drove Jesus into the wilderness for the treatment He received from satan there. *"Then Jesus was led up by the Spirit into the wilderness to be tempted by the devil"* (Matthew 4:1).

Why does God permit satan to run loose? Because He uses the evil enemies to test us, and to help us mature into proven spirits.

We can fail the test. Saul and Ahab did. David did also (1 Chronicles 21:1–8). Peter did, and Jesus had to rebuke him once and restore him three times (Matthew 16:23, John 21:15–19). We can also pass the test as Apostle Paul did.

> Therefore, most gladly I will rather boast in my infirmities, that the power of Christ may rest upon me. Therefore, I take pleasure in infirmities, in reproaches, in needs, in persecutions, in distresses, for Christ's sake. For when I am weak, then I am strong (2 Corinthians 12:9–10).

Some Christians take an inordinate pleasure in this intercourse with spirits. Jude 8–9 warns against this pride, which belies their poverty of spirit. A meek person cannot engage with spirits lightly. When we are meek, we have the attitude of archangel Michael.

> Likewise also these dreamers defile the flesh, reject authority, and speak evil of dignitaries. Yet Michael the archangel, in contending with the devil, when he disputed about the body of Moses, dared not bring against him a reviling accusation, but said, 'The Lord rebuke you!'

Spirit and Miracle-Deception

These realizations amplify hints and perceptions I've had for years.

In the past chapters, I've repeatedly cited Matthew 7:21–23, which says, *"There Jesus says, Depart from Me, you evildoers; I never knew you."* He is at least saying that these works—casting out demons, prophesying in His name and doing many mighty miracles—are not a sufficient sign we know Him. Their presence does not validate that we are on His side, nor that it is His Spirit behind our works.

Jesus' word for those people is *evildoers*. The allegiance of those people is to evil, and it is evil spirits which do the spirit-level works that deceive. Paul wrote of such deceiving masqueraders.

> And no wonder! For Satan himself transforms himself into an angel of light. Therefore it is no great thing if his ministers also transform themselves into ministers of righteousness, whose end will be according to their works (2 Corinthians 11:14–15).

Would the kingdom of darkness actually drive their own demons out of people? Yes. Jesus said in Luke 11:18 that the kingdom of darkness will fall because it is divided.

President Lincoln used the principle to justify saving the Union: *"a kingdom divided against itself cannot stand."* That's not the use Jesus intended for His principle. Jesus knew the kingdom of darkness would fall and He wanted it to fall. He said what would happen (its fall) because it is divided. That's precisely what we want for our unseen enemies and their kingdom.

If Matthew 7:21-23 evildoing characterizes the kingdom of darkness, what, by inverse, must characterize the kingdom of light?

The first and foremost contrast is relationship. On our Judgment Day assessment, He will say to us faithful, "Yes, I have known you," in contrast to "I never knew you." For Him to make that statement to me on Judgment Day signifies that He and I are intimate. My primary spirit-attention was on Him in my lifetime.

John 17:3 means that knowing Him is the primary driver in every respect of everything that is done by my spirit. *"This is eternal life, that they may know You, the only true God, and Jesus Christ whom You have sent."*

The spirit world is so potent and so mysterious to our natural selves! It is possible for evil spirits to trick us—that, we know. But to cast out demons, to do miracles, and to prophesy in His name? Jesus says: yes, darkness can use those to do evil.

Jesus identified this in the Jewish leaders who ultimately crucified Him. By saying to them, *"You are of your father, the devil,"* (John 8:44) He exposed their spiritual paternity. Jesus saw their allegiance to the Bible—and also identified that as evil, in John 5:39–40.

You search the Scriptures, for in them you think you have eternal life; and these are they which testify of Me. But you are not willing to come to Me that you may have life.

We can cooperate with darkness in Bible study, deliverance, prophecy, and miracles. Our capacity for this evil partnership is well-documented—in the Bible, in history, in church, and in our lives. It's one reason the Bible warns repeatedly about false teachers, false prophets, and false shepherds. The things of God are useful to darkness to fool Christians.

And darkness is useful to God. He is testing and proving us: is He our first love?

Our primary attention must be to God Himself and not to His things. It is very clear that if our living spirit is to remain holy and stay consecrated, there is only one thing to pay attention to. That is Him, the knowing of Him, the recognizing of His voice, the obedience to His commands, the readiness and the attentiveness to His commands. *"No one engaged in warfare entangles himself with the affairs of this life, that he may please him who enlisted him as a soldier"* (2 Timothy 2:4).

IOU'S

> Through your widespread trade you were filled with violence, and you sinned. (Ezekiel 28:16 NIV)

Lucifer became satan by rebelling against God. Ezekiel 28 tells us of that time.

There, God reveals the activity of trading in heaven—but how? He tells how, comprehensively, in two related passages, Ezekiel 27 and Revelation 17–18. Deeper study is in Book Nine of the *Unseen* series, *Nobody Sees This Victory Yet: Defeating Darkness*. Here, we will only introduce trading in the unseen. We want to expose the backing of this tapestry.

Trading can create IOU relationships. As true as it is in the natural, it is even more true in the spirit. Spirit beings operate according to obligations—a first principle of their being. "I owe you" is a statement of obligation. We also call them tit-for-tat relationships.

In Ezekiel 28, Lucifer's widespread trade occurred before there was mankind. Who did he trade with? Angels were the only beings then created outside the cherubim. He had the most prized privilege to offer them: access to God, whose throne he guarded.

But what could they offer him? He was created perfect and already had full access to God Himself. He could only require them to write IOUs—a payment to be determined later. Plausibly, it was the IOU relationships with Lucifer that obligated a third of heaven's angels to support his rebellion.

The contrast in God's responses to the fallen angels and us mortal people is vast. God accepts us graciously. He places no IOUs on us for access to His throne. He welcomes us. *"Let us therefore come boldly to the throne of grace, that we may obtain mercy and find grace to help in time of need"* (Hebrews 4:16).

Like the father of the prodigal son in Luke 15, He embraces us as if we had never sinned at all. The Son of God fully satisfied the price of our sin. Jesus gave Himself to receive the penalty for all our sins.

We therefore are under grace, not under law and its system of obligations. Our only obligation is the appropriate honor for such love; all else we freely give Him.

For this One has been counted worthy of more glory than Moses, inasmuch as He who built the house has more honor than the house (Hebrews 3:3).

I have been crucified with Christ; it is no longer I who live, but Christ lives in me; and the life which I now live in the flesh I live by faith in the Son of God, who loved me and gave Himself for me. (Galatians 2:20)

A spirit is capable of community and commitment. Thus, darkness can entice and seduce us living spirits into IOUs which obligate us to the dominion of darkness. That's how Lucifer roped a third of heaven's angels into his ill-advised rebellion. Their reward: eternal damnation.

We must be meek, with a proper estimate of our defenses. Our poverty in spirit makes us vulnerable to the IOU seduction of darkness. Although I am a living spirit indwelt by the Holy Spirit of God, I can choose the obligatory IOU relationships offered by darkness.

The kingdom of darkness sneaks them into my path, to erode my agreement with God. Whether fast or slow matters not to them, as long as there is erosion. The less I agree with God, the more I agree with them.

Testing exposes this. Surely, the trials of this life are beneficial. Will I be like the third of the angels that were seduced into Lucifer's IOU? Will my dullness to their seduction point me to hell, like theirs did?

No, I say: the blood of Jesus bought me, lock, stock, and barrel. I am a living spirit by the grace of God. Weak in myself, I rely entirely on His Holy Spirit to give me what I need. I repudiate the tit-for-tat relationship with Him.

> Oh, the depth of the riches both of the wisdom and knowledge of God! How unsearchable are His judgments and His ways past finding out!
> "For who has known the mind of the Lord? Or who has become His counselor?" "Or who has first given to Him And it shall be repaid to him?"
> For of Him and through Him and to Him are all things, to whom be glory forever. Amen. (Romans 11:33–36)

BOUNDARIES

I can bind spirits. You, Christian, can bind spirits. It's contained in being a living spirit that lives solely and entirely by the life-giving Holy Spirit of God. Binding is one family of action with boundaries.

So, Lord Jesus, can I set boundaries as a spirit, that other spirits must observe?

"Yes. You and other Christians fear that if you assert this binding authority, they will defy and even attack you—as the demons of Ephesus attacked the seven sons of Sceva in Acts 19. You are afraid of being exposed as weak if you set boundaries for evil spirits.

"But the evil spirits themselves see My authority in you and they fear your binding. So they deceptively promote fear in you—as if you are the weak ones. The seven sons of Sceva didn't know Me. The kingdom of darkness did not see any authority in them.

"They fear you because you are the carriers of Me whom they dread. That's why they knew My name and Paul's, who had demonstrated authority there previously. The spirits of darkness are nothing, less than nothing, so set your boundaries. The evil spirits must respect them."

This fits the Word of God. Wherever I set my boundaries, there is a flood of living water. Jesus said it, not merely as a promise but as a fact of unseen reality.

> He who believes in Me, as the Scripture has said, out of his heart will flow rivers of living water. (John 7:38)

For out of the abundance of the heart, the mouth speaks. A good man out of the good treasure of his heart brings forth good things, and an evil man out of the evil treasure brings forth evil things. (Matthew 12:34–35)

Agreed Boundaries

Not that we merely establish defensive perimeters! Nor do we set boundaries against evil so we can protect earthly comforts. Scripture is clear about the purpose for us to establish boundaries in the spirit.

Enlarge the place of your tent, And let them stretch out the curtains of your dwellings; Do not spare; Lengthen your cords, And strengthen your stakes. For you shall expand to the right and to the left, And your descendants will inherit the nations, And make the desolate cities inhabited. (Isaiah 54:2–3)

Your kingdom come. Your will be done On earth as it is in heaven. (Matthew 6:10)

When the Israelites invaded Canaan, they challenged and erased the borders of the previous occupants. We too challenge the boundaries of the evil spirits. They don't penetrate our boundaries; we penetrate theirs.

That was Apostle Paul's calling. As apostle to the Gentiles, he penetrated the territory of a different principality on every trip. At every stop, in almost every place, he challenged long-held property lines of darkness. The inhabitants were long-blinded by that territory's principality. Both he and his companions suffered greatly from them.

Acts 16:23 tells that Paul and Silas were locked deep in Philippi's Roman prison. There they sang and worshipped God—while they were in stocks, after harsh Roman whippings! How can this be? Paul and Silas knew that their mere presence was enlarging the tents of God's kingdom. We think jail is hellish; Paul and Silas agreed. They knew the unjust accusations and beatings had positioned them to push back the gates of hell in that jail. The miracle followed, not by petitions, but by confident praise.

The earthquake and the jailer's conversion were momentary miracles, but the lasting result was the new boundaries against darkness. The Philippian church prospered. Paul describes their amazing generosity in 2 Corinthians 8 and 9, and uses them as examples to Corinth and other churches.

We are the penetrators of darkness. Through our presence and ministry of the gospel, we force the boundaries of darkness into retreat: *"The gates of hell shall not prevail against it"* (Matthew 16:18).

ANGELIC HOSTS

Where do we stand in relation to angels? In the New Testament, Apostle Paul wrote the Corinthian church in his first letter that we would judge angels.

This is inconceivable to us. Book Eight of the *Unseen* series is *Nobody Sees These Friends: Partners in the Unseen*. There we will contemplate the Scripture about them in more depth.

My Spirit and Angelic Spirits

Angels: eternal spirits with physical bodies. Scripture is full of references to angels having both. The fallen angels physically mate with the daughters of men and produce babies (Genesis 6:1–3). The rebellious angels are physically bound in chains (Jude). The holy angels physically interact with people (such as Lot in Sodom).

Scripture does not indicate that they can die. The fallen angels with their leader satan had bodies before their fall. God's penalty for the rebellion greatly changed them. Though altered, their bodies still are able to be held in chains. They cannot die.

When Lucifer rose against God, Ezekiel 28 says he sinned. Angels have the power of choice and can choose to sin, even archangels like him. Revelation 12 describes war in heaven and implies that a third of the angels (using the symbol of the stars) sinned also, just as Lucifer had.

The Scripture gives no indication that angels can be forgiven. Presumably because they were created perfect and have access to God, any sin an angel may indulge is eternally punishable. For angels who sin, an eternal fire is prepared (Matthew 25:41).

Those angels who remained loyal to God are truly the holy ones! Always able to sin, they never do. No wonder their authority is so great.

Then there is me and my race. God created in us the ability not to sin, but now that our first parents chose sin, our mortal human nature is *not* able *not* to sin. He created our race as living mortal spirits, but our sin kills our spirits.

People both inherit sin, and choose sin themselves. People not following Jesus have no spirit—they are spiritually dead: *"Just as through one man sin entered the world, and death through sin, and thus death spread to all men, because all sinned."* (Romans 5:12).

Our bodies are so frail—no might at all—compared to the angelic bodies. Their bodies continue undiminished; my body requires constant maintenance, fighting age and other decaying forces. We are limited to the confines of our own skin, but angels can waft in and out of dreams (such as Jesus' father Joseph), appear and disappear (as to Manoah, father of Samson), and fly (as on Christmas night).

Yet despite these differences of magnitude, something mysterious occurred. Jesus, the Second Person of the Trinity, became one of us.

He did not become one of the angels. Aren't the fallen angels of a greater nature, more worthy of redemption, than mortal man? Wouldn't saving them be more fruitful for God? The fallen angels are eternal, never die, and have bodies. Why, just imagine what they could do if they repented and were saved!

Instead, He chose us—weak, frail, unable not to sin. By His incarnation and His substitutionary atonement for us, our spirit can be reborn through faith in Him! Our sins, past, present, and future, can all be forgiven. These are advantages that no angel has.

Jesus poured Himself out. What did He get for His effort? A slow-maturing Church, requiring thousands of years to "get it." The history of His Church is dominated by people like me—just out of tune with the spirit.

Yet these conditions of spirit poverty, He called *blessed* in the Beatitudes. He preferred us mortals over the well-endowed angels. Well did Hannah describe God's upending habit in 1 Samuel 2:4–8.

> The bows of the mighty men are broken, And those who stumbled are girded with strength. Those who were full have hired themselves out for bread, And the hungry have ceased to hunger. Even the barren has borne seven, And she who has many children has become feeble.
>
> The LORD kills and makes alive; He brings down to the grave and brings up. The LORD makes poor and makes rich; He brings low and lifts up. He raises the poor from the dust And lifts the beggar from the ash heap, To set them among princes And make them inherit the throne of glory.

Our Angelic Spirit-Servants

A kingdom of spirits welcomes us—we who are poor in spirit. Their welcome has one basis for our standing: the Son of God shed His blood for us. They knew Him as *"the Lamb slain from the foundation of the world"* (Revelation 13:8).

They saw the Lamb relinquish His place in heaven, sang at his birth, and watched as their dark enemy crucified Him. He did all this, not for the fallen angels, but for mortal man. Now His Holy Spirit lives in us. He delegated to us His authority; we rule the earth for His kingdom. And we are His judges for the other spirits in this kingdom,

> If you will walk in My ways, and if you will keep My command, then you shall also judge My house, And likewise have charge of My courts; I will give you places to walk among these who stand here. (Zechariah 3:7)

> Do you not know that the saints will judge the world? And if the world will be judged by you, are you unworthy to judge the smallest matters? Do you not know that we shall judge angels? (1 Corinthians 6:2–3)

They must wonder at God's wisdom. As they see it, the poor in spirit will judge them—the holy angels who can sin but never do.

For what will we judge God's house? How will we know what judgments to render? At least one basis: whether they served us well, in our pursuit of God's purposes. *"Are they* [angels] *not all ministering spirits sent forth to minister for those who will inherit salvation?"* (Hebrews 1:14).

Some Christians talk of angel interaction colloquially and informally. I cannot support that. Hebrews 1 roundly rebukes excessive focus on angels. Every biblical manifestation of angels shows their intimidating holiness. Jude 8–9 speaks clearly of the respect due the angels—not something to be trifled with.

There's no benefit in throwing out the baby with the bathwater, however. We are living spirits indeed, and God gives us *"places to walk among these who stand here"* (Zechariah 3:7). That's why our angelic spirit partners are perceptible to us and cooperative with us.

The God whose purposes we faithfully serve has put them under our agreement with Him. Jesus exhibited this faith after His arrest. In Matthew 26:53 He restrains Himself from calling upon the angels—with the faith that they would interrupt His death for our sins if He did call.

He did not. Instead, He chose death, separation from the Father for the sins of mankind. The kingdom authority to command, dispatch, and judge angels, He earned for us to exercise.

Unseen Wars of Words

Since awakening to my spirit identity, the attacks have been persistent—on my health, in my business, in my family, and even dreams. Lying half-awake this morning, I suddenly felt the presence and rush of armed invaders. They burst through the front door, fully armed. Then I switched from first person participant to third person observer.

I saw myself run from the kitchen to our bedroom, shut the door, get my gun, and push Diane onto the floor and into the corner. Immediately I saw an invader outside our bedroom window, with a direct shot at Diane behind the bed. I saw myself jump behind the red couch.

Gasping, I leapt up in bed to see that all was calm, surprised that the invasion was not real! But immediately You said within me it was real—the marauding invading spirits resisting me. You called me to further discussion, and I went onto the patio outside. The clock read 2:00 AM.

As the distinct winds brushed the trees ever so audibly, You told me two angels sat with me—their job was to execute Your and my concerted wishes. I knew You gave me authority to release them to accomplish Your will.

The angels made themselves known somehow. I didn't know how to act or respond. One suggested, inaudible to earthly ears, "Darkness could pay back to you for what they tried. In fact, you can make them pay back double." I agreed. Everything in the moment fit with the Bible. Clearly, the word had started with You. I agreed with it, and next it came out of my mouth. Off the angels went to exact the payback.

The day and the next four months were exceptionally good in business. I calculated the revenue: it was 204 percent what the previous period had been. Darkness paid me back double! The day was also good in family. These fruits validate that it really was You revealing such things.

Awakening to our spirit identities, we awaken to spirits. That's why I can sit with angels as I did after darkness' invasion in the 9/20/2020 dream.

Angel Self-Assessment

During night, whispers—definitely not the Holy Spirit, but holy spirits: "We can't create, and we do not initiate. We act only on the initiative and direction of God."

Then, Lord, why angels at all?

"I am Spirit. I multiply spirit. For the expression of My Spirit, I like participation of other spirits. Once they exist, I express Myself in a much more diverse and lavish array of freely agreeing spirits."

I ask: why didn't You just start with people? Why populate the heavens with angelic spirits first? If angels can't create or initiate, how satisfying could they have been? If You had created people first, there would be no satan.

"That is exactly correct. I seek partners. Those without free will cannot be partners. I made people as spirit partners in My image who had free will and free choice. Without the opportunity to rebel, free choice would not exist. Without temptation, free will could not mature.

"Without the kingdom of darkness, no one with a free will can be proven or tested. That's why I sent My Son Jesus into the wilderness for temptation after I endorsed Him.

"I've done this with human beings. I sent you people into the wilderness, casting you out of the garden even after I endorsed you with My own breath. Temptation has been your lot ever since. Through it, some emerge proven. The difference between Jesus and the rest of humanity is that He had a 100 percent success rate whereas humanity is 0 percent.

"Moreover, it was necessary for darkness to exist if any means of atonement could occur. Only the substitutionary death of Jesus would cover the sin of those who repent. The kingdom of darkness saw to His crucifixion exactly as I wanted them to.

"One more thing: I work in stages. Human history shows that I had an old covenant and a new covenant. Revelation was progressive until the Scripture was complete. Until then, I tolerated misunderstandings and behaviors that would ultimately be forbidden. Likewise, with individual disciples, I tolerate in your youth things that are intolerable in your maturity.

"The angelic host and all of My creating before the creation of humanity also shows My habit of working in stages."

The Judgment of Angels

As I slept, I received understanding. The Bible says angels are judged by men. We focus on the backwardness of it. The stated fact: they too will be assessed on Judgment Day. Angels are not permanently secure until then. Judgment Day is for the angels as well.

Also: last night with two, showing how they drink Your presence and sustain themselves without needs.

Suddenly, I saw the sin of Lucifer in Ezekiel 28:16, *"By the abundance of your trading, you became filled with violence within."* Lucifer was in Your presence, closer than any other. He was the exemplar of drinking Your presence and finding his sustenance in Your sufficiency. Yet he saw something in far-flung trading that was more desirable to him. The pride Lucifer showed was of one piece with his trading and its disdain for Your sufficiency.

The directional beacon of the holy angels is Your pleasure. Whomever You favor, they delight to serve, for Your pleasure. This fact requires us to believe that if You favor us, then angels are eager to serve us.

Conversations about Angels

I was wakened at 3:48 AM today, knowing that angels beckoned me. I was too groggy to act on it, returning to bed until 5:43 AM when I again perceived the invite and responded.

Two related to me, but many more, present. The two were charged to teach me.

"We stand ready."

I was too awed to respond, in the paralysis of my uncertainty.

"We serve God who has favor on you. You are a king. We are faithful to Him and those He favors."

I had to wait while intimidation fell away; if this is how they see me, then need I be intimidated? So I asked them things.

"How many are you?"

"More than you can accept."

I knew the answer had three digits.

"How do you stay holy? How have you avoided sinful choices? I respect that so much."

"We behold God and drink Him in. This is all the satisfaction we want. More than that, there is only the satisfaction when He commands, and we get to obey Him. That is the only additional satisfaction we seek."

Perception: like campers huddled around a fire on a cold night, the angels keep their faces toward God. Those campers only turn away to get more wood; likewise, the angels only turn away from facing God when that privilege requires a specific obedience.

Father, why do You work through angels, when you can simply declare a thing and it is so? Why do You use means of any kind?

"Because it is all My self-expression. You and your race in My image are My self-expression. And My acting through willing partners such as angels is My self-expression. Working with partners reveals My nature in ways that acting alone does not do."

And I see: You like partnership and agreement. Even with the kingdom of darkness, You work in partnership—albeit excluding them from Your inner counsels. (Job 1–2, 1 Corinthians 2:8).

"People are My self-expression. Paul, you being a king is My kingship in a flesh-and-blood living spirit, moving about and interfacing with others whom I have made for My self-expression—even the wicked for a day of disaster.

The destiny of every person is some expression of Myself—some by My blessing, and some by My wrath.

> The Lord works out everything to its proper end—even the wicked for a day of disaster (Proverbs 16:4 NIV).

> What if God, wanting to show His wrath and to make His power known, endured with much long-suffering the vessels of wrath prepared for destruction, and that He might make known the riches of His glory on the vessels of mercy, which He had prepared beforehand for glory, even us whom He called, not of the Jews only, but also of the Gentiles? (Romans 9:22–23)

Reflection and discussion questions for this chapter are in the back of the book

---

CHAPTER EIGHT

Darkness and Your Spirit

LUCIFER

Most of us prefer to think as little as possible about our enemies' leader. God must concur because He revealed very little about him in the Bible.

Lucifer a Spirit

What a surprise I received in the wee hours of reflection! You said, "See what Lucifer had as a spirit, and there you will see a fuller picture of spirit existence." Remembering this upon awakening, I realize this: we, the Spirit-born living spirits, are the ones with Your stature and authority in the unseen—not satan.

What do we see in Ezekiel 28? What did Lucifer have as a spirit?

Lucifer has a heart, lifted up in pride. With a physical body he walks on the stones on the mountain of God. That body makes possible his trading and far-flung sanctuaries. The specific day of his creation was known to God, who made Lucifer with an ornamental body that produced music. Splendor was visible to all; by that splendor, he and his wisdom were corrupted.

In Isaiah 14, we are told that Lucifer's body can decay like a corpse full of maggots. His original purpose of his body was to guard access to God on His throne. God gave Lucifer his splendorous physical condition to perform that function. Once he rejected that ordination, Lucifer's physique became bereft of the splendor to perform it. God ceased to sustain the archangel's beauty.

Our mortal bodies are frail, yes. Our spirits are mournfully poor and meek, yes. We are far less equipped for our function as mortal humans than Lucifer was for his. All the more reason to trust God. For us to function in His kingdom, we cannot rely on an exalted splendor, nor on our competencies.

Let the weak say, "I am strong." (Joel 3:10)

We can function there only because He gives our spirits life. The life He gives us, the poor in spirit, is more exalted than what He gave Lucifer and other non-mortal beings. To what angel did God ever say, "yours is the kingdom of heaven?" But that's what He says to human beings, in the Beatitudes: *"Blessed are the poor in spirit, for theirs is the kingdom of heaven.... Blessed are those who are persecuted for righteousness' sake, for theirs is the kingdom of heaven"* (Matthew 5:3, 10).

A spirit can refuse to trust God, as Lucifer did. A spirit, like Lucifer, can assert his intent to exalt his throne over God's. But God, the original Spirit, is unassailable. There is no potential for a spirit to rise successfully against Him. Perhaps this will be fully evident during the one-thousand-year reign, when Jesus is present and satan is absent.

Why Lucifer?

God has revealed that He is all-knowing, all-powerful, and good. People ask, "How can such a God permit evil?" Someone has said God can only have two of the three. We need not talk abstractly, because He has revealed the cause of the trouble: Lucifer. Why did God create Lucifer, knowing all the evil that would result?

I've read many Christian defenses over the years, all worthwhile. But in the final analysis, the availability of choice and rebellion makes it possible for God to show His nature as love. And what verse is more often quoted than 1 John 4:8? *"God is love."* Without the possibility of free choice, His creatures cannot perceive His love, nor enjoy it, nor reciprocate it.

There can be no love among people without free choice; love would be absent and only bondage would remain. God's Creation would be more characteristic of satan's prison and the lockstep rigidity in the kingdom of darkness.

When pain, evil, and tragedy affect us, God's love can be very hard to feel. Mary and Martha certainly questioned Jesus' love in John 11, because His purposeful travel delay resulted in their brother's death. This isn't to make light of our suffering. Apostle Paul himself says *"the days are evil"* (Ephesians 5:16).

Paul's list of sufferings shows that he knew evil much better than most people. Yet this same Apostle Paul encourages us that God's love trumps all. In the end, we are left with trust that our Father knows best. I am safe with My Father.

> In labors more abundant, in stripes above measure, in prisons more frequently, in deaths often. From the Jews five times I received forty stripes minus one. Three times I was beaten with rods; once I was stoned; three times I was shipwrecked; a night and a day I have been in the deep; in journeys often, in perils of waters, in perils of robbers, in perils of my own countrymen, in perils of the Gentiles, in perils in the city, in perils in the wilderness, in perils in the sea, in perils among false brethren; in weariness and toil, in sleeplessness often, in hunger and thirst, in fastings often, in cold and nakedness— besides the other things, what comes upon me daily: my deep concern for all the churches. Who is weak, and I am not weak? Who is made to stumble, and I do not burn with indignation? (2 Corinthians 11:24–29)

> If God is for us, who can be against us? He who did not spare His own Son, but delivered Him up for us all, how shall He not with Him also freely give us all things? Who shall bring a charge against God's elect? It is God who justifies. Who is he who condemns? It is Christ who died, and furthermore is also risen, who is even at the right hand of God, who also makes intercession for us. Who shall separate us from the love of Christ? Shall tribulation, or distress, or persecution, or famine, or nakedness, or peril, or sword? As it is written:
> "For Your sake we are killed all day long; We are accounted as sheep for the slaughter."
> Yet in all these things we are more than conquerors through Him who loved us. For I am persuaded that neither death nor life, nor angels nor principalities nor powers, nor things present nor things to come, nor height nor depth, nor any other created thing, shall be able to separate us from the love of God which is in Christ Jesus our Lord. (Romans 8:31–39)

Imperfect Perfection

God created Lucifer in perfection, as a perfect spirit with the body, the power, and the authority to match. We, in contrast, are born dead in the flesh—no spirit at all. Then we are born again; we come alive in spirit. Perfect? Far from it. We are reborn as babies in spirit; all our spirit's senses and functions are present in potential only.

Why did God do this? Why aren't we born as perfect spirits?

He did that with Lucifer—but the outcome? Clearly, being created perfect is no guarantee. Lucifer demonstrated that! His story shows the consequences of rebellion by a perfect spirit; they are eternal and inescapable. The cherub himself was deformed into satan. Lucifer, created in perfection, is beyond repentance. He now is eternally evil.

Therefore, God has now ordained that human spirits must be tested and proven. He intends that we will rule His kingdom with Him—but not in an unproven condition, exposing us to Lucifer's fate. Never again will He endanger the kingdom of heaven with corruptible leadership. God loves us and seeks to protect us from that fate, so He requires our testing and maturing in a process of time.

Exile from Eden

God formed Eden's garden with two prominent trees right in the center, practically impossible to avoid. One was the forbidden tree, placed right next to the most desirable tree—the tree of life. Then He gave the garden to our first parents as the intended starting point for the human race.

> The tree of life was also in the midst of the garden, and the tree of the knowledge of good and evil.... "Of every tree of the garden you may freely eat; but of the tree of the knowledge of good and evil you shall not eat, for in the day that you eat of it you shall surely die" (Genesis 2:9, 16–17).

The threat of their spirit's death, God Himself created. The threat of death stood right before them, in the middle, unavoidable—right next to the most desirable tree. Whatever perfection they originally had, it didn't include good decision-making. Adam and Eve made their poor choice, and immediately their spirits died—just as God had warned.

Immediately a new threat loomed. God did not tolerate it in the least, and quickly neutralized it for all human history. The threat was the tree of life, which had previously been a tree of promise. If they had eaten of that, Adam and Eve would have eternal bodies that could not die—eternal life without living spirits. You and I would be like Dorian Gray, except no portrait needed.

> Then the LORD God said, "Behold, the man has become like one of Us, to know good and evil. And now, lest he put out his hand and take also of the tree of life, and eat, and live forever"—therefore the LORD

God sent him out of the garden of Eden to till the ground from which he was taken (Genesis 3:22–23).

God clearly wants us to live forever. He paid the infinite cost of incarnation and substitution so we could. But not in that way, in Adam's condition of spiritual death.

Compare Adam and Eve to Lucifer and the fallen angels. Like the rebels of heaven, our first parents suffered *physical* consequences in their bodies. Any splendor that obscured their nakedness vanished. God added the pain of childbearing to our original mandate to multiply. People's spread over the earth decelerated. In place of our built-in physical endurance came aging, decay, and death. God declared, *"Dust you are, and to dust you shall return"* (Genesis 3:19).

Relational consequences followed their sin. It dismantled whatever prevented shame. The bond that inspired Adam's encomium about Eve was replaced with bitter blame, and passed down to their progeny. Their walks with God in the garden in the cool of the day—no more (Genesis 3:8).

All these degradations to His image-creature, God tolerates. One threat only is prevented—that they should also eat the tree of life. If they ate of it, all of us would live forever with eternal bodies and dead spirits. So severe is that fate, God prevents it immediately.

Lucifer and the angels have bodies that cannot die. After they sinned, their eternal fate was enmity with God. He did not protect them, but only us, His image-creature. He prevented us from living forever with bodies that could not die.

> So He drove out the man; and He placed cherubim at the east of the garden of Eden, and a flaming sword which turned every way, to guard the way to the tree of life (Genesis 3:24).

So adamant was God that we should never have undying bodies with dead spirits, that He dispatched His most exalted creatures, the cherubim, to prevent it. This fantastic garden and tree of life was on Earth, but accessible no more.

Now what is our situation? God gives us rebirth as spirits when we believe and follow His Son, Jesus. He Himself comes to live inside our skin. The Holy Spirit generates resurrection vitality in our bodies. Yet despite these positives, these bodies still age, decay, and die.

This is for our good. He will replace them with perfect, undying bodies like Adam and Eve originally had. But we must die first.

In his first letter to the Corinthians, chapter 15:42–49, Apostle Paul dwells on these truths at some length. When your body creaks and aches, and medical visits multiply, you will know the why of it all.

> So also is the resurrection of the dead. The body is sown in corruption, it is raised in incorruption. It is sown in dishonor, it is raised in glory. It is sown in weakness, it is raised in power. It is sown a natural body, it is raised a spiritual body. There is a natural body, and there is a spiritual body. And so it is written, "The first man Adam became a living being." The last Adam became a life-giving spirit.
>
> However, the spiritual is not first, but the natural, and afterward the spiritual. The first man was of the earth, made of dust; the second Man is the Lord from heaven. As was the man of dust, so also are those who are made of dust; and as is the heavenly Man, so also are those who are heavenly. And as we have borne the image of the man of dust, we shall also bear the image of the heavenly Man.

Replacing Lucifer

Lucifer: created a perfect, eternal spirit with a body.

Us: created mortal with a body, able to be a spirit, but since Eden spiritually dead.

Lucifer: no testing, no challenges, but a perfect situation, the best possible to any spirit.

Us: born dead in spirit, wounded immediately, tested and challenged without refuge.

Lucifer: endowed with a free will, with which he sinned, and can never choose repentance.

Us: endowed with a free will, able both to choose sin and to choose repentance toward God.

Lucifer: irreversible downward decay of body.

Us: born into decay but potential for renewal of body and transformation into a perfect body.

MINIONS

Lucifer, now satan, retained his cherubic nature. He commands the vast number of spirits turned rebels.

Evil Spirits

Are evil spirits excluded from Jesus' statement in John 4:24? God seeks worshippers *"who worship Him in spirit and in truth."*

Evil spirits are spirits, and they do know the truth about God. But they fail the first test: they are not worshippers of Him. They also fail the truth test: while possessing facts about God, they misuse them to deceive.

This warns all of us who may love our faith, our traditions, our routines, and even the wealth of our spiritual resources, such as Scripture and the power of the Spirit. Even in all that, we can be like evil spirits—knowing about Him, doing His things, and yet not worshipping Him.

Half-Breed Demons

This is another reason why the wicked half-breeds of Genesis 6 and 1 Peter 3:19–20 are the most likely candidates for demons.

> Being put to death in the flesh but made alive by the Spirit, by whom also He went and preached to the spirits in prison, who formerly were disobedient, when once the Divine long-suffering waited in the days of Noah, while the ark was being prepared, in which a few, that is, eight souls, were saved through water.

Peter says Jesus preached only to those living before the Flood. Why not preach to all unsaved dead people? Why stop at the Flood? And who was it? Peter identifies them: *spirits in prison*. But the human spirit died in the Garden, so that excludes the dead mortal humans from before the Flood, plainly. So, what spirits did Jesus preach to? And what prison was it, anyway? Who had a prison for spirits? God reveals it in Isaiah 14:17; Lucifer had a prison of spirits.

Combining the timeframe—before the Flood—and satan's prison for spirits brings us to Genesis 6:1–4. There the Bible reveals the origin of satan's prisoners.

The *sons of God* mated with mortal women who bore them children. I believe this identifies fallen angels described from a human point of view, with the semi-divinity typically ascribed to angels when seen by people.

These children were a race of half-breeds. They had mortal human bodies from their mothers, but eternal spirits from their paternal angelic ancestry.

God did not want us to have eternal spirits in fallen mortal bodies.

He had exiled our race from Eden and the tree of life so we would not. But these half-breeds with paternity by spirits now thwarted that exile's purpose. Without immediate action, the half-breeds would breed into the entire race of men. With their spiritual connection to the kingdom of darkness, the potency of these half-bred human spirits would be great.

> There were giants on the earth in those days, and also afterward, when the sons of God came in to the daughters of men and they bore children to them. Those were the mighty men who were of old, men of renown (Genesis 6:4).

In fact, it was their presence on the earth that stimulated God's two decrees. The first was to reduce man's lifespan to 120 years. The second was to cause a global flood and destroy humanity. Never since has the union of angels and mortal women threatened humanity at large, perhaps because of the shorter duration of human life.

Although God destroyed their mortal bodies in the Flood, their eternal spirits continued. As half-breeds, they formed the underclass of darkness, hell's lowest caste. Kept in satan's prison, they gained release only as needed. (This explains the swarm of demons in Israel during Jesus' three years, to be considered in depth in Book Six, *Nobody Sees This Warrior: God's Secret Ambush*.)

The half-breeds were not the lowest caste to God, however. These half-breeds had eternal spirits by their paternity, by no choice of their own. Jesus preached to themthem, as Apostle Peter wrote above.

Imagine it! Jesus gave opportunity for freedom and for conversion to true living spirits. His gracious descent to rescue them from hell is in Ephesians 4:8–10, citing Psalm 68:18. Tradition artfully names it The Harrowing of Hell.

> Therefore He says: "When He ascended on high, He led captivity captive, And gave gifts to men."
> (Now this, "He ascended"—what does it mean but that He also first descended into the lower parts of the earth? He who descended is also the One who ascended far above all the heavens, that He might fill all things.)

Who was in that prison? What was their most recent assignment? Oppressing people in Israel for the last three years—so, many of them would be demons He had cast out. We know from the gospels that demons recognized who He was. How shocking to them: Jesus, whom satan had crucified, preaching in satan's prison! Jesus, whom they themselves had pestered and opposed, offering eternal redemption of their spirits!

After Jesus preached to them, what happened? The Bible does not say. The apostles knew about the preaching in hell because Jesus told them in His forty days before ascending. It's possible that Jesus chose not to tell anyone the results.

Presumably some spirits in prison chose to go with Him. Sadly, we know a large number chose darkness—those who oppress people up until today.

DELIVERANCE FROM EVIL

Jesus gave us a short, simple pattern for prayer. Among its few petitions for ourselves is that we be delivered from evil. When Jesus announced His ministry in Nazareth, He chose Isaiah 61:1–2 for the purpose. One phrase refers to the prison of darkness: *"the opening of the prison to those who are bound."*

Demonic Oppression

The minions of darkness oppress people today. I know; they have oppressed me for most of my adult life. This oppression was not an overt kind, such as horror movies might portray. The oppression of demons in our time is more likely to be subtle.

A central, if not first, component of demonic oppression is a curse. Unfortunately there are plenty to go around. The first is God's own curse, revealed in Zechariah 5. It is a self-operating force of nature no less than gravity and stands against everyone on earth. Specific curses follow family lines, so that the sinful choices of my ancestors make it easier for me to repeat those choices. Curse also accompanies our spiritual failure, as God pronounces a curse on all who fail to keep the words of His law (Deuteronomy 27:26; Galatians 3:10).

Curses do not rob us of our free will, but they support our flesh in choosing our own way over God's way. Demons are required to have a doorway into our lives and who gives them that doorway? We do. Everything God made turns on agreement, and we enter agreements with demons. We don't do it on purpose. Demons don't approach us at a negotiating table. Instead, they trick us in our infancy. They do not fight fair.

A primary way we agree with our own demonic oppression is our ungodly beliefs. This refers not to doctrine but to disagreements with the God who blessed mankind at our creation. Demons oppress us by enforcing these ungodly beliefs which oppose and neutralize God's blessing.

The curses and ungodly beliefs we bring into painful situations set us up for further, deeper oppression. Our basic instincts say to avoid hurt, to predict how it might occur, and to behave so as to avoid it. A cycle of expectation, fulfilment, and belief is established through our hurts, and the natural effort to avoid repetitive pains. This includes efforts to bury painful emotions, but these efforts fail as the emotion will manifest throughout our behaviors whether we know it or not.

All this occurs to us before we even contribute our own sinful behaviors. Illicit relationships can create soul-ties which are exploited by darkness. Unholy behavior creates pollutants which ricochet inside us and put similar bullet holes in all our experiences. We refuse God's love and salvation and isolate ourselves thereby in a holding tank of all-around oppression.

The walls of the holding tank are called strongholds in the Bible—hard to identify, heavily defended and tightly impregnable. And when a Christian is born in spirit, these strongholds stay in place. They have permission from the Christian's past. The newly born spirit has to mature within this hostile environment: oppression with origins even before we were born as babies.

Deliverance Ministry

Many Christians have been left to their oppressors by churches and pastors unwilling to provide deliverance ministry. I know; my wife and I were. The repetitive problems manifested in widely diverse areas of our lives. We knew something unseen was at work to oppose us. We laid these persistent struggles before our pastors in each of our church stops. Not until we had been wholeheartedly pursuing Christ for forty years did we learn about deliverance ministry, through Christian International. The ministry we received was offered by an international, interdenominational organization called Restoring the Foundations.

With their help my wife and I surrendered our religious Christian pride. We accepted that we had entered in agreements with the kingdom of darkness—unwittingly of course, but agreements, nonetheless. Such an admission is befitting to the poor in spirit who recognize their defenselessness in the unseen. And once we admitted it, we could not get out of it fast enough.

The stronghold in my life was revealed and it explained how people responded to me in an uneven way. The demonic oppression in my life created a major blind spot: I did not know how I affected others and could not appreciate their personal boundaries. Whenever I was with people of similar boundaries, I prospered. But I never understood how I could prosper with some and alienate others, all the while acting the same way.

My wife and I were so greatly changed that people around us didn't know how to respond. Some friends left and new friends came. Some family members became more distant. But our love for each other was exponentially increased. Our enjoyment of life exploded. Though fewer, our relationships with others were amplified, deeper than we had ever dreamt possible.

And we have a competency now to recognize demonic oppression when it is attempted—against us and against others.

Your Spirit is Superior

If you are born in spirit, you are far superior to demonic oppressors. They can only hope and pray you refuse to see it—because when you do, you will seek deliverance ministry and become free of them. Jesus pronounced the disciples (and therefore us) superior to demonic oppression in Luke 10:19, *"Behold, I give you the authority to trample on serpents and scorpions, and over all the power of the enemy, and nothing shall by any means hurt you."*

This does not mean you can do it yourself. Deliverance isn't a D-I-Y proposition, because you can't see what oppresses you. The oppression affects your perception. To be free of your own strongholds, seek out deliverance ministers.

Earlier in my Christian life, I did not think it possible for Christians to experience demonic possession, because the Holy Spirit possessed us. When I heard of deliverance ministry, I supposed it was for the hard cases—not me. Then I read Derek Prince's 1998 book, *They Shall Expel Demons*[6]. His exposition of the Greek words in the New Testament showed me that I was half right.

Someone filled with the Spirit of God cannot be possessed by a demon—correct. However, our idea of possession was created by fiction like *The Exorcist*, not the New Testament. There, God revealed that people could be oppressed by demons. Thus Jesus' ministry announcement in Luke 4:18 included the phrase, *"to set at liberty those who are oppressed."*

My belief in Jesus as my Lord required me to admit that His statement included my need. I had indeed brought long-established demonic oppression into my life with Him. In true repentance, I wanted them out of my life.

And they leave when told to because the authority of Jesus in our superior spirits is evident to demons. He answers our prayer: *"Deliver us from evil."* Now that you know you are a living human spirit, do as I did: seek out deliverance ministry.

HELL

Hell is the opposite of heaven. The word has made its way into our language of exclamation: *What the hell?! Get the hell out! Hell's bells!* This ploy of darkness has made our worst nightmare into a laughing matter—all the easier to hide its true terror.

Jesus' Hell

My college honors thesis was half the credit hours of my senior year. The thesis began with hell as revealed in the Bible, and then surveyed the historical development of our popular caricatures of hell.

The religion professors ridiculed hell as punitive retribution, as primitive and vindictive. They did not regard all the Scripture equally; they discredited teaching regarding God's holiness, wrath, and judgment. To them, Jesus was about loving acceptance and the brotherhood of man. He would never teach such a backward retributive justice like hell, they thought.

My review of church history was a big hit with them! The 120-page thesis identified significant influences in our present-day notions of hell. But my first chapter, titled *The Biblical Basis for Hell*, assumed that the Scripture was reliable and truthful. It so angered my religion professors that they refused to grant the twenty-four credit hours—unless I removed the Bible chapter from my 120-page historical survey.

One tried to be nice about it and told me, "Paul, all you have to do is renumber the remaining chapters." God gave me the needed backbone during that time. I noticed He answered my prayers, but professors did not—so I chose Him. And He impressed me with His severity of accountability, such as Matthew 10:32-33, *"Therefore whoever confesses Me before men, him I will also confess before My Father who is in heaven. But whoever denies Me before men, him I will also deny before My Father who is in heaven."*

Chapter Eight: Darkness and Your Spirit

I refused their habit of choosing what parts of God's Bible to discard; I did not take out the first chapter. The professors who said they rejected retribution then denied me honors and twenty-four hours credit—half my senior year course load. They did this one week prior to my college graduation.

Ironically, it was they who attempted punitive retribution. But they failed; I graduated on time. God gave me favor before my church history professor and the college dean. With the professor, my good grades helped. With the dean, my contention over Scripture made me someone to help out, as in, out of the college.

Together, these two men retroactively created a twenty-four-credit-hour class only three days before my graduation—as if I had been in the class for the previous nine months. I walked in the ceremony with a blank diploma, until a new one could be printed without the honors designation.

By including Scripture citations as authoritative, I knew the professors would chafe. But I was not prepared to discover that nine of every ten references to hell in the Bible are from the lips of Jesus Himself.

This defies the popular concept of Jesus as teaching love and acceptance, does it not? All but two hell statements are in the New Testament, and 90 percent of those were Jesus' own statements. Most of what we know about hell, we know from Jesus' teaching.

It makes sense that Jesus taught hell. Why would He die to save us, otherwise? What would warrant God's incarnation and death as a mortal human being? There is a hell awaiting every mortal human soul. The most loving thing is to warn us and save us by providing escape. So yes—Jesus is love and acceptance.

He paid the highest cost anyone could conceive to keep you and me out of hell. He died as my substitute, and yours. The full punitive retribution, which I deserve, was poured out on Him. God's justice upon me is satisfied by Jesus' death. Now God accepts me because Jesus totally satisfied the divine wrath my sin earns for me.

Jesus repeatedly described hell as fire and outer darkness. These are both physical sensations requiring bodies. Accordingly, Apostle John saw all history's dead people, standing in their bodies before God to be judged, in Revelation 20:11–15, *"Then I saw a great white throne and Him who sat on it... And I saw the dead, small and great, standing before God... And anyone not found written in the Book of Life was cast into the lake of fire."*

I want no uncertainty on that day. When the eulogy is given over my casket, may there be no guessing whether I am saved. May God grant that my name, and yours, is in His Book of Life.

It is imperative that we encourage one another to pursue Christ wholeheartedly. The alternative is unthinkable.

Hell of the Dead

Here's what I think right now, from the Scripture. There are no human spirits in hell, because those who go there are dead in trespass and sin, and their spirit never even lived.

A human spirit exists only in relationship with God. Hell is populated with human souls created at mortal birth that never came into relationship with God and never became living spirits, or who did not persist as living spirits.

> And do not fear those who kill the body but cannot kill the soul. But rather fear Him who is able to destroy both soul and body in hell. (Matthew 10:28)

Historical Hell

A primary reason that hell has become a laughing matter is its history as a belief. In today's culture, hell is just an expression for emphasis. Our time greatly contrasts with the vast bulk of Christian history. Belief in hell dominated Christians' understanding and fears.

Pope Gregory I served fourteen years as pope, dying at age sixty-four in 604 AD. His influence was seminal and long-lasting, shaping the beliefs and practices of the medieval church. His writings spread through Christendom, preached in all its corners. People called him Gregory the Great.

To strengthen the church, Gregory wrote the visions of people supposed to have died and returned. These were no "light at the end of the tunnel" visions, such as people report today. Instead, demons torture people who were not faithful Christians.

Thumbscrews, the rack, disemboweling, boiling in oil—these horrors fed the popular imagination of hell for centuries. The unending inescapability of hell fed the superstitious, poorly educated medieval imagination. These manipulative caricatures still have a life of their own, persisting today.

When the Enlightenment brought the scientific movement, this medieval sensationalism made hell's reality easier to dismiss and ignore. The revival preaching of the early 1800s continued the long-held beliefs about hell. The terror of hell gave rise to Christian behaviors that were easy to disdain. The rapid adoption of the scientific method throughout Western civilization marginalized Jesus' teaching about hell to the wing-nut section.

Now laughter has replaced the terror of hell—even with braggadocio. There's even an anthem, Highway to Hell by AC/DC.

But Jesus assured us: it is no laughing matter.

YOUR STANDING

Many Christians and churches fixate fearfully on what the devil and his dark kingdom can do to them. If such a Christian musters up the fearlessness, they charge in, with emotional words or steeled resolve.

But why would darkness fear a Christian who defines darkness as the primary influence on Earth? That's honoring the kingdom of darkness, agreeing with the boundary lines they draw. It's like trying to play basketball on a football field.

We drive them back, Jesus said—not vice versa. To pray and act with desperate fear is substandard for us. He has drawn the boundary lines for this contest. We play within His field—not theirs.

God Almighty lives in us—could He ever *not* be the primary influence? If His Spirit fills us, can any spirit in the unseen resist us? When we cooperate with Him, what can darkness do?

> Yet in all these things we are more than conquerors through Him who loved us. For I am persuaded that neither death nor life, nor angels nor principalities nor powers, nor things present nor things to come, nor height nor depth, nor any other created thing, shall be able to separate us from the love of God which is in Christ Jesus our Lord (Romans 8:37–39).

The fallen, evil spirits are eternally bereft of the only source of spirit life—God. We, in contrast, have full access to Him; we are His home on Earth. My spirit is His temple here, and so is yours. (1 Corinthians 6:19–20)

In Matthew 16:19, the disciples had just professed that He was the Christ. Their faith represented all of us who, like them, follow Him as our Lord. Next, Jesus said this, to them and also to us, *"I will give you the keys of the kingdom of heaven, and whatever you bind on earth will be bound in heaven, and whatever you loose on earth will be loosed in heaven."*

Our standing in the unseen world is supreme, excelled only by God Himself. Binding and loosing are not a Christian commodity, skill, or position, nor merely a key to answered prayer. It is our standing which He has decreed. Authority to bind and loose is our position, which Jesus' death earned for us.

To all who believe in Him, He gives the power to become children of God. Rebirth as a spirit causes this authority in heaven and earth.

As stated at the outset: every Christian longing is satisfied by maturing as a living spirit.

Reflection and discussion questions for this chapter are in the back of the book

---

CHAPTER NINE

Discipleship of Your Spirit

SPIRIT MATURING

The maturity of your spirit is easily identified: to be under God and in agreement with Him. This simple statement is what a maturing spirit always returns to. Jesus put it this way, in the fourth New Testament book, John's gospel—5:19, 7:16, and 12:49–50 (NIV).

> Jesus gave them this answer: "Very truly I tell you, the Son can do nothing by himself; he can do only what he sees his Father doing, because whatever the Father does the Son also does."

> Jesus answered, "My teaching is not my own. It comes from the one who sent me."

> "For I did not speak on my own, but the Father who sent me commanded me to say all that I have spoken… So whatever I say is just what the Father has told me to say."

Spirit and Agreement

The life of the saved human spirit comes by faith in Jesus Christ. To live as a reborn spirit is solely a matter of walking with God. The living spirit can contribute nothing except a vacuum for the All-Sufficient One to fill. We can agree with His love nature and rule this earth on His behalf.

Thus, our prime choice is to agree with our Divine Lover. Should we argue with Him instead? Those are the only two choices.

Many foolish, deceiving voices whisper that other things matter more. Many values seduce us to love them more than we agree with our unseen God. A short list includes deeds, achievement, goods, fame, money, power, and influence. Our natural selves seek just about anything where we can feel at least like contributors, if not captains of our own fate.

Dangerous behavior, sickness, and loneliness often originate in our stubborn choice to be master of our own lives.

We do these energetic and self-willed things when what God wants most is agreement—just like in the Trinity (John 17:21–23). All the while, He simply wants us to increase our agreement with Him.

> That they all may be one, as You, Father, are in Me, and I in You; that they also may be one in Us ... that they may be one just as We are one: I in them, and You in Me; that they may be made perfect in one.

Could it be any clearer that Jesus wanted agreement?

Spirit Is Easy

> Come, all you who are thirsty, come to the waters; and you who have no money, come, buy and eat! Come, buy wine and milk without money and without cost. Why spend money on what is not bread, and your labor on what does not satisfy? Listen, listen to me, and eat what is good, and you will delight in the richest of fare. Give ear and come to me; listen, that you may live. (Isaiah 55:1–3)

Paul described striving in Philippians 3:12–14. Jesus said in Luke 13:24, *"Strive to enter through the narrow gate."* So how is spirit easy?

In natural striving, we work for gain. The striving of our natural selves has multiple levels and differing achievements.

Our striving as a spirit has one object only: increased intimacy with God. Isaiah 55 describes above how easy life is, when our spirit is born, and therefore in relationship with God. The food that our spirit craves is free and ample. It comes from listening to Him.

Our only effective striving is toward God. When I listen to Him, all is well. If I lay aside lesser cares and treasure Him, He is pleased. Father recognizes my choice of Him, and encourages my momentum. Out of all proportion, He covers 99.99 percent of any distance between Him and me. That's how Jesus described the father of the prodigal son in Luke 15:20, *"But when he* [the son] *was still a great way off, his father saw him and had compassion, and ran and fell on his neck and kissed him."*

That's my Father.

The Claw

The arcade game with the drop-down claw is a parable for my spirit maturing. Its owner wants our quarters (or dollars), offering a challenge in exchange. His profit requires he collect as much as possible and pay out as little as possible. So his machine makes it very hard to attain the desired prize. Not only is the claw insufficient to grasp the prize; he also limits the attempts or the time. Either way, I've won nothing.

The parable is the persistence for the prize. How many parents keep giving money to children who persist trying for the prize they wanted?

God wants us to persist likewise, but operates the game differently. He wants to us to keep putting money in and to get the prize. It's for our own benefit. He wants us to pay a cost, but our money is not His object. Our persistence to mature as spirits—that's what God wants, and that's the prize.

That's why He doesn't limit the game to one drop. Jesus, the Judge, sets a time limit—but it is your lifetime, hopefully years or even decades, not seconds.

The Lord also knows how to keep each one of us working the claw. He calls our attention to a prize, helps us grab it, and enjoy it. But after we have done so, He shows us an even greater prize that was buried, hidden from sight until we had grabbed and enjoyed the previous prize.

What our God wants is not our money, but rather our persistence. Will my spirit choose Him and what He has for me? Every time a prize and its cost present themselves, what will my choice be?

May I always put my "quarters" in, holding nothing back.

Spirit and Jars of Clay

Paul described our bodies with a telling phrase, in his second letter to Corinth's church: *"But we have this treasure in jars of clay to show that this all-surpassing power is from God and not from us"* (4:7 NIV).

Compared to being filled with the Spirit of God, our bodies are a fragile jar of clay. Is Paul consoling us for our mortal sufferings? Is he describing our inadequacy for things of the spirit? Yes, but there is much more. Christians who settle for consolations will miss it.

Our inadequacy is not a consolation, but a basis of hope and promise. All-surpassing power is in me. Who cares if I am a jar of clay?!

Paul applies our inadequacy this way. *Therefore we do not lose heart.* And why not? Because our struggles in the natural have a payoff for our spirit. *"Though outwardly we are wasting away, yet inwardly we are being renewed day by day"* (4:16 NIV).

Later in 5:1 (NIV), Paul continues, *"For we know that if the earthly tent we live in is destroyed, we have a building from God, an eternal house in heaven, not built by human hands."*

Why didn't we get a reborn body when we got a reborn spirit? Because the heavenly body comes after He has proven us in the jars of clay.

How do we know this? Our spirit itself is the evidence, filled with His Holy Spirit. *"Now the one who has fashioned us for this very purpose is God, who has given us the Spirit as a deposit, guaranteeing what is to come"* (5:5 NIV).

COST-BENEFIT ANALYSIS

The Paycheck for Our Spirit

These days, self-regulation is regarded as self-repression. Our society views Christian self-denial negatively, as inauthentic, not being yourself. Sports or military self-denial is okay, but otherwise, self-denial is crazy.

Why do we Christians do it? No one has a bigger paycheck or a better country than us living spirits. On the day of our judgment, Jesus will say, *"Well done, good and faithful servant. Enter into the joy of your lord"* (Matthew 25:21, 23); and *"Come, you blessed of My Father, inherit the kingdom prepared for you"* (25:34).

Paul described it well in 1 Corinthians 9:25, comparing our self-denial to that of athletes.

> Everyone who competes for the prize is temperate in all things. Now they do it to obtain a perishable crown, but we for an imperishable crown.

Spirit Rewards

Salvation, *a.k.a.* being born as a living spirit, is free, earned by Christ. So why are rewards still described all over the New Testament?

Our rewards come from maturing as a spirit. Our spirit constantly has to assert superiority over our flesh. For our spirit to rule our flesh, we pay many costs. How do you know you are maturing as a spirit? Apostle John wrote his first letter to explain that, using the repeated phrase *"this is how we know."*

The Obstacles

As a Christian, you face obstacles to maturity constantly. Your maturing process provokes the appearance of each one. The kingdom of darkness originates one set of obstacles. Your threat level to them escalates when you mature as a spirit. To neutralize you as a threat in the unseen world, they will use any obstacle needed to disarm your effectiveness in the unseen. If they fail to disarm you, they try to obstruct and retard your maturing as a spirit.

There is another instigator of obstacles to your spirit maturity: God Himself. His tests are positive; they develop, test, prove, and confirm you as a mature spirit. If you are a maturing spirit, you face more and more headwinds to your maturity. It's a sign of animosity from darkness. These tests also signal your welcome into the front lines of God's kingdom advance.

> But also for this very reason, giving all diligence …. be even more diligent to make your call and election sure, for if you do these things you will never stumble; for so an entrance will be supplied to you abundantly into the everlasting kingdom of our Lord and Savior Jesus Christ. (2 Peter 1:5, 10–11)

Never take a perverse pride in your trials, as if you are better or more effective than other Christians. Such attitude is at odds with the meekness which signals a maturing spirit.

Spirit Knows No Cost

When my identity is in the natural self, everything I do with my Lord is a cost to me. As a result, we often tell Him. "I'll do this for you, God—but I expect XYZ in exchange." There is a sure sign we are imposing an IOU on Him: we don't stop, wait, and see if He agrees to it.

A Christian is a reborn spirit. Yet we may consider ourselves merely a natural soul. That's why we remain ensnared in the IOU system of darkness, a system of negotiated exchange and obligation. This IOU trading is the original cause of Lucifer's fall.

> By the abundance of your trading,
> You became filled with violence within,
> and you sinned;
> Therefore I cast you as a profane thing
> out of the mountain of God. (Ezekiel 28:16)

In truth, imposing your IOU upon God is not possible. Your spirit only exists because God spoke it and you followed Christ Jesus. Your spirit either is, or it is not; there is no in-between.

Someone born only in the flesh cannot enter the kingdom of God, Jesus said. Without a spirit, exchange and negotiation with God are impossible. Once a human spirit comes alive by God's saving, there's no cost to pay. My spirit owns nothing and is rather in debt to God for everything. There is no cost to my spirit. The freely willed death of Jesus paid all the cost once for all. The second Person of the Trinity fully satisfied the justice requirement of the Triune God. Scripture is plain about the full satisfaction of all costs to God by Jesus' death.

> All have sinned and fall short of the glory of God, being justified freely by His grace through the redemption that is in Christ Jesus, whom God set forth as a propitiation by His blood, through faith, to demonstrate His righteousness, because in His forbearance God had passed over the sins that were previously committed, to demonstrate at the present time His righteousness, that He might be just and the justifier of the one who has faith in Jesus. (Romans 3:23–26)

> For what the law could not do in that it was weak through the flesh, God did by sending His own Son in the likeness of sinful flesh, on account of sin: He condemned sin in the flesh, that the righteous requirement of the law might be fulfilled in us who do not walk according to the flesh but according to the Spirit. (Romans 8:3–4)

> For such a High Priest was fitting for us, who is holy, harmless, undefiled, separate from sinners, and has become higher than the heavens; who does not need daily, as those high priests, to offer up sacrifices, first for His own sins and then for the people's, for this He did once for all when He offered up Himself. (Hebrews 7:26-27)

The natural man in contrast is a bean-counter. "What must I surrender to have the rewards of God's fellowship?" The Bible replies that I must surrender every natural right and expectation. Thus, the flesh resorts to

IOUs, in a spiritual capitalism. We may not even recognize the primal capitalistic mantra in our effort: "God, You give me that which I want, and I will give You that which You want."

Jesus repudiated that with many such statements as Luke 9:23–25. He does not want His disciples in the negotiation business, either.

> If anyone desires to come after Me, let him deny himself, and take up his cross daily, and follow Me. For whoever desires to save his life will lose it, and whoever loses his life for My sake will save it. For what profit is it to a man if he gains the whole world, and is himself destroyed or lost?

Jesus encountered three would-be disciples in Luke 9:57–62. Each one said, "I will, but first." They attached strings, but not abnormal or unrealistic ones. Yet Jesus didn't accept them, because they tried to exact an IOU. *"But Jesus said to him, 'No one, having put his hand to the plow, and looking back, is fit for the kingdom of God.'"*

THE PROCESS AND THE PROGRESS

Have you noticed that we don't mature as Christians overnight? We have heavenly moments of deep insight and intimate love with our Father, yet they give way to the daily grind, to disappointing self, to un-heavenly life.

Maturing seems like the path of a Yo-Yo in the hands of someone walking upstairs: gradually and certainly up, but with lots of downs along the way. That's why we need admonitions, like coaches yell at players.

> And let us not grow weary while doing good, for in due season we shall reap if we do not lose heart (Galatians 6:9).

Spirit Progress

The living human spirit has continual alternatives for choosing. These choices are presented to us by God's design. Spirits made alive, given the power of choice, choose differently. The Bible exhorts us what choices to make, because we can make wrong choices with our free will. Our powerful minds rationalize our poor choices. An old saying is "the heart chooses and the mind excuses."

Therefore, the choices made among living spirits vary widely.

Second Peter 1:5–11 twice exhorts us to *"make every effort"* and to *"show all diligence,"* in order that we may abound in divine qualities, and receive *"a rich welcome"* into Christ's kingdom. Will unique spirits therefore receive unique welcomes? Will the welcome I receive depend on my choice to be diligent?

Can a saved human spirit—a Christian—decide to settle? Choose to slack off? Aim at something less than the highest? We have all seen it, because each of us spirits can make different choices about following Christ and personal maturity.

Apostle Paul affirms this repeatedly, such as in Philippians 3:7–11, which we have cited often to describe pursuing God. All Paul's past accolades and achievements are rubbish. What anyone else thinks is of little consequence to his choice. All the excellence that he once relied upon, he relinquished—his heritage, his service, his passion, his fruitfulness, his merits. Building on them instead, Paul adopts an active, passionate, no-holds-barred pursuit of knowing God. After describing this pursuit, he says, *make note of my example and join me—only let us all hold on to what we have attained* (author's paraphrase).

Our spirit's power of choice does not merely affect our walk with Jesus and relationship with God. The choices made by a living human spirit are very influential in the unseen kingdom of God. This influence is in part because of God's nature as a rewarder. He likes rewarding our choices that please Him.

Maturity in Jesus Christ

Paul described his desired outcome in his letter to the Colossian church, chapter 1:28: *"Him we preach, warning every man and teaching every man in all wisdom, that we may present every man perfect in Christ Jesus."*

Over centuries, "perfect in Christ Jesus" has taken many forms. Monastic traditions have defined it as union with Jesus. In the holiness community, perfection has meant "without sin." Evangelicals measure it by thinking right doctrine. Many Christians focus on social justice; they identify perfection in Christ as herding society to provide a better life for more people.

These qualities are not undesirable—but they are incomplete. Throughout history, church and religion almost always discount the Holy Spirit and His filling—even today.

> Most assuredly, I say to you, unless one is born of water and the Spirit, he cannot enter the kingdom of God. That which is born of the flesh is flesh, and that which is born of the Spirit is spirit. Do not marvel that I

said to you, 'You must be born again.' The wind blows where it wishes, and you hear the sound of it, but cannot tell where it comes from and where it goes. So is everyone who is born of the Spirit (John 3:5–8).

To be perfect in Christ Jesus, we each must be a living spirit. To be perfect in Christ, we must be filled with the Spirit of God. The activation of our spirits is a *sine qua non* ("without which, nothing") of being like Jesus. For Paul to desire everyone to be perfected in Christ is saying that he wants everyone to be filled with the Spirit of Jesus. *"Do not be drunk with wine, in which is dissipation; but be filled with the Spirit"* (Ephesians 5:18).

These two go together: perfection in Christ Jesus and the filling of the Holy Spirit. A Christian cannot be mature in the Holy Spirit, nor as an individual living spirit, without conforming increasingly to Jesus Christ. Only as a living spirit can a Christian mature in Jesus Christ. Only as we follow Him are we filled with His Spirit that He pours out.

Jesus Himself was filled with the Holy Spirit. He was the first upon whom the Spirit was poured out without limit (John 3:34). Becoming more like Him includes being activated as a living spirit—just like He was.

Spirit Babies in Church

When first saved and filled, a person is like a spiritual baby. He or she can see, but cannot interpret the elements of the new environment. The exoskeleton of church and Christian habits provides support for the maturing to come. The long process of testing is intended for the spirit to unfurl into its full design potential.

But that unfurling can be arrested; its speed, decelerated. In its place, reliance upon that exoskeleton often substitutes for real spirit activation. A new Christian usually has a sense of new life, which actually dissipates. Every religious tradition in Christianity manifests this dynamic. One reason is the uncontrollability of our spirits filled with the Holy Spirit of God.

The Protestant tradition has suppressed spirit. Even after the Pentecostal outpouring, many packaged the filling of the Holy Spirit into a predictive code of religious measurement. The Catholic tradition has used different methods at different times with the same result: control for preservation's sake. The Orthodox church is no exception, either; they rigidly attribute both their doctrines and their practices to the apostolic succession, protecting themselves from anything new.

Sadly, someone can be born in spirit, yet receive no instruction on living as a spirit filled with God's Spirit. The powerful opposition of the flesh, the world, and the kingdom of darkness can go into overdrive to keep the person babyish and neutralize the threat. Spiritual babies can look very unspiritual and fail many tests, victims of religion's powerlessness against such unseen enemies. The maturity of the Church will render this tragedy a thing of the past.

A living spirit places primary attention on the relationship with God, not the relationship with the Church. Thus, those who would exercise control find maturing spirits to be an irritation. Like Jesus' wind, we living spirits can be heard, and our influence felt. But religious institutions cannot blackmail, cajole, or harness us under their control, nor direct us by their priorities. *"The wind blows where it wishes, and you hear the sound of it, but cannot tell where it comes from and where it goes. So is everyone who is born of the Spirit"* (John 3:8).

Attentiveness, Pass/Fail

This unseen world of our spirits is no trifling matter, nor is it elective and subject to our individual discretion. Yes, we have a choice. But once we have enrolled in the class, it is pass/fail. There are no degrees of success and no "trying;" there is only pass or fail.

In the world of spirit, everything hinges on the relationship with God. Only He makes our spirits alive and if He does, we pass! The class has only one very simple requirement, very easy to understand: our attentiveness to Him. Well, as they say, simple—but not easy.

The distinction between our spirit and an evil spirit is not capability, nor is it moral. We Christian spirits differ from evil spirits by a single hairline: obedient attentiveness to God.

Yes, *"blessed are those who are poor in spirit,"* but the Beatitudes signify a maturing process, in the end of which we will be *"called sons of God."* Jesus says, *"Great is your reward in heaven"* (Matthew 5:12). This presumes that we will mature as spirits.

Maturing spirits have more receptivity to God Almighty, more room for His domination, and more honor for His will. We have more alertness for our own self-will. We quickly recognize in ourselves the *"I Will"* attitudes that led Lucifer off the cliff into eternal damnation. As a spirit becoming perfect in Christ Jesus, my maturity produces more meekness.

His meekness explains why the much-proven Apostle Paul used a conditional term when describing his own salvation in Philippians 3:11: *"if by any means."* Likewise in 1 Corinthians 9:27, he wrote conditionally: *"lest, when I have preached to others, I myself should become disqualified."*

We pass the class because God made our spirit alive—but we never underestimate our ability to reject Him and fail the class.

The Outcome, Not the Method

I was reflecting on the gospels' prayer promises that Jesus made. So many believe those promises present the way to get what we ask for. I disagree. Jesus teaches us confidence in our prayers, but not to get what we want. His target is to implement the will of God on Earth.

Listen for that in the Lord's Prayer from Matthew 6:9–10. That's how He prayed and how He taught his disciples to pray.

> Our Father in heaven, Hallowed be Your name. Your kingdom come. Your will be done On earth as it is in heaven.

He would say that faith *alone* is inadequate, and the outcomes we expect, sometimes off target. Jesus used "faith" to describe the state of affairs that results as we mature and pray. We misread faith as a *method* when, in fact, it is a *precondition*.

> So Jesus answered and said to them, "Have faith in God. For assuredly, I say to you, whoever says to this mountain, 'Be removed and be cast into the sea,' and does not doubt in his heart, but believes that those things he says will be done, he will have whatever he says. Therefore I say to you, whatever things you ask when you pray, believe that you receive them, and you will have them." (Mark 11:22–24).

The faith that Jesus describes is a precondition: *"have faith in God."* It comes about as we mature in the Holy Spirit and the fellowship with the Father—just as Jesus did. When we are spirits matured to that certainty with Him, then we pass the threshold for mountain-moving faith. We then know the Spirit to dominate all.

What people call miracles and effective prayer are in fact the natural order for our spirit-dominant life. Our vocabulary uses "miracles" to mean unusual interventions in a natural reality. This definition requires the beliefs that natural reality is superior, and its immovability, fixed. But neither belief is true when the kingdom of God is at hand and its citizens mature. The new normal is living human spirits imposing the superior *"Thy kingdom come"* upon the inferior natural order. And our kingdom is the definitive kingdom in all reality. That's why Jesus' prayer promise in Mark 11:22 begins with the simple phrase, *"have faith in God."*

This understanding of Mark 11:22–24 explains Jesus' next statement about forgiveness in 11:25–26. To us it seems unrelated when we read the faith promise as a method. But as a precondition, forgiveness is of one fabric with faith in Jesus' mind. It is not a different subject, but is unified with the above promise.

> And whenever you stand praying, if you have anything against anyone, forgive him, that your Father in heaven may also forgive you your trespasses. But if you do not forgive, neither will your Father in heaven forgive your trespasses.

The same spirit maturity that produces mountain-moving faith also produces an immunity to unresolved hurt. That faith protects us from unforgiveness.

Inversely, if our spirit harbors unforgiveness, that reveals little faith. Unforgiveness reveals our priority upon the natural world; that's where the offense occurred. Cherishing our hurts signals that we cherish the natural world; it reveals an impaired attentiveness to the unseen world of our spirit.

Any prayer from that inappropriate imbalance is a handicapped prayer. Such "asking" signals a friendship with the world. As discussed earlier in James 4:1–2, this agitates God's jealousy; it makes our prayer target into one He may not support.

RESISTANCE

We are each given opportunity to fall away when the resistance is more than we wanted.

The Martyrs

How potent, how persuasive, how inarguable is life as a living spirit! This potency explains the many martyrs throughout church history.

What produces so much power, in so many numbers, against such frequent persecution, in so many places, for so many centuries? Think of their powerful sacrifice—millions over the centuries. No mere evangelical mental formulation, no mere charismatic gifts, no apologetics or theology can produce martyrdom.

Only the potency of spirit life explains why each Christian followed Jesus through their death. Life as a spirit forms the background to Hebrews 6:4–6.

> For it is impossible for those who were once enlightened, and have tasted the heavenly gift, and have become partakers of the Holy Spirit, and have tasted the good word of God and the powers of the age to come, if they fall away, to renew them again to repentance.

This might not apply to many of today's nominal Christians. So few have experienced anything like *"the powers of the age to come."* But when we mature as spirits, we experience the resurrection vitality of Jesus' Spirit within us. Foreswearing it would truly render us irredeemable.

Faced with persecution, may I continue to choose like my forebears in faith. The choice is simple: either safety for my spirit or safety for my flesh. Either martyrdom or irredeemable falling away. Either denying the Lord Jesus and foreswearing our spirit safety in favor of safety for our natural selves.

Training to Rule the Unseen

To function as intended in the unseen world requires strength in our spirit. When our spirit is newly born, it has to gain strength, like the butterfly emerging from its cocoon. Our newly born spirit has to kick against the cocoon to strengthen. That cocoon is our body, our mind, and our soul—collectively, the natural self, the flesh—everything we were before our salvation.

Resistance training builds muscles. Lifting weights develops capabilities. Our flesh is the weight that our spirit pushes against. Our spirit muscle grows capabilities for the unseen world.

All that God has made is *"to be received with thanksgiving"* (1 Timothy 4:3–5). We enjoy life in this body, with our minds and emotions. Life is rich, and many moments bear the imprint of Eden's intended harmony. Yet we are still to beat our body and make it our slave, the slave of our spirit (1 Corinthians 9:27). How do these go together?

The question is, which rules us? There is a warfare within us for supremacy—our flesh and our spirits are contrary to each other and have contrary desires (Galatians 5:17). Paul next says to *"keep in step with the Spirit,"* he exhorts us to live spirit-based lives, not flesh-based lives (5:25 NIV).

Our unseen spirits occupy the exalted position God has given us, who expects us to wield His authority on His behalf. But why should He entrust us with it if we are unwilling to rule our own flesh? When we do not identify and rule the cravings of our flesh, should we expect to be trusted with the unseen?

The Holy Spirit could make us holy instantly. But He leaves us imperfect so we can learn to rule. The first thing to rule is our natural self. Our flesh becomes our spirit's testing ground. We must pass the test if we want the rewards. People pass them at different rates. No basis of judgment exists because God's tests are individualized.

In Matthew 25:20–21, Jesus told a parable of three servants trusted by their master according to their abilities and aptitudes. What the master says to the first is why we war to rule our flesh.

> So he who had received five talents came and brought five other talents, saying, 'Lord, you delivered to me five talents; look, I have gained five more talents besides them.' His lord said to him, 'Well done, good and faithful servant; you were faithful over a few things, I will make you ruler over many things. Enter into the joy of your lord.'

A baby has to rule gravity if it is to walk. The baby learns to use gravity to its advantage, rather than fall to the floor under gravity's pull. Likewise, we must resist the gravity of the flesh if we are to walk in the spirit. The baby doesn't escape gravity, and the spirit doesn't escape the flesh. Instead, we rule our flesh and turn it to the purposes of the Lord Jesus.

THE WORD OF GOD

The discipleship of our spirits is impossible without a thorough engagement with what God says. Book Two in the *Unseen* series, *Nobody Sees This Unseen Realm: How to Unlock Bible Mysteries*, is devoted exclusively to our attentiveness to what He says.

The Word of God—Logos

By every human measure, my spirit is totally defenseless in this society of the unseen. But in fact, I am armed with the most powerful force: the Word of God.

If I am, that is. A living spirit may choose not to mature. I can choose instead to be victimized by unseen enemies and to incorporate their deceptions into my identity. Hebrews 5:12–14 presumes this capability for choosing not to mature.

> For though by this time you ought to be teachers, you need someone to teach you again the first principles of the oracles of God; and you have come to need milk and not solid food. For everyone who partakes only of milk is unskilled in the word of righteousness, for he is a babe. But solid food belongs to those who are of full age, that is, those who, by reason of use, have their senses exercised to discern both good and evil.

Jesus was a living spirit like us. Immediately after the Holy Spirit filled Him, Jesus was thrust into direct contention with satan himself (Matthew 4). His weapon was the Scripture, but there's more: it was the Scripture in His heart and in His mouth.

Had He not meditated on its principles, had He not memorized its words, had He not uttered the well-digested Scripture verbally, His weapon would have lain ineffective. Likewise, to deploy the Logos Word of God, we must know it and have it in us.

I thank You, Father, for planting a hunger for Your Word in me. *"He who looks into the perfect law of liberty and continues in it, and is not a forgetful hearer but a doer of the work, this one will be blessed in what he does"* (James 1:26).

The Word of God—Rhema

The appointed method of operation: my spirit doing and saying what You want, Lord Jesus. With Your Word in me, I am certainly not defenseless.

Your Word is not only the Word of the Scripture. The Scripture is Your abiding word and does not vary with circumstance, person, time, or place. The Bible's Greek word for this is *logos* such as in John 1.

But there is Your personal, circumstantial, and specific word to individual believers and churches. You speak specifically to our here and now. These words do not replace or augment the Bible, Your *Logos* word, but rather apply it in time and space. The Bible's Greek word for this is *rhema* ("ray-ma") which is used throughout the New Testament. You continually speak *rhema* words to us. *"When he brings out his own sheep, he goes before them; and the sheep follow him, for they know his voice"* (John 10:4). When You speak, I can take that word to the bank. "Father, You said what You were going to do." In the courts of the unseen, I can exert the authority of Your *rhema* word. I tell *You*, "Your will be done." I also tell *heaven's unseen citizens* as well: "I stand with the Father for His will to be done."

And Your *rhema* word in my mouth echoes throughout *Creation*, "This is what Father said. So be it: all that He made, align with it now." Is any power greater than declaring what You have said?

Christians who are growing without training can misuse prophecy. They use prophecy and *rhema* to relate directly to Creation, to the unseen angels, or to other people. Protective guidance can be found in *Prophets and Personal Prophecy*[7] by Dr. Bill Hamon. Using Your words as tools apart from You, whether *logos* and *rhema,* makes us like the seven sons of Sceva in Acts 19. Your jealousy is activated, and You permit us to be exposed for our protection.

Despite Your steps to protect us, Christians can still become enamored with the power of Your words. They forget that their spirits exist only by the life You delegated them. They take Your words and use them in self-directed ways, for self-appointed outcomes.

We can have mercy on them as we want mercy ourselves. They may not know that there is only one direct relationship, with You and You alone.

We do not declare Your Word to manipulate reality. We do not use it like a magic talisman. I declare Your Word because what You say is my spirit's life. My greatest joy is being in agreement with You. Whatever authority You want me to exercise comes from that.

> Man lives by every word that proceeds from the mouth of the LORD. (Deuteronomy 8:3)

> It is the Spirit who gives life; the flesh profits nothing. The words that I speak to you are spirit, and they are life. (John 6:63)

The Word of God—in Tongues

We've enrolled in a class with one simple requirement: attentiveness to God. This includes speaking in tongues. His Holy Spirit is expressing things through us and we pay attention.

> Likewise the Spirit also helps in our weaknesses. For we do not know what we should pray for as we ought, but the Spirit Himself makes intercession for us with groanings which cannot be uttered (Romans 8:26).

We also are praying in our spirits, as Paul says in 1 Corinthians 14:2–4 and 14. While correcting that church's misuse, Paul says we speak mysteries to God and strengthen ourselves when we are praying in tongues. With speaking in tongues comes an interpretive ability, which Paul also described briefly to the Corinthian church. Paul also described it as the *"tongues of angels,"* which suggests that angelic beings comprehend what we pray in tongues.

Our spirit language and its interpretation are among the most mysterious elements of being a Christian. Yet it aligns with what Jesus said we would be. Using the unaccountability and uncontrollability of the wind, He said, *"So is everyone who is born of the spirit"* (John 3:8). Another image of lavish wildness is John 7:38, where Jesus said, *"out of his heart will flow rivers of living water"* (John 7:38).

As a result, the Scripture doesn't convey much detail or give explicit outlines. And yet it is the Holy Spirit's specific gift to the Church of Jesus Christ. Many want to keep it at arm's length because it is uncontrollable. If He thought it so important, who are we to disdain it?

Like God's *rhema* words, speaking in tongues helps us apply the *logos* Word of God to a specific situation—and possibly not our own. He intercedes for people and places globally, and for times past, present, and future. He invites us to join with prayer in tongues.

When we pray in tongues, our focus is on intimacy with Him. Our understanding is not necessary. We are sharing our mouth with the verbal God who created everything by speaking it. There is great joy of being so intimately aligned with God—a joy that more than offsets the mystery and the desire to understand.

When we pray in tongues, we edify or strengthen our spirit. Speaking in tongues is an extremely beneficial element of spirit discipleship for that reason. This is particularly true in our modern world. All our education and media appeals to our minds. Simultaneously, rationalism and scientific ideologies have decried faith and spirit. For boosting our immunity to these negative forces, praying in tongues is unexcelled.

Reflection and discussion questions for this chapter are in the back of the book

---

CHAPTER TEN

Church of Spirits

NEW TERRITORY

We, the Church of spirits, are told to expand. We are not told that the existing territory is bad; quite the contrary. God announced through the prophet Isaiah that the pattern of His Church is to expand.

> Enlarge the place of your tent, And let them stretch out the curtains of your dwellings; Do not spare; Lengthen your cords, And strengthen your stakes. For you shall expand to the right and to the left, And your descendants will inherit the nations, And make the desolate cities inhabited. (Isaiah 54:2–3)

God revealed three distinct dynamics by saying that. First, the territory we already have will increase. We are not moving away; we are moving out. Second, we are not to conserve our resources, nor to be modest in our expansion. Supply will not be an issue.

Third, *the nations* and *the desolate cities* target both the seen world and the unseen. Throughout the Old Testament prophecies, these two signify the control of the kingdom of darkness. The cities are desolate because the devil comes to steal, kill, and destroy (John 10:10). Book Four of the *Unseen* series, *Nobody Sees These Enemies: How to Discern and Disarm Unseen Tempters,* reveals the biblical teaching about darkness' rule over nations.

God revealed that we, the Church, will replace darkness in their zones of control. He authorizes us in both zones of influence, the seen and the unseen. In the visible world, the exact form and timing varies as He leads each church. The lavishness of the expansion defies and discourages measurement in this seen world. Our primary expansion is in the unseen world, where the battle is fought and won. The natural will express the victories achieved in the spiritual world.

Nor is this the only such Scripture; there are many. Jesus defined the expansion, right into the territory of hell. No matter the strength of hell's gates, no matter their permanence or endurance, they will yield to us in a continual retreat.

Jesus punctuated this officially when He first announced the Church in Matthew 16:18, *"I will build My church, and the gates of Hades shall not prevail against it."* And those gates are giving way to our expansion today as well.

THE RULING BODY

Spirits are unseen—both ours and the heavenly hosts'. The substance of spirit influence is agreement. We are alive as spirits now. We Christians are each filled with the Holy Spirit.

Jesus described fatherhood in the third New Testament book, Luke's Gospel chapter 11. A child needs daily sustenance and asks his father, who gives bread, fish, and eggs. These were daily staples of the local diet. Jesus applies it to us with this question in verse 13: *"How much more will your heavenly Father give the Holy Spirit to those who ask Him?"*

How often do we ask for the Holy Spirit to fill us? As frequently as children ask fathers for food. The Holy Spirit is our daily bread, fish, and eggs.

The Ekklesia

The gospels record only three times that Jesus used the word *church*. Each time, we see the Greek word *ekklesia*. As a result, the apostles and New Testament authors used *ekklesia*. Every time an English translation has the word "church," the original language has that word.

That Jesus and the apostles chose this word for church speaks volumes. Their hearers and readers well knew the meaning of *ekklesia*. The word was used to denote the ruling body of a city or region. When the Roman Empire began to rule an area, they charged the *ekklesia* with enforcing compliance and maintaining the peace.

The Lord chose the word *ekklesia* to describe the assembly of living spirits, and thus communicated His intentions for His Church. We are the ever-expanding kingdom. Each place we go, He means us to conform our region to His kingdom's values and conduct.

He imparted to us the tools needed for this charge—authority in the unseen world. *"I will give you the keys of the kingdom of heaven, and whatever you bind on earth will be bound in heaven, and whatever you loose on earth will be loosed in heaven"* (Matthew 16:19).

The Spirit of Church

This world and its captives are dead in spirit; we are the alive in spirit. We are in the seen world but not of it, as Jesus said (John 17). Our spirits are unseen by any natural eyes. How do we function as a church here in the seen?

The typical church in the twentieth century American style has a pastor, Bible studies, Sunday School, buildings, outreach, fellowship, and giving. People attend in their best clothes and act their nicest. In the latter part of the century, this list came to include prophets, benevolence, and prayer groups.

Church was also the guardian of our social mores. Influence in past society required at least a pretense of church participation. Such behavior lists make it easy to conform without being transformed. Thus, many confessed Christians lived unholy lives and gave the lie to all that Church stood for.

In the early twenty-first century, there is an emphasis on authenticity, leading to a dress-down informality. No longer is church participation necessary to function in society. No longer are Christian values the underpinning of America. Witness the rise in unmarried couples and out-of-wedlock children.

In past centuries, the church in America was the guardian of culture. In contrast, the position of the twenty-first century church is underdog outreach. She has gone from confident answers to apology, and from gatekeeper to outcast.

In Chapter Two, *Getting to Know Your Spirit,* we saw that spirit has identity without reference to an external point. The same is true for the Church. What the seen world thinks of us neither impairs nor enhances our identity. We are of another world: the unseen world.

Apostle Peter's first letter shows his reflection on the spirit of Jesus' Church. Jesus' choice of *ekklesia* must have been in Peter's mind when he wrote 1 Peter 2:4–5: *"Coming to Him as to a living stone, rejected indeed by men, but chosen by God and precious, you also, as living stones, are being built up a spiritual house, a holy priesthood, to offer up spiritual sacrifices acceptable to God through Jesus Christ."*

We welcome influence when we are given it. Local American society generally welcomes good contributors. In politics, schools, clubs, neighborhood associations, and business, Christians who do good can exert influence.

But when our influence is eroded, we do not clamor desperately. We do not claw our way back into their good graces. We are not of their world—we're only in it. (John 17:14)

In American culture, the church doesn't presently enjoy the influence we once had. This is no impairment; *"rejected by men"* is in our DNA. Our house is spiritual, our sacrifices are spiritual, and the One we seek to please is a Spirit.

The *ekklesia* has a will, because He made us living spirits, each deriving their life from God. Everyone in such an *ekklesia* must school themselves in Scripture about the things of the unseen. Our will is singular: to agree with Him. That is how we function.

As a body of living spirits, we constantly invite everyone to become a living spirit. Membership drives for religious organizations have a place. But our appeal is personal. We love the dead in spirit with winsome persistence. Our message is truth.

Doctrines, beliefs, feelings, and practices provide necessary guidance as we mature. They cannot make someone a spirit. Only following Jesus as Savior and Lord can; that is the open door we show the dead.

Our simple presence in society as a spirit body is itself a constant invitation. First Peter 2:11–12 describes its full revealing on Judgment Day, the fruit of our spirit living.

> Beloved, I beg you as sojourners and pilgrims, abstain from fleshly lusts which war against the soul, having your conduct honorable among the Gentiles, that when they speak against you as evildoers, they may, by your good works which they observe, glorify God in the day of visitation.

Discounting the Holy Spirit

We are the only living human spirits on Earth. The Holy Spirit of God has filled us. In us, the fullness of God dwells; we partake of the divine nature—and how do we respond?

The Father poured out the Holy Spirit upon Jesus at His baptism by His cousin John. At Pentecost, the ascended Jesus poured out the Holy Spirit on His Church. But often this receives little thought because of the mysteries we've reviewed. Having the Holy Spirit in my body isn't subject to mental analysis or outlining. Sometimes we skip to something more meaty, something we can grasp with our minds. Why? Maybe we don't yet believe the seminal nature of God's Holy Spirit filling us.

Knowing ourselves unequal to this truth, the natural in us fears it. Instead of meekly accepting our exalted status, we can pridefully set limits on the Holy Spirit's influence—such as the limit of understandability. We keep these realities at a safe, controlled distance. We can even identify the Spirit's leadership as a threat to our preferences.

We have used our traditional religious perspectives, practices, and protocols as boundaries for God. We thus place the qualities of our inborn spirit on the other side of a church-approval fence, subject to passing grades on Christian achievement tests. So we distance the truth about ourselves as Christians; we keep Him at arm's length. It costs us to do this; it costs God; and it costs the dead in spirit all around us.

If we truly believed that we are the only people on Earth filled with the Holy Spirit, could anything intimidate us? hold us back? deter our momentum?

No.

If we accepted Peter's words about partaking with the divine nature just like the baptized Jesus, would faith for moving mountains be any difficulty at all? Paul said we are filled with all the fullness of God; what if we believed it? There would be no world that could contest us.

Sure, darkness, the world, and our flesh all persistently attempt to beset us. We can use that as our excuse, but it is a very weak one. After all, can anything in all Creation successfully beset spirits like us?

We are transparently afraid to be who we are: dominion-mandated image-creatures filled with our Creator.

Spirit Church Function

Jesus primarily spoke of born-again individuals, not born-again churches. He used *ekklesia* or "church" only three times. So how does a local church function as a group of spirits?

The primary function of a Christian church is in the unseen world. It is expressed in the visible world. Therefore, a Christian church conducts God's business in the unseen and influences the natural as a result. The natural world is subordinate to the unseen world.

Agreement is how God organized all Creation, seen and unseen. The primary business of a church is to be in agreement with God about what He wants done—following the example of our Lord Jesus. *"Most assuredly, I say to you, the Son can do nothing of Himself, but what He sees the Father do; for whatever He does, the Son also does in like manner. For the Father loves the Son, and shows Him all things that He Himself does"* (John 5:19–20).

The *ekklesia* is to function as an assembly of living spirits to whom God delegates His authority on Earth. Ours is a rulership conducted by spiritual means of influence.

We rule on behalf of God Almighty. The fuel for the proper exercise of His authority is to listen to Him. Like our Lord Jesus, we believe God shows us all that He is doing, in which we have a part to play.

Therefore, our methods are not bound to time or space, nor to the normal channels of the flesh. The methods of the unseen are superior to natural methods; we use both as He directs.

Paul presumes this unbound authority when instructing the Corinthians how to respond to the incestuous adulterer in 1 Corinthians 5:3–5. We actually can hand over someone to satan, much like God permitted satan to test Job.

> For I indeed, as absent in body but present in spirit, have already judged (as though I were present) him who has so done this deed. In the name of our Lord Jesus Christ, when you are gathered together, along with my spirit, with the power of our Lord Jesus Christ, deliver such a one to Satan for the destruction of the flesh, that his spirit may be saved in the day of the Lord Jesus.

The church has business to be conducted when they are together, and it is spirit business. We use, but are not limited to, building renovations, budgets, personnel, and programs. But our spirits' values and methods are always of God's kingdom.

Apostle Paul also faced this spectrum of opportunities. He taught that our spiritual authority is how we conduct kingdom business; he renounced reliance upon worldly methods, as in 1 Corinthians 2:1–5 and 2 Corinthians 4:2.

> And I, brethren, when I came to you, did not come with excellence of speech or of wisdom declaring to you the testimony of God. For I determined not to know anything among you except Jesus Christ and Him crucified. I was with you in weakness, in fear, and in much trembling. And my speech and my preaching were not with persuasive words of human wisdom, but in demonstration of the Spirit and of power, that your faith should not be in the wisdom of men but in the power of God.

We have renounced the hidden things of shame, not walking in craftiness nor handling the word of God deceitfully.

Agreed Spirit Will

Although our only direct relationship is to Jesus Christ, as living spirits in community with one another, we can have a single will—as a community or group. This "group will" results from the agreement of spirits. The spirits might be people. It might be you and angels assigned to your service.

Jesus first described this group in Matthew 6:10–11, commonly known as the Lord's Prayer. The subject of each petition is plural because we, the group of living human spirits, are praying. There Jesus gives us our primal urges. Just as creatures in the natural have survival instincts, so we the human spirits of the unseen have a basic instinct: *"Hallowed be Thy Name, Thy kingdom come, Thy will be done."*

He later described this group will in Matthew 18:19–20. This does not provide a magic talisman called "two or three." Instead, it signifies the unified will of those two or three with Jesus—one super-enhanced group will. *"If two of you agree on earth concerning anything that they ask, it will be done for them by My Father in heaven. For where two or three are gathered together in My name, I am there in the midst of them."*

People living in the flesh can have a group will also; this is well-known to anyone who has been in a sports stadium or worked a polling precinct. The Bible treats cities and nations as if they have a group will.

So how do you tell the difference between the group will of people in the natural and the group will of living spirits? One symptom is the primal urge manifested by our group will as living human spirits. Agreement centers not on getting our way, nor on our own advancement. Instead, our group will represents agreement on our basic instinct: *"Hallowed be Thy Name, Thy kingdom come, Thy will be done."*

The delight of angels may be perceptible as well, when living human spirits unite in one will. They delight in serving God, and the combined will of spirits that God has made alive. We may perceive it, as the shepherds saw the angels' joy at Jesus' birth.

Blessing Church

Our Father blessed our first parents, and in them, all humans ever to live. God is love, and He far prefers to use His divine power in favor upon us. Sin has scarred humanity so badly that we can look at our depravity and wonder if blessing is still appropriate. It is, and He has provided a body of living human spirits to express His blessing on mankind.

The primary means that Jesus established for His blessing on humanity is the Church. In whatever form we find it, one purpose for His Church on Earth is to convey His blessing on humankind.

When God established His Church of spirits to represent His blessing on mankind, He did not terminate His holy judgment. Quite the contrary—judgment is certain, and the judge is Jesus the Son of God and the Son of Man. Included, as Jesus Himself instructed, is wiping the dust off our feet when people reject His gospel.

Therefore, His *ekklesia* declares the gospel and demonstrates it so that all can escape judgment. Luke described the message in Acts 2:40.

> And with many other words he testified and exhorted them, saying, "Be saved from this perverse generation."

Awkward Church

> [Jesus] sent messengers before His face. And as they went, they entered a village of the Samaritans, to prepare for Him. But they did not receive Him, because His face was set for the journey to Jerusalem. And when His disciples James and John saw this, they said, "Lord, do You want us to command fire to come down from heaven and consume them, just as Elijah did?" But He turned and rebuked them, and said, "You do not know what manner of spirit you are of. For the Son of Man did not come to destroy men's lives but to save them." And they went to another village. (Luke 9:52–56)

Is Jesus saying that their spirit is bad? No. The word Luke uses for "manner of spirit" is the Greek *poiou,* meaning "in kind or manner." First, that is not Luke's typical usage of the Greek word *pneuma*, which means "spirit" in English. Second, in our age of "tolerance," we think only bad people would call down fire on an entire town.

Jesus' statement is not belittling their spirit but emphasizing "you do not know." This is the Greek phrase *ouk oidate.* He recognized they did not yet understand being a living spirit. James and John were immature. They thought having a spirit meant they could call down fire like Elijah did. But Jesus corrects: that's not the point of being alive as a spirit.

Jesus' statement includes rebuke for James and John. They did not yet understand the impact of their living spirits in arousing the hostility of others, such as the Samaritan village. Instead of being gracious, they adopted an antagonistic, retributive tribalism behind their chosen leader. James and John had become living spirits without understanding—same as we do. *"You do not know what manner of spirit you are of"* (Luke 9:55).

Jesus next expresses His purpose: *"the Son of Man did not come to destroy men's lives but to save them."* Jesus called them, not to call down fire on hostile towns, but to be fishers of men. The disciples would carry the message that saves the world, not so it could be condemned. The larger the great company of Holy Spirit-born spirits (Ezekiel 32, Joel 1), the more salvation there is—and the more resistance the spiritually dead express.

STATUS

We evaluate. We compare and contrast. These habits classify people and give rise to separation. In the spirit, this is not the way. These habits originate the divisions in the natural world. In the spirit, there is no basis for evaluation.

The Ranks of Spirits

Is there a rank of spirits in the kingdom of God? After all, the kingdom of darkness has ranks for their spirits. The Bible describes those ranks in Ephesians 6:12, Revelation 12, and Isaiah 14.

But what about our kingdom? What measure could rank the spirits in God's kingdom? No earthly measure! Only one measurement would exist: a spirit's relationship with God. But by definition, someone who has a spirit has a relationship with God, so there is nothing for us to measure.

In His kingdom, is there any basis for status? Is there any rationale for rank? The poor in spirit are the blessed ones who become royalty in His kingdom; how could there be rank or status or nobility?

In the kingdom of God, any ranking favors the poverty-stricken in spirit. On Earth we rank things based on superior achievement, character, or nature. But even miracle workers we rank as spiritually impressive might not even be saved. *"I will declare to them, 'I never knew you; depart from Me, you who practice lawlessness!'"* (Matthew 7:23)

Isaiah 32:1–2 and the army of Revelation 19 reveal that the organizational structure of the kingdom of God is very flat. It has no hierarchy and no ranks. Each of us has a direct relationship with the Captain-King.

Evaluation among ourselves is thus unnecessary. Comparing ourselves to each other is thus unfruitful. The poor in spirit would never attempt comparison or competition. Only one thing is needed which each spirit born by faith in Jesus Christ has: a living spirit. The receptivity and attentiveness of a spirit to the Holy Spirit of God is beyond comparison.

Spirit Measuring

The same Paul said, *"I do not even judge myself"* (1 Corinthians 4:3). Evaluation belongs to God alone. Religion, however, excels at measurement. Lucifer's iniquity includes self-measurement. Measuring habits can ensnare the Christian into unhealthy trading.

The trading that darkness promotes requires measuring—but a beneficial exchange of value is not the result. Instead, it is the enervating kind of trading. It's portrayed by the blood of the saints in the cup of Babylon, the Queen of Wickedness: *"I saw the woman, drunk with the blood of the saints and with the blood of the martyrs of Jesus"* (Revelation 17:6).

A living, saved spirit recognizes his spiritual poverty. This recognition comes not from self-evaluation, but from seeing God. We mourn when we realize His requirements are so far out of reach for us. Meekness is that humility that claims no merits. It protects us from the snares of evaluation and IOU trading.

No yardstick is big enough to measure how far we have come: Our Creator saved us when we were dead in spirit, made us living spirits, and gave us a spiritual kingdom.

LEADERSHIP

The characteristics of spirit include community and covenant. God collected us into His Church where those characteristics flourish. God has ordained that there be leaders for His Church. How do leaders of living spirits perform their service? After all, our spirits are unseen; how do you lead something unseen?

God appoints individual Christians to lead others in His Church. The Christians appointed to follow him or her perceive God's authority. A thorough review of the Bible's teaching about this vital subject is presented in *Spiritual Authority*[8], the teachings by Watchman Nee compiled by his listeners after his death.

Spiritual Authority

For our times and our variety of maturity, God provides leaders to help His Church mature.

Everyone who follows Jesus and receives Him is born again and has a living spirit. There is great variety among us. Not all Christians choose to mature. When you do, you follow an individualized sequence that God crafts for you as your Father.

Isaiah prophesied in chapter 32:1–2 of God's system of authority in His kingdom.

> Behold, a king will reign in righteousness, And princes will rule with justice. A man will be as a hiding place from the wind, And a cover from the tempest, As rivers of water in a dry place, As the shadow of a great rock in a weary land.

You may have worked in a corporate setting where organizational charts are used. For a kingdom as global and as powerful as God's, we would expect many levels. Isaiah's prophesy reveals the organizational chart of God's kingdom, with only three levels. Between the King and the kingdom's citizens is only one level, the princes.

How can this be? Here's how: we are spirits just like Him. We worship Him in spirit and truth. His authority commands each of us. As we mature and become functioning spirits, our obedience to His voice matures as well. The King lives in His citizens directly, and we can hear His voice.

> Your ears shall hear a word behind you, saying, "This is the way, walk in it," Whenever you turn to the right hand Or whenever you turn to the left. (Isaiah 30:21)

The Origin of Authority

Jesus' teaching about servanthood is a favorite today. But how does that permit the exercise of leadership authority within a church of spirits?

The answer is simple. Your spirit does not *exercise* authority. Instead, God *expresses* authority through you. Your spirit *receives* authority, as Jesus said in Luke 10:19, *"I give you the authority."*

Authority is always granted. In the kingdom of God, we have one Lord. Consider His title: *King of kings and Lord of lords* (Revelation 19:16). It is to His glory that under His rule are many kings and lords—namely us. When we cast our crowns at His feet, we are granting Him authority over us.

The rulers of the earth use scheming and political ploys. They seize authority through self-promotion and campaigns of conquest. But in Jesus' kingdom, He imparts authority as He wishes. None of the visible world's schemes result in spiritual authority.

Jesus expresses His authority through you. The prerogative is His. You do not own His authority and it does not become your possession. He reveals His authority in you when and how He wants. If He places you in authority as a leader, it is not your permanent possession. Nor are you identified by your authority.

Day by day, we watch for His authorization to speak, act, and demonstrate His kingdom. Whether in a church setting or a grocery line, whether in a car at a stoplight or in the media spotlight, maturity brings us the ability to recognize the authority He gives us for that moment and that person. He influences others authoritatively through His home in you.

American Authority

Authority is granted to leaders in America, where governance is by the people. We have regular opportunity to elect new leaders; we grant them the authority to lead us by electing them.

Governmental leaders are accountable to us to perform. Kingmakers scheme to win elections for their preferred candidate: the news media, big donors, and campaign professionals. The corporate and religious realms have their own kingmakers as well. Yet in each realm, followers are free to leave the leaders; without followers, the leaders stand alone.

Work as we might to improve our systems of governance in any arena, we must have mercy on our leaders. In the fifth of the nine Beatitudes, Jesus said, *"Blessed are the merciful, for they shall obtain mercy"* (Matthew 5:7).

The Conduct of Authority

The last night before His crucifixion for our sin, Jesus taught the twelve disciples about leadership in His kingdom by washing their road-dirtied feet. John records it in his gospel, 13:12–15.

Do you know what I have done to you? You call Me Teacher and Lord, and you say well, for so I am. If I then, your Lord and Teacher, have washed your feet, you also ought to wash one another's feet. For I have given you an example that you should do as I have done to you.

These same disciples abandoned Jesus, who had washed their feet only three hours previously. After He permitted Himself to be captured without resistance, they ran away and denied Him, disillusioned and disoriented. To all natural appearance, this movement was as dead as its leader.

Only ninety-three days later, these same quavering, disillusioned disciples manifested world-changing authority. They spoke with persuasive certainty to thousands, and organized the new Church with authority. They taught the Bible, they prayed, they appointed officers. By Peter's shadow and Paul's handkerchiefs, the lame and sick were healed, the dead were raised and the oppressed were delivered.

Their authority was evident to everyone, including their enemies—even to the point of falling dead at the apostles' words!

Now when they saw the boldness of Peter and John, and perceived that they were uneducated and untrained men, they marveled. And they realized that they had been with Jesus. And seeing the man who had been healed standing with them, they could say nothing against it. (Acts 4:13–15).

Then Ananias, hearing these words [of Apostle Peter], fell down and breathed his last. So great fear came upon all those who heard these things... "Look, the feet of those who have buried your husband are at the door, and they will carry you out." Then immediately she fell down at his feet and breathed her last. (Acts 5:5, 9–10)

Jesus taught these men to be servants. They neither took authority nor lorded over others. They simply expressed the authority of God. The Holy Spirit of God had filled them and placed His authority within them. They paid attention to His voice and expressed it in concert with Him.

Apostle Peter stated it this way in 1 Peter 5:2–3. *"Shepherd the flock of God which is among you, serving as overseers, not by compulsion but willingly, not for dishonest gain but eagerly; or as being lords over those entrusted to you, but being examples to the flock."*

The Hindrance to Authority

Until we are at full maturity, our spirits do not always perceive His commands. We can even perceive His voice and disdain it. In fact, to our shame, we can actually ignore His voice within us. This is the influence of the flesh. The book of the prophet Jonah accurately depicts our resistance to His voice.

Disobedience does not alter the security of salvation, because we are born again. There is no turning back. But when we tolerate within ourselves a disdain for what God says within us, it deafens our ears to Him.

It's costly to our spirits when we disregard His voice. Without listening to Him we lose His exact and intimate knowledge of the people in our lives. When we isolate ourselves from His voice, we act as we think best. Well-meaning Christians hurt too many people by acting in their own wisdom. Let us not add to the number.

For any willful disregard for God's voice, there is judgment. In fact, our accountability is greater even than Lucifer's. A full exploration of the following summary will be found in Book Three of the *Unseen* series, titled *Nobody Sees This Creation: The Origin of the Devil and His Replacements*.

The prophet Ezekiel was told in 28:14 that God lamented the loss of Lucifer, who beheld God directly and lived in His presence.

> You were the anointed cherub who covers; I established you; You were on the holy mountain of God; You walked back and forth in the midst of fiery stones.

Despite this face-to-face privilege with God Almighty, Lucifer jealously considered his own discernment and capabilities to be superior to God. Isaiah was told in 14:12–15 that Lucifer actually thought himself qualified to replace God, and is suffering eternally for it. He has become satan.

> How you are fallen from heaven, O Lucifer, son of the morning! How you are cut down to the ground, You who weakened the nations! For you have said in your heart: "I will ascend into heaven, I will exalt my throne above the stars of God; I will also sit on the mount of the congregation On the farthest sides of the north; I will ascend above the heights of the clouds, I will be like the Most High." Yet you shall be brought down to Sheol, To the lowest depths of the Pit.

Chapter Ten: Church of Spirits

Lucifer beheld God and interacted with Him, but that was his limit. In contrast, God lives directly in each of us by the filling of His Spirit. We are welcomed to partake of the divine nature (2 Peter 1:4), a privilege never offered to Lucifer. Shall a spirit in whom the Holy Spirit has made His home repeat the disdain of Lucifer for His voice? God forbid.

And yet I do. So often I forge ahead, thinking my judgment sufficient. Therefore, Jesus identified mourning, meekness, and mercy in the Beatitudes. They are the only appropriate response to my extreme poverty of spirit toward God. What excuse can suffice when we disdain the voice of God Almighty? Only mourning and repentance will do.

The Trigger for Authority

God desires our meekness. By placing us in churches and groups with many needs, He tests that meekness: will we take authority because a need is present? We are commanded to expand and opportunity to minister abounds everywhere. But the presence of opportunity does not outweigh His priority on attentiveness to His leadership and authorization.

Just because leadership is needed does not mean God authorized you to lead. Your ability and spiritual gifts do not place you in authority. Your education, title, recognition, and requests of others—none of these impart God's authority.

A meek person is alert to God's grant of authority. The Holy Spirit does not tell us to rise and take authority. That is not His way; instead, He is willingly under the authority of the Father and Jesus. *"He will not speak on His own authority, but whatever He hears He will speak; and He will tell you things to come. He will glorify Me, for He will take of what is Mine and declare it to you"* (John 16:13–14).

Instead, authority appears before us. As our spirit matures, we can recognize our influence upon others. It just happens. There is no visible trigger for authority. The meek discover it with surprise.

Identifying Authority

Because we are alive in spirit, we can recognize the authority of God in someone else. He equipped us to identify His leaders among us. We can discern and submit to those He placed in authority over us. *"Obey those who rule over you, and be submissive, for they watch out for your souls, as those who must give account. Let them do so with joy and not with grief, for that would be unprofitable for you"* (Hebrews 13:17).

As spirits, we can perceive the authority of God. But inaccurate thinking, personal wounds, and misuse by others all dull that perception. We seek natural identifiers of authority, with many to choose from: personality, gifts, vestments, titles, endorsements, and the like.

Our ability to discern God's authority in someone can mature. The New Testament letters of 1 and 2 Thessalonians, 1 and 2 Timothy, 2 Peter, 2 and 3 John, and Jude all presume this. The clarity of those letters also identifies the self-promoting, misleading, and abusing leaders. By maturing as living spirits, we can perceive the source of someone's authority.

Substandard Authority

If you perceive ungodliness in a church leader, that does not give you the authority to rectify anything. God places such leaders in your life for your testing. Will you follow His voice or the measuring voice of your ideal?

Your discernment about your leaders is not an authorization to act. Your leaders are as poverty-stricken as you are. Any replacement leader will be as well. The only leaders available are other Christians like you, with flaws, awaiting further maturity.

First and 2 Samuel in the Old Testament describe three kings: Saul, David, and Absalom. Gene Edwards wrote *A Tale of Three Kings*[9] in 1992, and gives a great cautionary lesson.

Leaders who are like Saul can only see usurpers like an Absalom. They cannot see a David whom God had anointed for authority. Inversely, ambitious leaders like Absalom can only see terrible leaders like Saul. They cannot see a David bearing the authority of God, nor can they have mercy for flaws.

When you see a poor leader, don't be like Absalom. When you see a usurper, don't be like Saul. Be like David: accept authority as God gives it. Respect His choice of authority over you.

Spirit and Leadership

As discussed above, the organization structure in the kingdom of heaven is very flat. Every spirit-citizen is alive solely because of a direct relationship with God. Extensive hierarchy is not needed, even though His kingdom spans the globe.

Isaiah 32:1 indicates that there is only one level between each of us and God. Revelation 21:14 affirms that there is only one level of leadership, with the apostles' names on the gates and foundations.

That leadership is a foundational one, not a controlling one. As such, it provides the shoulders for other spirits to stand upon. Apostle Paul described the foundation of God's Church of spirits in Ephesians 2:20, *"having been built on the foundation of the apostles and prophets, Jesus Christ Himself being the chief corner stone."*

Control of Spirits

Leadership among spirits is not about dominating or controlling. Not even Jesus does this. Not even God imposes salvation on anyone. Spirit leadership is foundational, not controlling; it supplies the shoulders for other spirits to stand upon. Followers come voluntarily.

The relationship of leader and follower is even more than voluntary. True leadership is one of agreement in spirit. A leader in spirit makes clear his own agreements and identity plain, and other living human spirits enter into agreement. Thus they grant him or her authority to lead them.

Controlling leadership originates in darkness, where leadership is top down with multiple layers of hierarchy. They are legalistic to the extreme in their structure and their purposes. Darkness victimizes those with no relationship to Jesus, no spirit, and no recourse.

Their legalism affirms that God's principle of agreement is inescapable. Hell itself requires agreement to function.

The agreement that reigns each kingdom differs starkly. In the kingdom of darkness, spirits use power *against* other spirits. In God's kingdom, spirits use power *for* other spirits.

CHURCH MARKETING

Living human spirits comprise the Church or *ekklesia*. No others can be in it. The outreach of the Church is to awaken more living spirits through faith in Christ. The methods for this vary widely. Some worldly methods betray our very nature as the *ekklesia*, God's ruling body.

Need-Based Marketing

Churches and religion often work within the same boundaries laid down by evil spirits, the world, and the flesh. How can this be?

One example of darkness' boundary lines is the widespread belief that Christianity exists to meet our needs. Many confessed Christians remain at that starting point. Churches can limit their mission to meeting peoples' needs. The needs may vary but the boundary line is the same, drawn by darkness.

This starting point is a thinly disguised invitation to the IOU exchange system of darkness. A church that majors on meeting needs can manipulate donations and volunteers with guilt. When meeting needs is uppermost, both churches and believers fall into patterns of exchange and compensation. It confines our living spirits into a system established by the world, the flesh, and the devil. It's like trying to play God's ball game on a field chalked by His enemies.

What about the charismatic and Pentecostal movements? They may practice a fuller gospel yet still on the same playing field, with the same belief, chalked out by the same principalities. When this happens, the Pentecostal message becomes the Holy Spirit exists to meet our needs.

There are many motivated needs that church marketing can target, all true needs but misused as a church's reason for existing:

- make ourselves feel better,
- address our insecurities,
- enjoy recognition and respect,
- give us a break from children,
- make sure our kids turn out well,
- be part of a big movement that succeeds,
- be close to God or feel His presence,
- fix our nation, and
- have fame, power, and money.

Much need-based marketing uses those longings to manipulate Christians. The preacher-and-program solution shunts aside our inborn longings as spirits.

Once we presume that the traits of our spirit are obtained, rather than inborn, the Christian life becomes the striving of the natural. It's tempting to use God rather than love Him. The training, the Bible studies, the giving, the deacon service—all the sacrifice can be manipulation rather than love. We are not alone in this temptation, nor is it new; Job's ancient complaints reveal that he used God as well.

Traits, powers, and gifts that have to be obtained are necessarily separate from us, and not in us already. This belief puts the Christian spirit under earthly IOUs, tit-for-tat efforts, and mechanistic works.

Whether a televangelist is building his personal ministry kingdom, or a regular believer in the pew is simply wanting to feel happier, the danger is similar. They both can be in agreement with the boundary lines set by our enemies. The televangelist and the regular believer both can try to play God's ball game on the devil's playing field.

Boundary Change

Being in agreement with darkness thus gives them authority to dictate limits. It is not simply the boundaries of our spirit, but also the boundaries of our expectations. We settle for what satisfaction we can get, and disdain to strive for the upward call of God.

The kingdom of darkness is always attempting to limit and frustrate us living spirits. Therefore, everyone has to be pushed onto God's playing field with God's boundary lines—even Jesus the Son of God. The Holy Spirit drove Jesus out past those boundaries with forty days in the wilderness.

Apostle Paul lived within the boundaries darkness had drawn for him all his previous life. God also pushed him out—not for forty days but for fourteen years (Galatians 2:1).

When we feel the Holy Spirit driving us out past these long-accustomed boundaries, we can feel conflicted. The need-based marketing that got us into the churches of today leaves us in fear of self-denial for the sake of pursuing God.

Our Father loves us, and forces us to choose the same rest Jesus learned that forty days in the wilderness. *"Come to me, all you who labor and are heavy laden, and I will give you rest. Take my yoke upon you, for my yoke is easy and my burden is light, and you will find rest for your soul"* (Matthew 11:28–30).

The "Presence"

Darkness tricks churches into desiring and clamoring for something they already have: the presence of God. Motives vary among churches, but the kingdom of darkness does not care. The result is the same.

Many anointed church leaders have unwittingly traded the New Testament gospel for the Old Testament system. Their reference to *the presence of God* betrays it.

In the Old Testament, the presence of God is rare—a signal indicator of His pleasure, commitment, and favor. During the forty years of wilderness wandering, His presence was visible, described in Numbers 14:14:

"You, Lord, are seen face to face and Your cloud stands above them, and You go before them in a pillar of cloud by day and in a pillar of fire by night."

When King Solomon led Israel in dedicating the newly built Temple, God's glorious presence was a physical obstruction to sight and body alike, in 2 Chronicles 5:13–14: *"The house of the Lord was filled with a cloud, so that the priests could not continue ministering because of the cloud; for the glory of the Lord filled the house of God."*

The presence of God could fill the Temple. It could depart the Temple as well. After God judged with the exile from their land, Ezekiel saw God's presence leaving Jerusalem also, and recorded it in chapters 10–11 of his prophetic journal.

When Christians consider the presence of God as a thing that comes and goes, they are back in the Old Testament system of relating to God. When a church chases the presence of God, it becomes manipulative. God seeks worshippers in spirit and truth. Experience-chasing is not worship—it is using God.

Jesus taught that the presence of God is constant in us and not variable. God is unchanging and faithful. His presence in us is unrelated to our merits or our placating efforts. Jesus plainly buried that old system in John 14:21–23.

> 'And he who loves Me will be loved by My Father, and I will love him and manifest Myself to him.' Judas (not Iscariot) said to Him, 'Lord, how is it that You will manifest Yourself to us, and not to the world?' Jesus answered and said to him, 'If anyone loves Me, he will keep My word; and My Father will love him, and We will come to him and make Our home with him.'

If God Almighty has made His home with you, the "presence of God" is no longer a come-and-go variable. God is present in you on this earth. Every person who encounters you comes into the presence of God, because you are where God has made His home.

In the Old Testament, the Temple was the residence of God's presence on Earth. In the New Testament, it prefigured us. We living spirits are His residence on Earth now. When we congregate, as Jesus said, where only two of us are gathered, there He is in our midst.

> Do you not know that you are the temple of God and that the Spirit of God dwells in you?... For the temple of God is holy, which temple you are. (1 Corinthians 3:16–17)

> Do you not know that your body is the temple of the Holy Spirit who is in you? (1 Corinthians 6:19)

> For you are the temple of the living God. As God has said: "I will dwell in them And walk among them. I will be their God, And they shall be My people." (2 Corinthians 6:16)

> In whom the whole building, being fitted together, grows into a holy temple in the Lord, in whom you also are being built together for a dwelling place of God in the Spirit. (Ephesians 2:21–22)

Only immature spirits can prefer the Old Testament concept of God's presence over Jesus' teaching that His presence is constant with us.

Spirit Church Marketing

Jesus Christ is all-sufficient. Everything Christians want becomes available when we put our faith in Him. We are born as living human spirits.

Every longing you have is obtained by maturing as a living spirit. Apostle Paul wrote in 2 Corinthians 1:20, *"For all the promises of God in Him are Yes, and in Him Amen, to the glory of God through us."* All the Bible promises are Yes for the living spirit. We manifest their fulfillment as we mature.

When a church teaches this, an entirely new perspective develops for the Christians and their teachers: God is in me. What need could possibly remain?

> And he who loves Me will be loved by My Father, and I will love him and manifest Myself to him.... My Father will love him, and We will come to him and make Our home with him (John 14:21, 23).

A church of living spirits is a constant invitation to all around. What the Father gives us is what everyone wants. The only question: what cost will a person pay to be a living spirit?

Our Lord made the cost quite plain. To His Jewish listeners, who had regularly seen Rome's crucified rebels lining Israel's streets, He said it this way in Luke 9:23.

> If anyone desires to come after Me, let him deny himself, and take up his cross daily, and follow Me. For whoever desires to save his life will lose it, but whoever loses his life for My sake will save it.

By today's marketing standards, this cost is guaranteed to scare people away. But by kingdom marketing standards, this benefit is worth any cost.

---
*Reflection and discussion questions for this chapter
are in the back of the book*

CHAPTER ELEVEN

Spirits in the World of the Dead

THE THREAT OF PEACE

The birth of your spirit brings you into the society of living spirits. By definition, this removes you from the society of the dead. Thus, Jesus described us as *"in the world but not of it"* (John 17:14).

Our community of living spirits is imperceptible to the dead in spirit. Jesus knew we would be like the wind to them. We seem unaccountable and unpredictable to them. They can neither relate to us nor control us. We are like the wind. *"The wind blows where it wishes, and you hear the sound of it, but cannot tell where it comes from and where it goes. So is everyone who is born of the Spirit"* (John 3:8).

Every person was born with a potential spirit. Few find spiritual life alluring—at least on God's terms. The majority finds spiritual life threatening, as Jesus said in John 15:18 (NIV): *"If the world hates you, keep in mind that it hated me first."*

The Threat of Spirit

If you were of the world, the world would love its own. Yet because you are not of the world, but I chose you out of the world, therefore the world hates you. (John 15:19)

We living spirits pose an existential threat to the spiritually dead. They respond negatively to us. Because their spirits are dead, they cannot perceive they have a potential spirit. By resisting us, they confirm themselves in spiritual death. *"He who hears you hears Me, he who rejects you rejects Me, and he who rejects Me rejects Him who sent Me"* (Luke 10:16).

God honors the choice that each person makes. He will cooperate with it—even if that choice is to remain spiritually dead. He will support our choice.

The Bible says that darkness deploys deceptive miracles to confirm the choice of death, and God endorses this activity.

> The coming of the lawless one is according to the working of Satan, with all power, signs, and lying wonders, and with all unrighteous deception among those who perish, because they did not receive the love of the truth, that they might be saved. And for this reason God will send them strong delusion, that they should believe the lie, that they all may be condemned who did not believe the truth but had pleasure in unrighteousness. (2 Thessalonians 2:9–12)

We have evangelistic fervor and want all potential spirits to be born. But just like God supports people's choice, so must we—even if their choice is their own eternal death. Jesus was plain about this also, in Luke 10:10–12. We must accept the choice of those who refuse the kingdom of God.

> But whatever city you enter, and they do not receive you, go out into its streets and say, 'The very dust of your city which clings to us, we wipe off against you. Nevertheless know this, that the kingdom of God has come near you.' But I say to you that it will be more tolerable in that Day for Sodom than for that city.

Peacemakers

> Blessed are the peacemakers, for they shall be called sons of God. (Matthew 5:9)

> That they all may be one, as You, Father, are in Me, and I in You; that they also may be one in Us. (John 17:21)

These two statements of Jesus describe the same reality in two ways. The oneness Jesus describes requires a constant peacemaking. With the innumerable variety of unique identities and wills among spirits, friction is the default. Peacemaking is therefore a determined choice.

Communion with the Father breathes our spirits into life; our spirits place intense priority upon oneness with You. Intimacy with You has a deeply illuminating effect.

When people think of religion, they fear the exposure of their moral failings. In contrast stands the peacemaking spirit, who wants to overcome every barrier unwittingly erected to intimate peace with You.

If we tolerate a division lazily, if we dismissively ignore impediments to intimacy—that is our flesh at work. Our spirits are magnetized to You; by maturing, we perceive divisiveness wherever found. We make peace by agreeing with You about it.

All who endeavor toward You make peace. You call us Your sons in both the heavenly realms and on Earth.

Blessed are the peacemakers, For they shall be called sons of God. (Matthew 5:9)

SIGHT UNSEEN

When you are a living spirit, you can perceive other spirits. Spirits perceive, express, and communicate. This includes the unsavory spirits of darkness.

Identification

The gospels are full of Jesus' miracles. Their display of power is more comprehensive than we might realize. One apparent power of spirit is accuracy in identifying unseen influences.

In our miracle service to others, we expect to be accurate in identification as well. We perceive all the participants in the moment: both the holy and unholy spirits as well as the human.

Inability to speak is an example. In Luke's eleventh chapter, a mute man is brought to Jesus, who identified the origin as demonic. That's why He cast out the demon; then the man spoke.

Not all muteness was demonic, however. The priest Zechariah was righteous, long faithful in prayer, and honored by God with the visit of an archangel. Yet he became mute for nine months (at least) until his son, John the Baptist, was born. His muteness resulted from his own unbelief; the archangel Gabriel declared Zechariah's muteness (see Luke 1:20).

Not all ailments originated in demonic oppression. When the friends lowered a paralytic through the roof in Mark 2, Jesus did not cast out a demon. Instead, He said, *"Your sins are forgiven you"* (v 5). In John 5:14, Jesus healed the man lame for thirty-eight years by the pool of Bethesda, then said to him, *"See, you have been made well. Sin no more, lest a worse thing come upon you."*

Jesus identified unseen spirits at work in a wide variety of situations. When Peter showed bravado and forcefulness, Jesus affirmed it. An example is Peter walking on the water in Matthew 14:28–29, at Jesus' affirmative welcome, *"Lord, if it is you, command me to come to you on the water."* He also discerned the Father's action in Peter's confession of faith in Matthew 16:17.

But Jesus also discerned when the same Peter was speaking for satan himself. In fact, Jesus says exactly the same thing to Peter that He said directly to satan when tempted in the wilderness. *"Get behind me, Satan!"* (Luke 4:8, Matthew 16:23).

You also, as a living spirit, have access to Jesus' skill for identifying the unseen influences. You are poor in spirit—it is not a capability that belongs to you. He does not install such discernment in you like an aftermarket auto part.

The meek spirit does not take over His discernment and wield it like a sword among people. Instead, it remains His capability. Your meek intimacy with Him is how you practice it as well.

The Old Testament Is How He Knew

Jesus consistently identified the causative spiritual reality. How did He know?

The life study of Jesus was His Bible, now our Old Testament. That is where He learned this discernment. The very portion of the Bible often disdained as irrelevant was useful to Jesus; it was all He had. That's why He quoted and alluded to it so often. The Bible explained what His Spirit perceived.

The Word of God is the exclusive focus in Book Two of the *Unseen Series*, titled *Nobody Sees This Unseen Realm: How to Unlock Bible Mysteries*. The Bible was Jesus' key to identifying the unseen, and it is our key as well.

> For the word of God is living and powerful, and sharper than any two-edged sword, piercing even to the division of soul and spirit, and

of joints and marrow, and is a discerner of the thoughts and intents of the heart (Hebrews 4:12).

Perception for Dominion

Our living spirits, filled with the Holy Spirit of God, inherit His original mandate in Genesis 1:28. His image-creatures are to rule the earth, as our Creator commissioned us at our creation. *"Be fruitful and multiply; fill the earth and subdue it; have dominion over the fish of the sea, over the birds of the air, and over every living thing that moves on the earth."*

He places only one boundary on our mandate: the edges of Earth. For us to receive such delegated authority requires the ability to discern the other spirits on Earth with us. How can we dominate them unless we can perceive them?

Spirit and Conviction

We are the source of the world's conviction. Everyone around us is like popcorn kernels. We are the oil, and we are very hot with the Spirit of Holiness, the heat. Wherever we go, whatever we say or do, people start popping.

Holy and unholy alike are everywhere we go. The one group is supportive; the other is hostile. All of them see the Holy One living in us. Every person born again as spirits is hot oil like us.

Jesus told us this would happen on His last night with the disciples in John 16:8–11. *"And when He has come, He will convict the world of sin, and of righteousness, and of judgment: of sin, because they do not believe in Me; of righteousness, because I go to My Father and you see Me no more; of judgment, because the ruler of this world is judged."*

The Holy Spirit is on the earth, doing a convicting work—but He does not do it from power lines, or from air, or from objects of any kind. His home on the earth is us. The Spirit of God is holiness personified; He lives in us.

Each of us is convicted also. Our own barriers to Him, He fingers. Oppression we once agreed to accept, He exposes. Sins we once excused, we now mourn. Then mix in the wide variety of people, personalities, and circumstances. Finally the last ingredient: the heat of the Spirit's convicting influence.

Mayhem arises around the newly born Christian spirit as a result. It can be discouraging, which the enemies desire, of course. God permits it to test and strengthen our spirits.

If that Christian passes the test, they will persist and mature in spirit.

Their identification ability awakens. He or she will start recognizing the unseen spirits on the earth, holy and unholy. Next is the learning, in order to fulfill our mandate for the earth.

Seeing Angels

As a Christian, born as a living spirit, your choice to mature includes seeing your unseen helpers. Book Eight of the *Unseen* Series is *Nobody Sees These Friends: Partners in the Unseen.* Your spirit sight for the unseen includes perceiving angelic ministers.

Everyone wants to see angels—but the meek know their favor toward us is conditional. The holy angels could as easily be our enemies because we sin. So natural is sin to us, we don't even recognize—but they do.

The angels favor us only because they serve God, and He chooses to love us. Their holiness protects them from being jealous when they see His favor upon men. Instead, it inspires their wonder (1 Peter 1:12) and they rejoice (Luke 2:13–14).

> And suddenly there was with the angel a multitude of the heavenly host praising God and saying:
> "Glory to God in the highest, And on earth peace, goodwill toward men!"

Therefore, we do not presume upon the holy angels. In meekness, we expect nothing from them. We relate to God; we request angelic help from Him. He honors us; the holy angels, seeing that, serve us with joy.

Threat

In contrast, the demonic oppressors of the unseen consider you a threat. Their antagonism does not await your maturity. They will not fight fair.

Because their doom is sure, the enforcers of unseen oppression will use every advantage available. That's why they oppress helpless babies who interpret the world with half-truths—just like satan helped Eve to do.

You are a threat to them for several reasons.

First, as a living spirit filled with the Spirit of God, you disarm their hiding habits. Paul described us this way in Ephesians 5:8–14.

> For you were once darkness, but now you are light in the Lord. Walk as children of light (for the fruit of the Spirit is in all goodness,

righteousness, and truth), finding out what is acceptable to the Lord. And have no fellowship with the unfruitful works of darkness, but rather expose them. For it is shameful even to speak of those things which are done by them in secret. But all things that are exposed are made manifest by the light, for whatever makes manifest is light. Therefore He says:

"Awake, you who sleep, Arise from the dead, And Christ will give you light."

Second, as a spirit redeemed by Jesus' death on the cross, you threaten their primary weapon: accusations of transgression.

And you, being dead in your trespasses and the uncircumcision of your flesh, He has made alive together with Him, having forgiven you all trespasses, having wiped out the handwriting of requirements that was against us, which was contrary to us. And He has taken it out of the way, having nailed it to the cross. Having disarmed principalities and powers, He made a public spectacle of them, triumphing over them in it (Colossians 2:13–15).

Third, as a spirit in Jesus' many-membered Church, you are a threat to what they consider their entitlement: dominion over sinners.

I will build My church, and the gates of Hades shall not prevail against it. (Matthew 16:18)

But if I cast out demons with the finger of God, surely the kingdom of God has come upon you. When a strong man, fully armed, guards his own palace, his goods are in peace. But when a stronger than he comes upon him and overcomes him, he takes from him all his armor in which he trusted, and divides his spoils. (Luke 11:20–22)

US-THEM

All people are born into sin with a sinful nature. In this, all are alike. All of us are subject to temptations common to man. We all sin. We all die. *"By one man's disobedience many were made sinners"* (Romans 5:19).

Our personalities mirror the wounds of our forebears and families. Generational lines transmit the sins of our forefathers. Curses follow families across centuries. Everyone is in this boat together—helpless.

There is none righteous, no, not one; There is none who understands; There is none who seeks after God. They have all turned aside; They have together become unprofitable; There is none who does good, no, not one. (Romans 3:10–12)

The Mass of Humanity

Amid this mass of seven billion people, we find varying degrees of morality and depravity, multiple manifestations of good and evil, and fluctuating divisiveness and union.

The mass of humanity, and the product of their culture, values, and patterns—the Bible calls "the world."

Then There's You

Among these billions, you believe in Jesus—you then become a living spirit. You instantly join a new race, the race of the spiritually born. You continue with your natural self, plus. Your newborn spirit matures gradually.

You are alive in both natural and spirit. You interact with the same peers, families, work colleagues, and merchants as before. This interaction is with the same life languages, the same personality, the same intelligence, and the same schooling as before—PLUS.

By believing in Jesus you have a new existence: a living spirit full of the indwelling God Almighty. Now living in you is Someone with *every* life language, *every* personality, and *supreme* intelligence. *"I have come that they may have life, and that they may have it more abundantly"* (John 10:10).

Us-Them

In Western society, an us-them attitude is regarded not highly but rather derisively—a defect of character. We like to get along with as many people as we can, to be respected wherever possible. Like Major Frank Burns famously said in the 1970s TV series M*A*S*H, "It's nice, to be nice to the nice." So we avoid acting or talking like we see things as us-them.

The American Declaration of Independence declared that "all men are created equal." The French revolution cry was "liberty, equality, and fraternity!" In both revolutions, patriots were regarded as brothers.

In the early 1900s, Walter Rauschenbusch and Charles Sheldon promoted the social gospel. God's fatherhood of the saved was redefined as God's fatherhood of every man He creates. The happy concept of humanity's brotherhood was born—brand new in human history, and not biblical.

The evidence soon disproved it. Within ten years, the century became the Century of Wars, the bloodiest in history. Nations saw enemies within and without; they killed and killed and killed. In violent death, the twentieth century excelled.

Yet the social doctrine persisted, happily and blithely ignoring the plentiful contrary evidence. "All men are brothers!"

Thus, in the 1960s it became fashionable to call anybody *brother*. Now in our day, any differentiation among people is met with hypersensitivity. (Even my editing software measures the inclusivity of my writing.)

The Bible does not teach that. Instead, God has revealed that there is definitely an *us-them* imperative for us who are living spirits.

Could it be otherwise? When we become spirits, born again, and filled with Him, we are no longer mere humans but another race of men, the race of the spiritually alive. We march to a different tune now (to use another 1960s phrase).

We have organs they don't have—ears, tongues, eyes, hearts—all alive in the spirit. God delegates to us responsibilities they can't bear, and powers they don't want. We have the favor of God, and they can only be jealous.

Trading in the World of the Dead

In Revelation 17–18, the trading system is symbolized as Babylon, and God reveals its fall. Apostle John is guided by an angel with these words in 17:1–2: *"Come, I will show you the judgment of the great harlot who sits on many waters, with whom the kings of the earth committed fornication, and the inhabitants of the earth were made drunk with the wine of her fornication."*

John sees the sight with spirit-eyes as well as flesh-eyes, and immediately knows what the golden cup in her hand contains (17:6): *"I saw the woman, drunk with the blood of the saints and with the blood of the martyrs of Jesus."*

As the scene unfolds for his spiritual perception, God's voice utters from heaven (18:4): *"Come out of her, my people, lest you share in her sins, and lest you receive of her plagues."*

He tells His people—Christians—to come out. Obeying this requires an us-them attitude. By disdaining the us-them of God's Word, we disobey Him. We surrender our unique racial identity as the spirit-born among the dead. Instead, we sacrifice on the altar of "the brotherhood of man."

What has it gotten us? We are ensnared by the trading system of darkness, the devourer of the saints. Its comforts are in fact alluring. The world's trading system provides us with many creature comforts. God knows that. In Revelation 18 and its parallel Old Testament passage, Ezekiel 27, He specifically names over fifty commodities and international trading contracts.

Business contracts themselves are not bad. But when they are used to seduce the unwary, to suck us into the golden cup, to compromise our holiness, to share in her sins—these all steal our energies and leave us lifeless.

Its threats also have frightened us from being *in the world but not of it.*

Christians polished age-old capitalism, which flowered in church-led nations as a system to serve mankind. The best capitalism fulfills mankind's mandate to dominate throughout Earth while elevating individual responsibility.

But the system that resulted now oppresses. "Either participate or go without," the great harlot says. The world's system of trading is an elaborate and refined network of IOUs, obligations, legal contracts, and financial exchange.

In 17:15, John perceives the seat of the woman as *"many waters."* The angel explains it as the worldwide system, in 17:15: *"The waters which you saw, where the harlot sits, are peoples, multitudes, nations, and tongues."*

She must oppress us. In her midst, our spirits carry the Holiest Spirit of all. To this world's trading system, we represent an eternally convicting force. Jesus said the Holy Spirit would have this effect in John 16:8—and He has it from within us. We are where He lives on Earth. *"When He has come, He will convict the world of sin, and of righteousness, and of judgment."*

The world's trading system cannot ignore us or treat us as the same. The drunk woman and her minions must dilute our effect, or isolate it, or eliminate it through persecution. Her efforts may be both active and passive.

Jeremiah's prophecies succinctly and frequently identify our threat to the world.

> Because you speak this word, Behold, I will make My words in your mouth fire, And this people wood, And it shall devour them. (5:14)

> I have set you as an assayer and a fortress among My people, That you may know and test their way. (6:27)

> Pour out Your fury on the Gentiles, who do not know You, And on the families who do not call on Your name. (10:25)

We can dislike the us-them, but it is forced upon us. First Peter 4:4 and 2 Thessalonians 2:10 say it plainly: the dead do not want to be born again.

> In regard to these, they think it strange that you do not run with them in the same flood of dissipation, speaking evil of you.

> They did not receive the love of the truth that they might be saved.

Jesus presumed an us-them distinction among men. One instance is in Matthew 17:25 (NIV). Peter returned after being asked about the temple tax. Jesus greeted him with this question: *"From whom do the kings of the earth collect duty and taxes—from their own children or from others?"*

Jesus taught the us-them plainly in Matthew 13:10–11. When His disciples asked, *"Why do You speak to them in parables?"* He replied, *"Because it has been given to you to know the mysteries of the kingdom of heaven, but to them it has not been given."*

He warned in Matthew 10:22, *"you will be hated by all for My name's sake."* And perhaps nowhere is His us-them discernment more evident than Matthew 10:34–37.

> Do not think that I came to bring peace on earth. I did not come to bring peace but a sword. For I have come to set a man against his father, a daughter against her mother, and a daughter-in-law against her mother-in-law; and a man's enemies will be those of his own household. He who loves father or mother more than Me is not worthy of Me. And he who loves son or daughter more than Me is not worthy of Me.

Culture

What about human culture? When a culture is transformed by Christians with living spirits, does it have a spirit?

The book of Revelation reveals the worship in heaven. John reports no cultural distinctions there, in the unseen world. All clothing, all purpose, all activity is uniform. God reveals no cultural distinctions in heaven.

What if two living spirits, from vastly different cultures on Earth, meet in the kingdom of heaven? Do their cultural differences bear upon their relationship as spirits? I have to think about that. My first intuition is no. See comments about marriage in the next chapter.

Culture is the product of our testing in the mortal body. People groups develop corporate mannerisms for communication. Wherever we congregate, we adopt civic patterns of self-regulation. These form culture.

We all have met Christians from other cultures. Experience testifies that our spirits know no cultural distinctions. We can bond with other Christians across the differences. When spirit has supremacy in us, then the power, the prohibitions, and the permissions of culture necessarily subside.

The Sent Spirit

Jesus wanted people to know that the Father sent Him. He said several things about it in John 5. Anyone desiring to honor the Father must receive someone sent by the Father (5:23). His sending by the Father was the template for all His actions and words (5:30). Jesus' miracles testified that God sent Him (5:36).

Jesus made a profound analogy multiple times. In John 6:57, He said, *"As the living Father sent Me, and I live because of the Father, so he who feeds on Me will live because of Me."* He said it a second time in John 17:18. *"As You sent Me into the world, I also have sent them into the world."*

A third is John 20:21. *"As the Father has sent Me, I also send you."* This is called the divine analogy, and says you are in the same position to Jesus as Jesus was to the Father—sent. Your sending is just the same as Jesus' sending. That is the equivalence.

God has given life to my spirit. Contained in that is my sending. By making me a living spirit, He sent me into the world just as Jesus was sent into it.

People need to know I am sent. Jesus spoke of His sending, not to brag, but for the benefit of His hearers. They needed to know He was sent. He never exhibited the slightest modesty about it. No one was qualified to question it. There was proof—John the Baptist, the miracles Jesus did, the obedience He gave to the Father.

He wanted the world to know He was sent by God. What He prayed for us in John 17 was a means to an end: *"that the world may know You sent Me."*

When we become living spirits, the Holy Spirit of God makes us His home. By Jesus' definition, we are sent. The people we meet need to know that, for their benefit. We are sent by God into each and every encounter—His living spirit emissaries (2 Corinthians 5:20).

Our message of salvation in unseen realms must have a basis of credibility. Our own confidence gives it. Meet every person knowing that God sent you to them; the other person is blessed when you express that confidence. They feel it as love from God, that He sent you to them. But you have to believe it first, and say so.

As Jesus experienced, some welcome you; others reject you. That is rejecting Him. *"He who hears you hears Me, he who rejects you rejects Me, and he who rejects Me rejects Him who sent Me"* (Luke 10:16).

INFLUENCE

Given our nature as a living spirit, do we have an influence on the dead in spirit? or between our spirit and the things of the natural? How does my unseen spirit cause things in the natural?

Rivers of Blessing

God overflows with blessing. He portrays this in the Bible with rivers. In the garden of Eden, the headwaters gushing from the ground split into the four mightiest rivers of the ancient world. Imagine the sights, sounds, and smells in Genesis 2:10–13 (NIV).

> A river watering the garden flowed from Eden; from there it was separated into four headwaters. The name of the first is the Pishon; it winds through the entire land of Havilah, where there is gold. (The gold of that land is good; aromatic resin and onyx are also there.) The name of the second river is the Gihon; it winds through the entire land of Cush.

The passage next describes the Tigris ("Hiddekel") and Euphrates, lifeblood of the Fertile Crescent where civilization arose. The geographical breadth of influence is emphasized. The four rivers illustrate our own widespread, potent influence as living human spirits, blessing every place we go.

Several rivers in the Bible illustrate God's blessing on mankind. The first is Psalm 46:4. Because Jerusalem sits on mountaintops with no rivers, this is a spiritual river. *"There is a river whose streams shall make glad the city of God."*

What is the spiritual river? Jesus reveals it in John 7:38; Apostle John explained it in verse 39. It is you and me, filled with His Spirit, born again as living spirits. We, the body of Christ-lovers, are His river of influence on the earth.

'He who believes in Me, as the Scripture has said, out of his heart will flow rivers of living water.' But this He spoke concerning the Spirit, whom those believing in Him would receive; for the Holy Spirit was not yet given, because Jesus was not yet glorified.

The most exhaustive Bible description of the river is Ezekiel 47, an entire chapter rewarding Christian reflection for generations. The level of detail is astonishing for a prophecy, but the effect is singular. No physical river fulfills this prophecy. It is God's revelation of what we will do—the spirit-born.

And it shall be that every living thing that moves, wherever the rivers go, will live.... Along the bank of the river, on this side and that, will grow all kinds of trees used for food; their leaves will not wither, and their fruit will not fail. They will bear fruit every month, because their water flows from the sanctuary. Their fruit will be for food, and their leaves for medicine (Ezekiel 47:9, 12).

Be the Hose

Our God is the fountain, gushing blessing, and we, like the rivers, carry His overflow. With a more modern metaphor, we are like firehoses. We don't make the water; we carry it. By pointing us, He points His water.

We have a phrase to describe overwhelming input: *"like sipping from a firehose."* This saying has to be modified for the poor in spirit. In meekness there's no pretense: we cannot control His influential hose of blessing. We cannot hold it, whether to sip from it or point it somewhere. But one thing we can do: we can *be the hose*.

Father, I consecrate myself to express Your blessing on mankind, both near and far.

Influencing the Dead

Yes, my spirit can influence the dead around me. It's the unstated principle in 1 Corinthians 7:14 about being married to an unbeliever: *"For the unbelieving husband is sanctified by the wife, and the unbelieving wife is sanctified by the husband; otherwise your children would be unclean, but now they are holy."*

First John 5:14–15 tells one way it happens: asking anything according to His will. When my influence is in alignment with God, then He will happily extend His influence. My agreement creates the highway for His unseen influence. *"Now this is the confidence that we have in Him, that if we ask anything according to His will, He hears us. And if we know that He hears us, whatever we ask, we know that we have the petitions that we have asked of Him."*

Spirit and Proximity

Think of our power. By agreeing with God, we can influence anyone. Our agreement with God is enforceable anywhere, anytime.

We are unbound by the limits of our geographic placement. We do not need proximity to those we influence. It is clear in both the Old Testament and New Testament that for a living spirit, proximity in the natural is unnecessary to influence.

We have to believe that if we think we are truly praying for someone.

Within us is a divine Spirit searching the globe. In contrast, unsaved people are spiritually dead, with no such resource. For them, proximity is required. All they have is their natural selves—their souls and their mortal bodies. For thousands of years, their spells and sorcery required proximity to a person and their articles.

Counterfeit Influence

From this perspective, there's a new view of the communications invented over the last two hundred years. They all appeal to people's desire to relate—from a distance, in a burst, and without intimacy.

- trains
- cars
- airplanes
- radio
- TV
- telephones
- cell phones
- internet
- personal computers
- email
- text messages

God's enemies saw an advantage in these counterfeit measures. They could eliminate the need for face-to-face intimacy with electronic communications. Now even the dead in spirit can counterfeit our freedom from proximity. These technologies enable our opponents to create an artificial satisfaction.

God outfitted mankind to exercise dominion spiritually without proximity. All our inventions now serve as the countermeasures of darkness. They seduce us into reliance upon digital interaction.

Darkness gains three advantages. First, it handicaps our unseen fighting ability. Christians, though alive in spirit, actually fear social media death-blows to our righteous causes—as if their power was greater than ours. Many Christians filled with the Spirit of Almighty God tacitly believe that social media has more widespread influence than He does.

Secondly, by controlling the artificial satisfaction, darkness can control people. Like drug dealers, they offer electronic communications to get people hooked on artificial intimacy. It seems there's no downside—until abject dependency takes over and counteracts true intimacy.

Darkness's third benefit from electronic communication: it deadens the longing of the spiritually dead. Their potential spirit yearns for intimacy; darkness supplies Facebook.

These artificial technologies counterfeit Christians' true freedom. They also blind the prisoners of darkness to the possibility of spirit life.

Influence throughout the Heavens

The Bible says that we will judge angels. This verifies our influence as spirits in the unseen world. Psalm 8 also alludes to it. Daniel 7 clearly portrays us as the judges of heaven. Zechariah 3:7 is quite plain about it:

If you will walk in My ways,
And if you will keep My command,
Then you shall also judge My house,
And likewise have charge of My courts;
I will give you places to walk
Among these who stand here.

To serve as God's judges of the angels, our *place* is superior to that of angels. All heaven's beings honor our place in His kingdom. Our seating is superior to the holy angels, and also to Lucifer, his fallen partners, and the host of demonic spirits.

They all see our exalted seating in the heavenly realms. Jesus described this in Luke 16:23 about the rich man in hell. *"And being in torments in Hades, he lifted up his eyes and saw Abraham afar off, and Lazarus in his bosom."* Apostle Paul says we are God's showpiece, visible throughout the heavenly realms, *a.k.a.* the unseen world.

> God raised us up with Christ and seated us with him in the heavenly realms in Christ Jesus, in order that in the coming ages he might show the incomparable riches of his grace, expressed in his kindness to us in Christ Jesus (Ephesians 2:6–7 NIV).

However, our *nature* is not superior to the angels. Our place in God's courts mustn't blind us to our spiritual poverty.

Like the original Lucifer, angels have a might and a spirit by nature. God made them that way. Some joined Lucifer's attempt to replace God, and with him, they lost their place. To replace them, God created mankind.

When God cast out the disobedient angels, He did not remove their angelic natures. Their devilish choices did not erase their nature. They remain eternal spirits. We, the poor in spirit, must respect that angelic nature and not defame it. We must not talk down to them. (Jude 8–9)

In contrast, we people have no internally enabled spirit power. People are spiritually dead. We cannot escape it or even perceive it. We are entirely at God's mercy to become alive in spirit. *"I thank You, Father, Lord of heaven and earth, that You have hidden these things from the wise and prudent and have revealed them to babes"* (Matthew 11:25).

He prepared the means by the blood and imparted righteousness of Jesus. He prepared the impartation by pouring out the vitality of His Holy Spirit upon people. And He initiated my spirit's birth by His gracious mercy upon me.

God likes it this way.

> For thus says the High and Lofty One
> Who inhabits eternity, whose name is Holy:
> "I dwell in the high and holy place,
> With him who has a contrite and humble spirit,
> To revive the spirit of the humble,
> And to revive the heart of the contrite ones." (Isaiah 57:15)

> In returning and rest you shall be saved;
> in quietness and confidence shall be your strength. (Isaiah 30:15)

> The sacrifices of God are a broken spirit,
> a broken and a contrite heart—
> These, O God, You will not despise. (Psalm 51:17)

In the kingdom of God, our poverty of spirit places us closer to God than the angels who have an eternal spirit in their created nature.

Topsy-Turvy Influence

God created angelic spirits with power in their nature. As His servants in the unseen world, they use their might to execute whatever He wills. They can also exercise it against God, as Lucifer and his partners do.

Therefore, in the world of angelic spirits, there is an honor that is due their nature by God's creation. This honor is due to both holy and fallen angels alike. Scripture reveals this.

But no honor is due us after *our* fall. Our fall was much more severe. Angels were not made in God's image—we were. Yet we reject this highest honor. We refused it in Eden, and we repeat the refusal globally. We are truly the lowest, the least, the meekest, the least capable, the poorest, the weakest, and the basest.

Because we are such jars of clay, His honor redounds when we are born as spirits. And as we gain function, His honor is even greater. We are intimate with our Father by faith that He lives in us. Unlike the angels, we do not have an inborn internal power of spirit. When we mature as spirits, the honor is His, not ours. As our spirit functionality grows, He is more honored, more praised, wiser, richer, and more capable of executing His will on this earth.

That is, if we will yield to Him and agree with Him.

---

*Reflection and discussion questions for this chapter
are in the back of the book*

CHAPTER TWELVE

THE DAILY LIFE OF OUR SPIRITS

CHOICE-POWER

Dear Sons,

As the father who raised you, I find you constantly on my mind as I go through life—and especially so during this weekend's funeral rites for our dear friends' daughter. She was thirty-five years old when she died on the next-to-last Saturday in October 2020.

You have been to funerals—they sure have a "wake-up-to-reality" effect on you, don't they? Because of my seven diagnoses of terminal illness, and my first teenage job in a cemetery, I have had that "waking up" many more times than anyone I know. God had purposes for me in those experiences which I understand better now. As they add up, you are in mind more than ever—my sons.

Everything in life influences our power to choose. We all have the power of choice. How do our decisions *strengthen* that power—and how do our decisions *erode* that power?

I now see that every choice *toward* God strengthens that power—as if He is the true fuel for our power to choose. Such choices yield more choice-power. When the power of choice grows, we have more alternative choices we can make. The world expands before us.

And the opposite is true as well: every choice to refuse Him weakens our power to choose. We have fewer alternatives that we can realistically choose. We may conceive alternatives mentally, but the power to choose them diminishes.

Each of you put your faith in Jesus and has a living spirit now, the one He birthed within you. But your present choices conflict with your living spirit. You run from God, and what are you running from? From *more* choices—*not* from fewer ones.

I first saw this with my mom. You know she was an alcoholic and died of the resulting liver failure. In the last four years of her life, my dad would search the house repeatedly and throw away all the alcohol. With the help of her "friends," she would get more and hide it in ever more clever places—and act as if she did not know about it. Her power to choose was very low. Her physiological dependencies overpowered it.

Our dear friends' daughter only began using heroin and other drugs (as far as her parents know) earlier in 2020. Almost instantly, her power to choose vanished, her physiological cravings fixed in one direction and one only. The cravings reduced her to near-slavery under an abuser. Mentally and emotionally, she despised herself for it, and entered rehab three times in the last ten months of her life. But once the drug use changed her physical chemistry, her power to choose diminished rapidly.

We always taught you three dangers of drug and substance use: being a liar, a lawbreaker, with only liars and lawbreakers for friends. Now for the first time I see the fourth, and worst, danger yet: you're killing your power to choose. The will of your natural self overrides the will of your living spirit. You become powerless to stop it.

Drugs and substances are not the only decisions that give away your power of choice. Every decision which refuses the Creator of choice, erodes your power to choose. Any choice that neglects your spirit is a choice that strengthens your natural self, and its ability to bury your spirit.

Please choose Lord Jesus, who gives the powers of the coming age to those who choose Him.

Dad

CONFLICTED

I wish life was easier. I really do. But conflicts keep arising. Just about anything is easier than conflicts with other people—for me, anyway.

Trouble with Others

I am on my way to a client meeting. This man and his wife are both losing their mental ability. Their resulting anxiety is at a fever-pitch. They are lifelong, avid Christians, yet anxieties persist. Their diminishing mental control permits the emergence of unrestrained anxieties—and I may be in its crosshairs.

As I go to the meeting, I have an acute sense of what could go wrong for me. A similar event occurred exactly twelve months ago today. Someone's tremendous favor for me suddenly became extreme and overt hostility. The timing is unmistakable, and not coincidental.

In this unwelcome training, I realize You are permitting me a repeat opportunity. You're teaching me to dominate in the spirit.

My spirit doesn't fluctuate. Its life comes from You, and You are consistent. What fluctuates is my engagement in the natural world with my natural capabilities. To be dominated by my spirit means that my spirit imposes Your steadiness and Your nature upon the natural circumstances and upon the potential outcomes. *"On earth as it is in heaven"* (Matthew 6:10).

I am seated in heaven with You (Ephesians 2:6) and my spirit enjoys full access to You (Hebrews 10:19–22). My living spirit has received authority from you to bind and to loose on Earth as it is in heaven (Matthew 16:18).

And now I face a potential conflict in the natural.

As I drive to the meeting, You inspired me to pray assertively and aggressively in the tongues of angels, among whom I have a place to walk (Zechariah 3:7).

While praying in tongues, my spirit senses the angels You've dispatched to prepare the way for my arrival. You reveal angel helpers are soothing the tortured anxieties of my client. And upon my arrival, all threat of hostility was absent.

Being a living spirit in these actual situations is the best!!

The Troubles

About trouble a month later: "Paul, trouble is not you." Okay—this trouble is "not-me." I believe that and will not let it into me or my identity.

Flesh-Busy?

Our natural selves, our flesh, cooperate with the kingdom of darkness. Together, they keep us busy, preoccupied, and distracted with lesser things.

Their aim is to suppress the superiority of our spirit over them. Friction occurs within me and produces conflicting impulses. *"Jesus answered and said to her, 'Martha, Martha, you are worried and troubled about many things'"* (Luke 10:41).

Stillness

I can sense my spirit most when I am still. It is slow and steady, compared to the fireworks of my natural self. Elijah's meeting with God on Mt. Sinai (Horeb) portrays this vividly.

> A great and strong wind tore into the mountains and broke the rocks in pieces before the LORD, but the LORD was not in the wind; and after the wind an earthquake, but the LORD was not in the earthquake; and after the earthquake a fire, but the LORD was not in the fire; and after the fire a still small voice. So it was, when Elijah heard it, that he wrapped his face in his mantle and went out and stood in the entrance of the cave. Suddenly a voice came to him. (1 Kings 19:11–13)

Attention to Holiness

I am finding out something: when I'm attentive to the superiority of my spirit, I can give the conflict to God Almighty. His Holy Spirit then "holifies" me and my spirit. Together, He and I commandeer and disarm my natural self. My flesh and its impulses, anxieties, purposes, and self-will lose their influence over me.

Inter-Spirit Conflict

Can a spirit experience conflict? Can Christians have conflicts, even when we live as spirits?

A spirit exists only in relationship with God. Our choice toward God is the most influential choice of all. All other choices our spirits can make feed off that one. Among Christians, there is an infinite variety of differing choices toward God.

Christians exhibit many differing levels of maturing. Some are far along and some just begun, but all are maturing forward. Yes, therefore, Christians living as spirits can have conflict.

The experiences of life produce conflict and friction by God's design. They enable our spirits to mature and be proven. Conflict with other spirits is one way that God proves our ability and desire to choose the relationship with Him.

Intra-Spirit Conflict

Even within my spirit, I have conflicts. Romans 7 affirms that also. Paul was deeply conflicted that sin's influence persisted in him, even as he grew. He also explained it to the Galatian church. *"For the flesh lusts against the Spirit, and the Spirit against the flesh; and these are contrary to one another, so that you do not do the things that you wish."* (Galatians 5:17).

Why is friction so constant, Lord? I'm grateful for the oases of calm, but they only punctuate the friction of life. Within and without, above and below, all around—friction gets so wearisome.

Why God Offends Us

How many losses and disappointments we endure in life! This is true of all people. Being a living spirit makes it more acute; many sufferings occur only *because* we are a living spirit. That's why I wrote *The Pains of the Christian: Desire, Glory Joy*[10].

Doesn't God know we are trying to win souls here? Why would He act in offensive ways? We can't explain what He does. Why does He make it hard? Why doesn't He prevent conflicts, tragedies, and losses? He could, effortlessly. Didn't He say He loves us? that He is our Father?

But what happens to us, we would never permit our own children.

God is resolute that my spirit should mature. He offends my natural self—my flesh—to provoke my cooperation. God is equally resolute in helping every person choose Him. He offends them likewise. He does it to free them from the domination of their hostile, spiritually dead self.

No one in Scripture manifests this more than Jesus Himself. Of all people qualified to expect the Father's kindness, Jesus was more forsaken than anyone: *"My God, My God, why have you forsaken me?"* (Mark 15.3).

But Jesus chose that forsaking so that you and I would be spared it. He Himself provoked the religious leaders. He wanted them to manifest the murderous rage of their father, the devil (John 8:44).

Paul spoke about the offense of the cross for this reason. In his first letter to Corinth, he described the weakness he felt bringing a gospel of offense there (2:1–5).

Contained in our gospel is the proclamation that God will wrestle us in a no-holds-barred contest. Why? Because He hates us? No, because He loves us and wrestles us for a good purpose: to release us into our fullness as living spirits.

Job's Offense

The book of Job poetically depicts God's willingness and ability to offend us. It begins with God's announcement to His fallen archangel Lucifer, *"There is none like him* [Job] *on earth.."*

The result is predictable; didn't God know what satan would retort? Yet instead of leaving Job unmentioned, God Himself called satan's attention to Job. Thus, it was God who instigated Job's suffering. To make matters more confusing, He authorized the prince of darkness to conduct it.

God acted offensively to rescue Job from sterile, perfunctory, and transactional religion. Our introduction to the man tells us *"he feared God and shunned evil"* (1:1). His stature in society is next described, followed by this glimpse into his religious habits:

> When a period of feasting had run its course, Job would make arrangements for them to be purified. Early in the morning he would sacrifice a burnt offering for each of them, thinking, 'Perhaps my children have sinned and cursed God in their hearts.' This was Job's regular custom (Job 1:5 NIV).

By offering the sacrifice, Job believed God would protect his children from bad things. They were not. A windstorm killed them all, collapsing the firstborn son's house.

Job's regular custom tried to put God in his debt. Job says as much in 3:25. *"What I feared has come upon me; what I dreaded has happened to me."* This is clearly the IOU exchange system of darkness, disguised as righteousness.

We all strike up deals with God unknowingly. The terms of exchange are never stated, and He never agrees to them. We just presume that He is bound to them. We give ourselves leeway, but not God.

The balance of the book is Job's struggle, but not with God. Picture the former caterpillar as it wrestles out of the cocoon. That is Job. He grows out of an IOU cocoon, the tit-for-tat relationship with God that he wanted.

Job began with an identity as someone rich in spirit. The first round of trouble in Job 1:20–2:10, he received without anger at God. But as his second round of physical and internal tragedy began, he realized God was violating the terms of exchange. Examples include 6:29, 9:17, and 29: *"Concede, my righteousness still stands!... He multiplies my wounds without cause.... If I am condemned, then why do I labor in vain?"*

Over the course of his trials, Job descended from the identity of the rich in spirit to one of spirit poverty, mourning and meek, such as 40:4 and 42:6 (NIV): *"I am unworthy—how can I reply to you? I put my hand over my mouth... Therefore I despise myself and repent in dust and ashes."*

God offended Job to mature his spirit, and the same is true for us.

SATISFIED

How elusive is satisfaction in the natural! Early in my Christian life as a virile young man seeking women, a pastor cautioned me about the Law of Diminishing Returns. I found it to be true and repented out of self-interest. The treadmill of finding satisfaction in sin was wearing me out. It keeps climbing and climbing, like a doctor's thallium treadmill test—less and less enjoyable until all your hope and pride lie in pieces on the floor.

The Easiest Satisfaction

Human personality has many unique sets of responses, filters, motivations, and distresses. Each personality also feels satisfied differently.

My primary life language is Mover. I am satisfied when beneficial innovation is implemented. My secondary language is Doer, satisfied when everyone does their part in getting things done. (For more about communication with other languages and coaching, see LifeLanguages.com.)

Satisfaction differs so widely! The diversity of people, cultures, and circumstances reflects God's unbounded and lavish imagination.

Changes in our lives can change what satisfies us. Having children, turning thirty, and surviving near-death experiences are just a few powerful examples. The most powerful change happens when you are born as a spirit. You find decreasing satisfaction in this world.

As living spirits, what satisfies us? My spirit only exists because He gave me spirit birth. I didn't do it. Nor can I keep my spirit alive; only one Person can speaks me into existence and keeps me there. He, and He alone, satisfies my spirit. *"When You said, "Seek My face,"My heart said to You, "Your face, LORD, I will seek"* (Psalm 27:8).

Jesus expressed this frequently. Once you see it, you can't not see it. Two examples are His statements in John 5:19 and 7:18.

> Most assuredly, I say to you, the Son can do nothing of Himself, but what He sees the Father do; for whatever He does, the Son also does in like manner.

> He who speaks from himself seeks his own glory; but He who seeks the glory of the One who sent Him is true, and no unrighteousness is in Him.

When the multitudes of followers abandoned Him, Jesus invited His twelve disciples to stay or go. Peter answered for them all, and for me. He vocalized the craving of my spirit as well: *"But Simon Peter answered Him, "Lord, to whom shall we go? You have the words of eternal life"* (John 6:68).

The Westminster Confession wrote that man's chief end is to glorify God and enjoy Him forever. Enjoyment means satisfaction. The Christian's destiny in a race of living human spirits is to be satisfied by God, The Spirit.

When we live as spirits, being satisfied is much easier.

The Satisfaction Test

Your shift to the easiest satisfaction also strengthens your discernment. As your experience of Jesus Christ brings more delight, rest, and safety, the failure of all other satisfactions stands in stark relief. You can prioritize satisfactions other than Him. Yet they grip the heart, and anxieties ensue. Controlling behaviors revive. Whether you see this happening in yourself or in other Christians, it signifies the same thing: the subordination of your spirit by your flesh.

You can use this like a diagnostic tool, a compass, a weathervane. As long as you are in this flesh, it is at war with your spirit. When the war within arises, discern yourself: am I seeking fleshly satisfactions? You may be, unawares.

When you are beset by anxiety, control, guilt, you can put the brakes on. Recalibrate yourself by time with God and in His Word. You can tell Him you are sorry and ask Him to help you readjust. You can refocus your satisfaction in the Spirit who made us and gives life to our spirit.

Spirit in Movies

I like superhero movies. There are certain common themes because such movies are good parables. They display the life of limits that unsaved people have chosen by refusing Jesus Christ.

Paul wrote in Romans 1:20 that mankind is without excuse, because everyone knows there is an all-powerful, holy God. Superhero movies all assume the fragility of human existence, that evil lurks close by, and no one is safe. They readily identify that this world does not offer permanent satisfaction. The movies agree a Savior is needed.

The superhero movies all show our innate knowledge of mankind's inadequacy. That's why superpowers are needed. We know the true SuperPower: the supremacy of God Almighty and His consistent loyalty to those who choose Him. He lives in us.

The superhero movies always agree about what is good. Whatever the hero, whatever the power, and whatever the villain, the superheroes always use their power of choice for good. The movies center less on the use of their powers and more upon the use of their choice.

The villains in contrast are always slaves—slaves of their power, slaves of their master, and slaves of their previous irrevocable choices.

If only the movie's viewers could see through the "movie" to God Almighty—the "Mover."

What Are My Limits?

Paul said he had learned *"the secret of being content in any and every situation, whether well fed or hungry, whether living in plenty or in want"* (Philippians 4:12 NIV).

I now see that contentment on the horizon of my maturity; it is coming toward me. When I understand that I am a living spirit, I also perceive that there is nothing I can possess. Possessing nothing, I can lose nothing. There's nothing that can threaten me.

I live because God Almighty has spoken the life of my spirit. I have one power, the power of choice, and one primary sense, the sense for His voice.

My sense of accountability for the vision given to me grows daily. Yet as I endeavor to obey Him, limits confront me from every direction. The momentary circumstances say, "Why change anything?" Obstacles say, "Just you try to get past me!" and barricade all discernible paths to fulfillment of the vision. The world says, "We don't want you to." The devil says, "You'd better not, or else!" My flesh simply says, "I can't." All voices limit me, resisting the fulfillment of what He shows me.

The issue is straightforward: I am a living spirit and as a spirit, I have power of choice. If I choose to obey my Father, He will help me obey Him. He will also change all my limits into His resources.

> Seek first the kingdom of God and all these things will be added to you. (Matthew 6:33)

One prophet could see nothing but limits everywhere he looked. Habakkuk saw the proud; he saw the marauding invaders; he saw the intimidating judgment of God. Habakkuk voiced his frustration to God and then recorded God's reply, in Habakkuk 2:2–4.

> Then the Lord answered me and said:
> "Write the vision And make it plain on tablets, That he may run who reads it. For the vision is yet for an appointed time; But at the end it will speak, and it will not lie. Though it tarries, wait for it; Because it will surely come, it will not tarry.
> "Behold the proud, His soul is not upright in him; But the just shall live by his faith."

Like Habakkuk, we too plant our feet in faith. We endeavor to make every choice in God's direction.

SPIRIT BOUNDARIES

Timeline

Our spirits are alive in the unseen world where God is. Everything is NOW to Him. Therefore, everything is NOW to us. Our NOW is continual and eternal for us, because His is.

He creates the NOW by His word of power (Hebrews 1:3). The world of memory (past) and plans (future) exists in a subordinate way to it. He is continually unrolling the totality of things, events, and circumstances through all existence, the all things of Revelation 4:11.

> You are worthy, O Lord,
> To receive glory and honor and power;
> For You created [past tense] all things [Greek τὰ πάντα, pantas],
> And by Your will they exist [continuing action] and were created.

In Him, our spirits are unbound by time because our home is in His word of power, creating each moment and its circumstances. Yet until our death, we live in a world of time. So how do we integrate our lives in these two worlds?

When He speaks within you, you can ask Him: *is this for now, or for a time yet to come? Or for a time that has passed?* He may be inviting us into actions of the past, the future, or the present.

This timeless NOW of the unseen world, where our spirits live, makes the past and the future equally accessible. The common factor is the God above time, the Spirit who gave birth to our spirit when we believed Jesus.

The prophetic movement spreading throughout the globe's Christians expresses God's timelessness, and our partnership with Him. Sometimes, He directs the prophecy of a future event. Those who are stuck in time limit it to the future. If we know the God of NOW, then we also know our place with Him above the timeline. We break out in thanks and praise therefore because the genuine prophecy is fulfilled even when it is spoken.

A good Bible example of our timeline freedom is the Old Testament prophets, who described past, present, and future simultaneously. In Book Two of the *Unseen* series, *Nobody Sees This Unseen Realm: How to Unlock Bible Mysteries*, we will explore the Time Trombone as a picture.

The best Bible example of the eternal NOW will be explored there: the Angel of the Lord.

Controlling Emergencies

We can assume that our natural response to perceived threats, crises, and emergencies is the best. We hide behind that with our excuses for not having faith. My natural response is like Jesus described in Matthew 6:27: *"Which of you by worrying can add one cubit to his stature?"*

Last night my laptop fell off my motorcycle seat! Landing hard on the concrete, it made a big metal thud—the thud of crashing on a screen-breaking corner.

I cussed about it. Immediately, I began to open it and see what happened. But my spirit immediately rose up. Something within me overruled those impulses of fear and I put my mouth in gear for the kingdom of God. "No, not that word. I declare the computer is fine and there is no emergency in actual fact."

The emergency impulse died away quickly, but my mind kept returning to the damage visible on my computer. After all, I need it on this trip.

Each time, the doer language in me reached for the computer. And each time it tried, my spirit rose up: "No!"

The moment finally came when all sense of threat was at ease. At last, I could accept that this was no genuine emergency. The fear in my heart was replaced by harmony of agreement with You. With that permissive safety, I opened the laptop. The visibly dented corner inspired no fear. Power on ... and it worked just fine.

This was a wonderful study in the spirit's ability to tame the natural self. I learned again that the will of my spirit can assert itself. The impulses and inclinations of my flesh can be subordinated in responding to circumstances. *"Therefore do not worry, saying, What shall we eat? or What shall we drink? or What shall we wear? ... For your heavenly Father knows that you need all these things. But seek first the kingdom of God and His righteousness, and all these things shall be added to you"* (Matthew 6:31–33).

The Disarming of Fear

Fear is a power. It vies to control me and contests the supremacy of my spirit. My flesh is very susceptible to fear's manipulation, without even knowing it. When a fear arose today, You helped me disarm my default response, and stay free of its domination. You reminded me to ask You about the fear.

"Paul, ten minutes ago you did not know about these facts. How did you stand in your spirit then?" Well, Lord, I was calm and cognizant of Your favor upon me.

"What changed, in reality?" Your piercing question illuminates the *fear acronym*: False Evidence Appearing Real.

"Paul, if you are a king for Me on Earth and if I am in you, then what truly is real? Who gets to speak the real into being? Who decides what is real, Paul?" I listened with the Bible in mind as always. Hebrews 1:3 says You uphold all things by the word of Your power. Colossians 1:16–17 put it this way:

> For by Him all things were created that are in heaven and that are on earth, visible and invisible, whether thrones or dominions or principalities or powers. All things were created through Him and for Him. And He is before all things, and in Him all things consist.

You are the Real, Lord, with us, Your partner kings. "Yes, and the more someone matures in their spirit, the more threatening they are to darkness, which responds with assaults on the natural self, both in fact and in fear. And that's how I ordained things to be.

"I cannot entrust the power of spirit to people I love, until they prove themselves safe with it. As much as I love you, I cannot give you full privileges in the unseen world until I'm satisfied you won't suffer the ruin Lucifer did."

Work as a Spirit

We are spirits contained within mortal bodies. Lord, in our world, You mandated that we work. How do we integrate natural work with our spirit identity? Does our spirit coordinate the responsibilities of our natural selves? I asked about it. You gave me this guideline and I now start each day by saying:

> You, Lord, decide my part. It starts with Your word, followed by my agreement, initiating unseen activity, concluding with the results You imagined.

So my primary job is to pay attention to what You say and agree with You. Sometimes Your direction involves me solely, and sometimes that it involves me corporately with others. As a living spirit in relationship with You, I can ask You: *is this for me alone, and/or is for me with others?*

God's Hands

What a delightful existence—being a spirit. Yet not always perceptible. I wish it was—how peaceful, to be one in spirit with the Prince of Peace. How contented! a living spirit in the heavenly realms under Your lordship.

What about when I am so busy, so responsible? when my mind, heart, and body are in full action? Lord, am I still a spirit then? Have I forsaken Your path for me?

"No—even if only because you asked. We are together, Paul, and nothing changes that. I am in you, period. There is no expectation that My presence will always be perceptible, nor that your spirit will be. Besides—I want you to be active in the natural. Of the two of us, you're the only one with hands."

SPIRIT'S FAMILY

"Who is my neighbor?" asked the man seeking to justify himself. Jesus' answer: ask not who is your neighbor, but ask who you can be neighbor to (paraphrasing John F. Kennedy).

Marriage of Spirits

> For in the resurrection they neither marry nor are given in marriage, but are like angels of God in heaven.

Jesus' statement in Matthew 22:30 is still mysterious to us who by long union feel one with our mates. But the truths about our spirit explain it.

God's purpose is to populate the unseen world with proven spirits in union with Him. He is proving our quality to express what He says and perceive what He sees. We each have a direct relationship with Him; we can each make choices in agreement with Him.

He made us as spirits in mortal bodies; this was part of being made in His image and likeness. Our spirits, like His, are capable of community and covenant. Our bodies manifest our spirits; they are the arena where our spirits are proven.

In our bodies, we are saved and born again as living human spirits. While in the body, we develop our spirits; we become secure; we can relate in the unseen world.

We are male and female in body to enable covenant marriage of two mortal-body spirits. God did not make us male and female because He is. He did it so that marriage of a man and woman could depict His multi-personal oneness as a Trinity. Male and female bodies enable variety, marriage, and reproduction, all helping to image Him and prove us.

Maleness, femaleness, and marriage in the mortal body are therefore for Earth. By them we are prepared and proven. Their purpose will be fulfilled when we are proven and fully at home in God's heaven. Physical reproduction will not continue in heaven. Likewise maleness and femaleness, if present, will be different. There will be no marriage.

> Then He who sat on the throne said, "Behold, I make all things new." (Revelation 21:5)

No marriage in heaven doesn't mean there is less unity! Heaven is not less satisfying than a good marriage in our natural selves. Jesus meant that we would have a superior oneness—a unity far more satisfying in both spirit and body.

He has not yet revealed the details. He has only revealed that mortal marriage is preparation for superior relationships in the kingdom of light.

In *Mere Christianity*[11], C. S. Lewis humorously illustrated how we discount what we cannot imagine. He told of a twelve-year-old boy who prized chocolate above all else. When his father gave him the pre-teen talk to reserve sexual intercourse for marriage, the boy listened patiently. When his father ended, the boy asked only one question: "Do you eat chocolate during intercourse?" Dad said no and the boy concluded, "Intercourse must not be very good, then."

Child Spirit

Can a young child who loves Jesus be born again, born of the Spirit? Even before they can grasp the full gospel?

I believe they can. The unseen enemies of children do not fight fair; we must welcome all our unseen helpers. Adults must encourage a child's spiritual attentiveness. Parents' vigilant discernment is necessary. Children can display sentiments motivated by affection. They desire to be included and fear rejection. A child desires to please or can manipulate for rewards.

Apostle Paul described his youth as a top student in the hardest Jewish training. The training, the compliance, and the discipline did not produce a powerful spirit. In fact, it produced no spirit at all but death, as Paul reported in Romans 7:9–11. He was not born as a spirit until Jesus saved him in Acts 10.

> I was alive once without the law, but when the commandment came, sin revived and I died. And the commandment, which was to bring life, I found to bring death. For sin, taking occasion by the commandment deceived me, and by it killed me.

If indeed a child can be a living spirit in agreement with God, what age is that spirit?

The same age as an older person's spirit can be. Not time, but maturity, defines the age of spirit. Thus, Samuel grew strong in spirit, as did John the Baptist and Jesus. The surrounding adults recognized each child as a mature spirit. All their peers took part in standard Jewish training, but those three children exhibited more strength of spirit than adults. Their memorable impact outlasted their lives and landed on the pages of the Bible.

Childhood growth as a spirit characterized Samuel, John the Baptist, and Jesus in ways that no other student had. Only God awakens someone's spirit.

And we know He loves the little children, all the children of the world.

Hello, Children

The first encounter anyone ever has is with their family. The second encounter is the kingdom of darkness.

The newborn child inherits death from Adam (Romans 5), with total insecurity suddenly thrust upon it. No wonder a baby cries at birth. The child misinterprets the environment its family provides. The child's fears are those of the natural flesh. A child of Adam's death, the infant does not have a living spirit.

These are not the only hurdles confronting the newborn human. There is also a voracious dragon making war on it and ready at the womb's exit to devour the child (Revelation 12:4, 17). This malevolent enemy is this fallen archangel Lucifer, become satan. So powerful is he that no child can escape his imprisoning.

How does satan imprison them? He feeds them the same misinterpretations he fed Adam and Eve; he stimulates self-doing and insecurity. Each descendant of our first parents manifests the generational impulse to hide behind some type of fig leaf: *"I was afraid because I was naked"* (Genesis 3:10). Shame, fear, and control form satan's prison chains, reproduced in every human child.

All this the infant faces without a living spirit. Children are raw meat for the kingdom of darkness—defenseless against them. How is anyone ever born as a spirit, then?

> When His disciples heard it, they were greatly astonished, saying, 'Who then can be saved?' But Jesus looked at them and said to them, 'With men this is impossible, but with God all things are possible' (Matthew 19:25–26).

We need not think satan's prison is inescapable. How does anyone ever become a living spirit but through rebirth into Christ?

> As for you, you were dead in your transgressions and sins, walking in the ways of the prince of the power of the air... But God, who is rich in mercy, made you alive. (Ephesians 2:1–6)

The Spirit of the Lord is upon Me, Because He has anointed Me... To proclaim liberty to the captives, and ... To set at liberty those who are oppressed. (Luke 4:18–19)

Children Who Die Young

One of the test readers asked how this applies to her stillborn son. My heart went out to her as I remembered our feelings over at least one miscarriage.

Catholic doctrine identified salvation with being baptized into the Church. For children who never are, they developed a doctrine of Limbo. Protestants identify salvation with personal faith in Christ and generally refer to God's mercy upon those who die too young. The Scripture does not present a clear outline about the death of the young and there is room to differ—but patterns are present to guide us.

With awareness comes accountability, as Paul described in Romans 7:9. *"I once was alive apart from the law, but when the commandment came, sin revived and I died."* The legacy of Adam's death-choice affects every person, and that sadly is why many die quite young through no fault of their own. The ripples of sin—whether Adam's or our own—can be widespread and long-lasting, affecting even the most helpless children. May we never take sin lightly.

In Matthew 18:7, Jesus pronounced woe upon those who cause children to sin. *"Woe to the world because of offenses! For offenses must come, but woe to that man by whom the offense comes!"* He clearly states God's compassion for children as the helpless, and simultaneously affirms they are born into a world of sin.

Yet in this world of sin, God wants the best for everyone as John 3:16 famously declares: *"For God so loved the world ... "* The gospel of the Kingdom clearly presents the mercy of God, such as Beatitude number five in Matthew 5:7. *"Blessed are the merciful, for they shall receive mercy."* Jesus often quoted Hosea 6:6 to His legalistic antagonists: *"I desire Mercy rather than sacrifice."*

Jesus said in Matthew 18:10 of the children coming to Him, *"In heaven their angels always see the face of My Father."* In Luke 18:16, He soundly rebuked the religious people who thought He should not be troubled by children: *"Let the little children come to Me, and do not forbid them; for of such is the kingdom of God."*

Each is judged according to what was entrusted to them. The character of our God in the Scripture reassures us that children dying young are favorably received. Since they may not have been born as spirits, the manner of His provision for them is not yet fully revealed.

Wounds

Parents do their best. They have the energy because they are young, but not the wisdom for the same reason. They raise their children into adults with wounds. The grown children then raise their own children with scars of past parents' failings and shortcomings. No child is immune to this cycle.

God has left parents imperfect, purposefully: to point the child to the perfect Father.

A parent who matures as a living spirit discovers their wounds from previous generations. Older Christians can perpetuate these wounds or seek healing for them. Although living spirits, we can unwittingly choose divisions because we tolerate these old wounds.

Children, once grown, can linger in the wounds inflicted by their parents. Many proven coping methods are available through the counseling profession. But only maturing as a living spirit can fully lay the wounds to rest.

The living human spirit seeks communion with God. In Him, spirit-to-spirit with others, the scabs of old wounds can fall easily away. Darkness keeps seeking to agitate the healed wound with familial memories and patterns. But we living spirits can resist those efforts; we can replace the pain of wounds with the health of trusting our Father.

The parent who is a living spirit looks back meekly on the years they parented in their natural selves and relied only on natural knowledge. That parent can humbly acknowledge the failings of the years to their children, and is not threatened by apologizing.

That meek parent can welcome God's purpose in parental imperfections: to point the child to the perfect Father.

Parent to the Dead

As living spirits, we have pains others cannot have. This is part of our proving process.

One such pain is being the parent of a child who is dead in spirit. Jesus warned us about this in Luke 12:51–53, citing Micah 7:8. Listen carefully to Him speaking. You can affirm His warning: generational conflict results from someone's faith in Him.

Chapter Twelve: The Daily Life of Our Spirits

Do you suppose that I came to give peace on earth? I tell you, not at all, but rather division. For from now on five in one house will be divided: three against two, and two against three. Father will be divided against son and son against father, mother against daughter and daughter against mother, mother-in-law against her daughter-in-law and daughter-in-law against her mother-in-law.

Conflicts between just two generations means heartache for the Christian parent. Your living spirit threatens the dead everywhere. Now add to that, the parent-child relationship. Friction results. The child is in proximity to living spirits (his parents). He or she is constantly agitated by the Holy Spirit. Further agitation results if in the same residence, or if helpless grandchildren are affected.

You are a spirit-born parent while such a child is somehow refusing the Holy Spirit. The pressure of the Holy Spirit in you creates a furnace of anger in the child, in friction with the refusal. A child under sin's captivity can't identify the heat source; they only feel the furnace.

The eruption may be overt, as they blame the parent and curse them. It may be covert; the child can deceive or misuse his or her parents. Forgiving seventy-seven times, parents can neglect Jesus' other teaching to wipe the dust off our feet, when it's our own child's dust. Parents reluctant to create a barrier to the child's repentance can keep casting their pearls before swine.

Your persistent pursuit of the Spirit of God also creates intense pressure upon the kingdom of darkness. While you are always seeking to make the child a living spirit, darkness is working to maintain their grip on each dead person.

Besides all this are the prayers of the parent who is a living spirit. God's nature is to show His love to a thousand generations of those who love Him. There may also be prophetic words over the child that are unconditional and will not be thwarted.

How can any grip of darkness prevent God's rescue? Answer: it can't.

When a strong man, fully armed, guards his own palace, his goods are in peace. But when a stronger than he comes upon him and overcomes him, he takes from him all his armor in which he trusted, and divides his spoils (Luke 11:21-22).

Therefore know that the Lord your God, He is God, the faithful God who keeps covenant and mercy for a thousand generations with those who love Him and keep His commandments. (Deuteronomy 7:9)

DEATH-TIME

Christian focus has been on the afterlife for decades. Jesus actually talked little about life after we die. Far more frequent was His use of the phrases *kingdom of God* and *kingdom of heaven*. When He spoke of eternal life, He did not mean what we mean; instead, it is an unending life beginning immediately when you believe and follow Him.

But in His society, death and disease were not antiseptically removed from daily life. Death-time was a common occurrence.

Finished?

Jesus only raised some of the dead he encountered. Where are they? They are not here with us now. They died again. Nor was everyone in Israel healed; people wouldn't have needed healing in the book of Acts if He had.

"It is finished," He announced from the cross. Yet humanity remains in the same tragic condition it had been in since Adam's fall: we die. Even Jesus wept about death. Why do we still die?

It is not God's purpose to spare us the consequences of Adam's deathful choice. To the contrary: God intends that we should die. Only by that means can we gain the eternal bodies to match our eternal spirits.

Yes, His work is finished. In fact, the trail He blazed is the only pathway to life. *"Whoever wants to be my disciple must deny themselves and take up their cross daily and follow me. For whoever wants to save their life will lose it, but whoever loses their life for me will save it"* (Luke 9:23–24).

Agreements while Aging

People age at different rates, but we all age. Our agreement with God, or lack thereof, has a powerful role in our aging.

God made my body. It is part of physical Creation, and like Creation, my body longs to awaken. Even in my dreams, its physical expression is heaven-equipped. But the march of time introduces an opposing force of decay. We call it aging, but how much of it will triumph over us? The longing to awaken, and aging—they enjoin a contest.

Many older people—Christians or not—agree with decay and aging. What they feel in their bodies is more influential than their agreement with God. Professionally, I've worked with retired people for nearly thirty years. I can emphatically report to you: when our stronger agreement is with aging, then ailments expand to fill the agreement available. My own aging concurs with that principle.

Many areas of life display this dynamic. For example, we build new and wider roads to accommodate overwhelming traffic, and then development expands to fill the roadways available. Or attempt a quick task, and watch the effort fill the day, because work expands to fill the time available.

Likewise, when you agree with your body's decay, then aging will expand to fill the agreement available. Of course, the kingdom of darkness wants to help you age and become decrepit.

Inversely, your spirit can impose agreement with God upon your body. The methods vary from simple prayer, to fasting, prayer partners, and the like. The result is the same: it releases the life of the Holy Spirit of God inside your skin. He expands within you to fill the space available.

The meek person easily recognizes this. Bereft of ability to control aging, a humble person recognizes spiritual poverty in themselves. The meek person cries out to the Holy Spirit. Apostle Paul did, in Romans 7:24–25: *"Who will deliver me from this body of death?"*

Like Paul, we answer aging with our stronger agreement. *"I thank God—through Jesus Christ our Lord!"*

Time to Die

I'm closer in time to my body's death than I am to its birth. My body could die soon; so could yours. Let's assume we die tonight.

Have you ever watched a show, knowing that the character would die in the next scene? It's an omniscient feeling. You see how they could have prevented death. The character on screen does not know they have little time left—only you do. And you coach them on screen: "Do this!" Don't go there!" You want to protect them from dying.

Apply this to us in the natural, visible world. We rarely live as if we might depart the seen world today. Is anyone rooting for us to see it? Death is always at hand: a careless driver, a physical failure, a marauder, an accident. All just seconds away.

Why not live every moment that way? Nothing sobers the mind like a firing squad, I've heard. It's true. Seven times in my life, doctors have told me I had a fatal ailment. Three were in 2018–2019. What was God teaching me? My seen body is not the chief thing. My spirit is my life. My body expresses my spirit.

Because we Christians are living spirits, our bodies aren't the source of our true welfare. The Holy Spirit of God lives in me! Yielding to my body's domination is beneath His dignity. I can permit the fear of physical death to impose itself upon me. I can give my natural body power over me. But that is a surrender.

When Jesus died, the Son of God incarnate, He opened up a gigantic treasury for us. The Second Person of the infinite Trinity endured the forsaking of the First Person. This infinite rift in the infinite God has infinite rewards—for us.

After Jesus died physically, He was resurrected physically. Is there any better evidence that dying in this world is not death in the unseen? The death of His natural body did not threaten the life of His eternal body. And the body He received was a heavenly body—walking through walls, crossing time and space.

After Jesus ascended to heaven with His physical body, he poured out His Spirit, the Third Person of the Trinity, upon people who believed Him. Now God has made His home on Earth within the physical bodies of us living spirits. Need we yield to the natural body's fear of death? The Author of Life Himself lives in me, inside my body. Surely that has a revitalizing effect!

Can my natural body and its conditions or diseases or handicaps impair this Triune God within me? No. Rather, it is God, a Spirit, to whom I offer my body. *"Do not present your members as instruments of unrighteousness to sin, but present yourselves to God as being alive from the dead, and your members as instruments of righteousness to God"* (Romans 6:13).

My natural body is no impairment to Him. He actually imparts resurrection life into my natural body. *"But if the Spirit of Him who raised Jesus from the dead dwells in you, He who raised Christ from the dead will also give life to your mortal bodies through His Spirit who dwells in you"* (Romans 8:11).

Whether I will die sooner or later, let me die every day. This is how the mighty influence of God the Spirit manifests within my spirit. *"For we who live are always delivered to death for Jesus' sake, that the life of Jesus also may be manifested in our mortal flesh"* (2 Corinthians 4:11).

Funerals

What is happening at a funeral? The mixture of bitter and sweet varies from funeral to funeral. What do they have in common where spirit is concerned?

If not following Jesus Christ, people die with soul only, and no spirit. These we can only remember and memorialize. Existing eternally, they never receive a living spirit. Eternal life only begins when we follow Jesus; the deceased never did. His or her eternal life never started.

Their mortal death occurred before their potential to be born as a spirit was realized. Biblically, every human being who dies without faith in Christ Jesus has perished. He or she is in hell. Jesus Himself warned about this in the Bible. Despite all His effort, the deceased never responded to God's wooing. *"He is patient with you, not wanting anyone to perish, but everyone to come to repentance"* (2 Peter 3:9 NIV).

We who are born as living spirits before our physical death have already begun our eternal life. We have a fuller function, greater than we can imagine, elevated to the full potential of perception and capacities.

What about the mourners? If they are unsaved, with soul only but no spirit, they have an opportunity. In the funeral, God may reveal to them their living deadness. They can desire spiritual life. They can fear judgment and repent.

Mourners who are alive in spirit through Christ have a meek fellowship. We accept our common mortality. The funeral reminds us somberly that this life is for testing and proving us. Our hope is strengthened. We resolve to endure to the end. *"He who endures to the end shall be saved"* (Matthew 24:13).

The wide human range of emotions, thoughts, and actions is available to all in attendance. Emotions show neither who is alive in spirit nor who is not.

Most people know the shortest verse in the Bible: *"Jesus wept"* (John 11:35). We assume He wept over His friend's death, like we do. That's not why; Jesus knew He would raise Lazarus up.

Jesus wept instead because death was the *unnatural*. None of us believe death was God's original plan, and rightly so: it was not. He wept that our first parents ate from the tree of death, rather than the tree of life.

And so also, we weep.

HABITS

I've been actively following Christ for forty-seven years. Only in the last ten have I understood His teaching about spirit. What preparatory habits did He give me to follow? If a Christian wants to mature as a spirit, what can they do?

The Evangelical Answers

When God called me, I put my faith in Christ. Curiosity exploded within me about this world of peace and hope I had entered. Simple habits immediately launched me into growth: fellowship with other Christians, tithing, Bible study, and prayer. And never since have they failed to stimulate my maturity. Never have they impaired my progress. I maintain these habits to this day.

After marrying my wife four years later, we devoted the first twelve years of our marriage to college ministry as staff of InterVarsity Christian Fellowship. The sacrifice was significant. Yet those years were spiritually lavish with godly input, deep study of Scripture, effective fruitfulness, and extended times in prayer. We also read Christian literature extensively and heard teachers of globally proven stature.

About fifteen years into my Christian life, my wife and I began feeling discord between the input from our church and the input from Scripture. No one had warned us this could occur, and we felt the problem was us. So we pursued God wholeheartedly in all that we did. We figured He would lead us in the right direction, whatever we might feel about it.

A Rough Road

While we pursued the knowledge of God, our various pastors sought us out for positions of leadership. We accepted and served to the best of our ability, with an effectiveness that others recognized. Yet we kept experiencing conflict with these same pastors. Again we concluded the problem was us, and our pastors were inclined to agree. Yet nothing we attempted would resolve the conflicts.

In two churches where our service included serving as founders, the pastors' hostility become overt and spread to others. The Scripture instructs us plainly in Romans 12:18, *"If it is possible, as much as depends on you, live peaceably with all men."* Despite our best efforts at reconciliation, the spreading disdain forced us out the door of their churches.

During this time, we sought counseling, so deeply wounding is church pain. One book that lifted us to a biblical outlook was *A Tale of Three Kings*[12], by Gene Edwards. We understood afterward that Sauls can only see Absaloms, so we resolved to be Davids. Instead of discrediting the Lord's anointed, we respected the pastors who mistreated us. Even among those who sought us out to lead separate efforts, we spoke honorably of the pastors and did not nurture discontent.

Whether the dissonance with pastors was overt or unseen, we kept maturing. And in each church we attended, we kept longing for more than it could offer.

As a Christian, you face the same choice we did. You can stay at a maturity level that your church approves. But the alternative is far preferable: while honoring their position and authority, you can pursue God. You can follow Jesus beyond what your church or pastor encourage.

Finally, in 2006, a friend in our charismatic Episcopal church recognized our longing and gave us the book *The Eternal Church*[13] by Dr. Bill Hamon. I dismissed the first reading with disdain. The Holy Spirit convicted me, and obediently I reread it. On the third reading, its point of view exploded within me. Dr. Hamon had described our life: constantly outgrowing what once satisfied us.

Intimacy with God

God honored our habits as we pursued Him. Fellowship, tithing, Bible study, and prayer are built into His system. We continue enjoying the fruit of our habits to this day.

Yet I sometimes used these habits to create IOUs for God. I came to Quiet Time with a list of things I wanted God to do. In my immaturity, He tolerated that, even as we often tolerate our children's manipulative requests. But parents want the child to mature into adulthood. Therefore, the time comes that parents refuse the child's manipulation. Likewise, God began exposing that I was using Him.

Through the assorted ministries of Christian International, founded by the same Dr. Bill Hamon, my wife and I began prizing intimacy with our Father above the things of this world. Many Christians have come to this maturity; God has used many ministries to get them there. *"Whom have I in heaven but You? And there is none upon earth that I desire besides You"* (Psalm 73:25).

Your spirit lives because God gives it life. Only from Him and in relating to Him are you alive as a spirit. What is eternal life, after all? *"This is eternal life, that they may know You, the only true God, and Jesus Christ whom You have sent"* (John 17:3).

How to Grow as a Spirit

The habits listed above are age-old gateways to intimacy with God: fellowship, tithing, Bible study, and prayer. But limiting ourselves to these is mechanistic. Some Christians even use them as Job did and as I did—an IOU system to obligate God, not welcome Him.

As intimacy with the Author of Life expands in your life, things pop. A force of divine life is in you: a love relationship with God, who is Spirit.

Some new habits form, which you cannot pick and choose. Babies can't decide not to grow their arms, and focus on leg growth. Neither can the person in love with Jesus Christ put limits on the growth they will accept.

You grow as a spirit by loving Jesus Christ. He leads you where your maturity lies. He will let you retreat to your secure, accustomed habits. But what if He wants to lead you in unknown places of maturity?

> He calls his own sheep by name and leads them out. And when he brings out his own sheep, he goes before them; and the sheep follow him, for they know his voice (John 10:4–5).

Habitual Meekness

> All we like sheep have gone astray; We have turned, every one, to his own way. (Isaiah 53:6)

Sadly, we go our own way; we abuse the power of choice God endowed us with. Therefore, to grow as a spirit requires a deeper entry into poverty of spirit, mourning, and meekness. Such people don't wonder how they have sinned. You just know you have, and you mourn it penitently.

Those who can only see God exalting us often disdain the teaching in James's New Testament letter. Yet it merely expresses the Beatitude qualities that Jesus called *blessed*. The promise James gives is that God will draw near to you and lift you up. Isn't that what we want?

> Draw near to God and He will draw near to you. Cleanse your hands, you sinners; and purify your hearts, you double-minded. Lament and mourn and weep! Let your laughter be turned to mourning and your joy to gloom. Humble yourselves in the sight of the Lord, and He will lift you up (James 4:8–10).

SPEAKING IN TONGUES

The Pentecostal denominations fix their organizational origin in 1905 when there was a weeks-long outpouring of the Holy Spirit on Azusa Street in Los Angeles. Those affected left the historic denominations such as Catholic, Lutheran, Presbyterian, Baptist, and Methodist. Each went their separate ways.

The charismatic movement of the 1970s saw many Christians in those historic denominations filled with the Holy Spirit, emphasizing spiritual gifts and speaking in tongues—and remaining in their denominations. No longer could the manifestation of the Spirit be an unspoken topic.

Christians formed opinions both pro and con, and as we have historically done, supported both extremes from Scripture. As theological battle lines were drawn, Christians at every level showed their immaturity, and that of the Church at large. In this context, speaking in tongues was the lightning rod.

The Resource God Provides

Jesus promised His followers He would fill them with the Holy Spirit. The day He ascended, His instruction was singular: wait and watch for the promise of the Father (Acts 1:4).

He poured out the Holy Spirit upon 120 people on Pentecost, and they in turn imparted the Holy Spirit to others by ministering the gospel. The apostles were not content for people simply to believe gospel assertions. They worked for people to be filled with the Holy Spirit, such as Peter's sermon on the day of Pentecost. *"Repent, and let every one of you be baptized in the name of Jesus Christ for the remission of sins; and you shall receive the gift of the Holy Spirit"* (Acts 2:38).

As the apostles saw it, the gift of the Holy Spirit was the point of the gospel. But in the centuries since, the organized church has dominated the lives of Christians and replaced personal reliance upon the Spirit's filling. Gradually, over the last five hundred years, the Church has grown and matured to welcome the Holy Spirit in our lives.

In the apostles' writing, they described three categories of resources which the Holy Spirit originates in us. First are spiritual gifts, capabilities for service as a spirit. These may be unrelated to our personalities, or may amplify them. The apostles wrote about them in Romans 12, 1 Corinthians 12–14 and 1 Peter 5.

The second category is comprised of character qualities that the Holy Spirit produces in every Christian who welcomes His influence. Paul labeled them the fruit of the Spirit in Galatians 5. These fruit are described throughout the apostles' writings.

The resources in the third category are not specific to our personality, character, or assigned positions of service. Chief among these resources is speaking in tongues. Miracle-working power is also included. Although many Christians today prize it most, miracle power was not the primary manifestation of the Holy Spirit's filling. Speaking in tongues was the primary evidence for the apostles.

When Tongues Begin

The apostles in the New Testament always ministered the filling of the Holy Spirit. What happened next varied. The apostles understood the work of the Holy Spirit as a process. Many Christians spoke in tongues when they were saved, and others, afterwards.

For me, it was much later. Saved in 1974, I regularly prayed to be filled with the Holy Spirit—not with a focus on tongues, but simply for the joy of having Him in me. In 1977, a respected leader laid hands on me and prayed for me to receive the baptism of the Holy Spirit. When I didn't speak in tongues, she said, "You just wait and watch."

One day ten years later, I spent a morning of prayer in a Kentucky bird sanctuary. Torrential rain began, and I retreated to the back seat of my compact car, fogging the windows. Suddenly, I heard another person in the car! Despite my complete view of the car's unoccupied interior, the voice was so real and audible. I instinctively looked all around the tiny interior to see who was speaking. Then I realized that was my voice, speaking in tongues. This was thirteen years after I first followed Jesus.

In some circles, they judge this delay harshly. Others claim that speaking in tongues was only for the first century. I'm satisfied the Bible teaches us to have this expectation. At some point, full of the Holy Spirit, He will impart this spiritual resource to us. The timing and means are determined by Him. We wait on Him. Wait and watch, just as I was told.

When Tongues End

Apostle Paul says in 1 Corinthians 13:8 that speaking in tongues will come to an end. *"Love never fails. But whether there are prophecies, they will fail; whether there are tongues, they will cease; whether there is knowledge, it will vanish away."*

The question is when? What time was he describing? The passage suggests tongues will end simultaneously with prophecy and knowledge. He's showing that love continues past the time the three resources are useful.

Obviously, we still know things, God still reveals things in our hearts, and prophecy still occurs. John writes in 1 John 2:20 that we know all things; is Paul talking about a time when we won't know anything?

I believe the end Paul's describing is after God has made everything new. We will be direct to Him, without the fallen world. Barriers we experience in this seen world will be obliterated. In their place will be unity with God Almighty, as John saw and reported in Revelation 21:3–5.

And I heard a loud voice from heaven saying, "Behold, the tabernacle of God is with men, and He will dwell with them, and they shall be His people. God Himself will be with them and be their God. And God will wipe away every tear from their eyes; there shall be no more death, nor sorrow, nor crying. There shall be no more pain, for the former things have passed away."

Then He who sat on the throne said, "Behold, I make all things new."

Why Choose Speaking in Tongues?

Few people ask why God manifested His filling as our speaking in tongues. Why choose that? We have been content over the centuries to mentalize the filling of the Spirit. Whatever it meant to a group of Christians, the limitation was what they could imagine.

My wife and I are very well read, yet until 2014 no book had explained to us why God chose speaking in tongues. Then Dr. Bill Hamon published the book, *70 Reasons for Speaking in Tongues*[14]. We highly recommend it for further study.

God is verbal. Scripture is clear that everything starts with Him speaking. So integral is speaking to God's nature that Apostle John, searching for the right word to describe Jesus, chose the word WORD. The Greek word is ὁ λόγος, transliterated *ho logos* and meaning simply "the word."

It's plausible that being filled by this verbal God's Holy Spirit would manifest in speaking. But why wasn't speaking in tongues prophesied in the Old Testament? Paul, the apostle most studied in the then-available Bible, cited in 1 Corinthians 14:21 only one Old Testament reference, from Isaiah 28:11. *"For with stammering lips and another tongue He will speak to this people."*

Did Jesus even teach them about speaking in tongues? Neither the gospels nor the apostles' epistles suggest He did. Did they see it in the Old Testament when the 120 followers studied the Old Testament ten days between Jesus' ascension and Pentecost? There is no sign they did.

The newly filled Apostle Peter readily explained Pentecost in his sermon that day, but he did not break it down into its component elements. He didn't pinpoint speaking in tongues, flames of fire, or the hurricane-force wind. He packaged the entire experience in one bundle by quoting Joel 2:28–32. In that passage is nothing about speaking in tongues nor about the other elements.

The total experience of the Spirit's filling was what he explained. That is the proper focus. Love Jesus Christ and let the gifts fall where they may.

Speaking in Tongues Makes Sense

For a living spirit able to communicate with God, speaking in tongues makes sense. As Paul says, it permits a verbal exchange with God even if we do not understand it.

> We also who have the first fruits of the Spirit, even we ourselves groan within ourselves ... Likewise the Spirit also helps in our weaknesses. For we do not know what we should pray for as we ought, but the Spirit Himself makes intercession for us with groanings which cannot be uttered (Romans 8:23, 26).

Paul also says in 8:27 that speaking in tongues helps us pray what God wants to do; the Holy Spirit *"makes intercession for the saints according to the will of God."*

To the Corinthian Christians, Paul describes what many have experienced by speaking in tongues, although he does not call it that in this passage.

> These things we also speak, not in words which man's wisdom teaches but which the Holy Spirit teaches, comparing spiritual things with spiritual. But the natural man does not receive the things of the Spirit of God, for they are foolishness to him; nor can he know them, because they are spiritually discerned (1 Corinthians 2:13–4).

He later alludes to speaking in tongues as *"the tongues of angels"* (1 Corinthians 13:1). This also is plausible, that speaking in tongues equips us for communication with the unseen friendlies.

Armies need encryption for their communications. Apostle John saw Jesus in Revelation 19 at the head of an army, composed not of angels but of us who are *"clothed in fine linen"* (19:14). Elsewhere, we considered Isaiah 32:1–2 and the flat organizational structure of God's kingdom. Isaiah also prophesied that the government would be on Jesus' shoulders. Speaking in tongues makes sense as an encrypted communication system within a kingdom at war with unseen enemies.

The Practice of Speaking in Tongues

My wife and I have discovered what Stephen pronounced against the religious pressure of his day: *"You always resist the Holy Spirit"* (Acts 7:51). No matter the denomination, the tradition, or the group, the urge to resist His expression is everywhere. My heart is no exception.

Therefore, as a habit of self-denial, we speak in tongues continually. Everything we do and say with God, we engage in tongues. We want to know what to pray. Why not let the Holy Spirit intercede first, by speaking in tongues? Usually we know what He is saying as we do so. That is what we then pray in our own language of English.

As the day rolls toward me, circumstances arise unexpectedly. By praying in tongues continually, I am prepped and ready for whatever situations may arise. People come into my path; praying in tongues reveals to me what the Spirit says for them. I am better able to receive them with His love. In evangelism, this is a fantastic resource; your gospel comments can pinpoint their exact, hidden need.

Religious systems always tempt Christians into conformity. Different traditions permit evidence of the Spirit in different ways. Wherever you are, you must respect the authority God has set in place, or permitted. But you can always pray in tongues under your breath. As He has led, I have also preached a sermon in tongues, and interpreted it in keeping with Paul's instructions to the Corinthian church.

The living spirit exists for intimacy with God and expression of His heart. If praying in tongues manifests the Holy Spirit to others, certainly it does to the speaker as well. Shouldn't we want the maximum?

The ministry of the Holy Spirit will be plumbed in far greater depth in Book Six of the *Unseen* series, titled *Nobody Sees This Warrior: God's Secret Ambush*.

---

*Reflection and discussion questions for this chapter
are in the back of the book*

CHAPTER THIRTEEN

THE REALITY FOR OUR SPIRITS

THE COMPREHENSIVE ORDER

The natural world seems normal to us, but only by our agreement. If we break that agreement and agree with God instead, what do we find?

Our reality is of a far more comprehensive order. The Creator and His world-dominating image-creature are now united. We pray *"Your kingdom come; Your will be done."* In will and in power, the human living spirit is unified with His purposes. As we mature as spirits, our fellowship with the Triune God matures. Thus, we increasingly reflect God. *"But we all, with unveiled face, beholding as in a mirror the glory of the Lord, are being transformed into the same image from glory to glory, just as by the Spirit of the Lord"* (2 Corinthians 3:18).

We, His Church of living spirits, increasingly reflect the multi-personal unity of God Almighty, as Jesus intently desired: *"Father ... may they be one, even as we are one"* (John 17:11 NIV).

God our Creator creates and sustains all that is. Our agreement with Him and filling by Him places Him everywhere we go. Can any other reality be superior? Can any other assessment be determinative? No.

We now have one all-comprehending order. The God who made man in His image now fills us. We are a new race of men, full of all the fulness of God (Ephesians 3:19, Colossians 2:9-10). We are the divine power manifested—as Jesus exemplified. *"As He is, so are we in this world"* (1 John 4:17).

He exemplified this, but not because He was the Son of God. That was the title most justified, but Paul wrote that Jesus emptied Himself of all that was God, and became man (Philippians 2:7). We call Him *Son of God* after the fact, but in His life, Jesus did not use it. He called Himself instead *the Son of Man*—and why? The race of men that sired Him could do everything he did.

The Father sent him to restore that which was lost: Creator, one with His image-creature. *"The Son of Man has come to seek and to save that which was lost"*—the order that was lost, not only the who that was lost (Luke 19:10).

This order has been restored. Jesus sought it, and He saved it.

The unseen reality has comprehensive power; it subsumes all measurements and overwhelms all standards. This order is not a higher order; it demeans nothing we have known previously. It is a more comprehensive order that explains more than the previous. The reality for our spirits resolves many mysteries, unexplained things, and unfulfilled promises.

It is this unseen reality that saved, living spirits can perceive and participate in.

The History of the Unseen

Once seeing that spirit is relationship, the unseen world and its history are very plain.

God Himself is a Trinity of three Spirits forming one Spirit, or One Spirit forming three Spirits (no one knows which or how, or both). He first created additional spirits—the angels, the cherubim and seraphim, and the archangels.

Among these classes of angels are differing ranks, and their rank is part of their nature. There is in Scripture no description of mobility among the ranks of angels. He designed them as spirits for relationship. Therefore, hell is the isolation eternally of an angelic spirit made for relationship, yet by itself eternally.

Evidently, after the rebellion in heaven, God created no new angelic spirits. He instead created a new mortal-body race of spirits—humanity. In their mortal bodies, He would test and prove this race of spirits. This race of proven mortal-body spirits would form a new rank in the unseen. This citizenry of human spirits would differ from the angelic spirits, whose spirit status was in their nature.

This new mortal-body race of spirits He placed on the earth to which He had exiled Lucifer and his evil cohorts. By doing this, God placed our race into direct conflict with the kingdom of darkness. He was prepared for Lucifer's deception of our first parents. The Son of God was crucified before the foundation of the world for just that reason (Revelation 13:8).

He intended that following Jesus would prove our spirits. This would provide proven mature spirits for the kingdom of heaven. For His co-regents, He wanted human spirits who *electively* chose Him and *electively* resisted the deception of the fallen Lucifer and his rebels. In the end, the proven ones shall reign over the other spirit classes of angels, archangels, cherubim, and seraphim.

The Story of Everything

God is populating the unseen world of spirits with more spirits like Himself. He is saving individual people from sin and making them alive in spirit.

He is proving these human spirits through mortal tests, challenges, and circumstances. We develop over time and process into mature spirits, in contrast to the angels, whose spirit is part of their created nature.

He wants to enjoy eternal and effective agreement with us. This new rank of spirits will be His co-regents throughout existence.

The Spirit Gospel

Therefore, the gospel is a means to an end. It is not the end in itself. The Christian religious institutions use the gospel as the end in itself. That's why the Church functions as a permanently immature infant, a collection of slow spirits.

Jesus died to produce a result. That result is the population of the kingdom of heaven with proven human spirits.

That's why the pouring out of God's Holy Spirit accompanies salvation. That's why we have a spirit-language, and why the long centuries of Israel's choosing occurred. He is building His *ekklesia* for this result.

The Intercourse of the Unseen

And immediately, coming up from the water, He saw the heavens parting and the Spirit descending upon Him like a dove. Then a voice came from heaven, "You are My beloved Son, in whom I am well pleased."

Immediately the Spirit drove Him into the wilderness. And He was there in the wilderness forty days, tempted by Satan, and was with the wild beasts; and the angels ministered to Him. (Mark 1:11–13 NKJV)

Jesus' endurance of direct testing by satan brought Him into the company of wild animals and ministering angels. If God fills you with His Spirit: 1) you please Him, and 2) you are going to interact with unseen entities, such as satan, the holy angels, and the forces of Creation, such as wild animals.

Our cooperative relationship with the holy ones of the unseen has a proper protocol. We do not seek angels. Rather, God grants us interaction with them, for His purposes rather than ours. It can happen more frequently as our spirits mature.

The purpose of being a living spirit is solely our relationship with God, which is the *sine qua non* of the living human spirit. The heavenly host comes with that package, but the package is Him.

Intercourse with the unseen is part of the package because God is Spirit. He seeks *"true worshippers who will worship Him in spirit and truth"* (John 4:24). This means that we are in the unseen kingdom of spirit when He makes us worshippers through salvation.

No wonder truth is equally central to spirit, for many in the unseen oppose the truth. The importance of truthfully following Jesus cannot be diminished. It's clear even in Jesus' statement to Pilate at his so-called "trial."

> You say rightly that I am a king. For this cause I was born, and for this cause I have come into the world, that I should bear witness to the truth. Everyone who is of the truth hears My voice (John 18:37).

Everyone who hears His voice and follows Him is a citizen of His kingdom. Truth, not power, marks that kingdom. What a contrast to the man who stood before Him that day!

Communication Barrier

How could Jesus communicate these things? He described Himself as the *"one who came down from heaven"* (John 3:13).

Our spirits do not lend themselves to formulaic outlines. Jesus used parables and questions, signs and miracles, testimony and sacrifice. He conveyed what He Himself knew from heaven. *"We speak what We know and testify what We have seen, and you do not receive Our witness"* (John 3:11).

His followers knew He was revealing a more comprehensive order. What allured them to the costly discovery adventure of following Him?

Peter put it this way in John 6:68: *"Lord, to whom shall we go? You have the words of eternal life."*

Imagine you have a new acquaintance. Your experiences are different from his, so you try to describe them to him. He breaks in to say, "Oh, I see what you mean." You ask him to feed it back to you—but what he says shows clearly that he does *not* see what you mean! What do you do, then? You can't really correct him, because he's doing his best to understand you. So you affirm the elements he has right and you wait for a later time to rectify his mistaken conclusions.

My five-year-old grandson asked why the building switched sides when we went back and forth on a local road. I attempted to explain perspective. But when you try to explain an adult knowledge to a child, long before you finish, they exclaim, "Oh, I got it!"

Then they proudly tell you what they've figured out. They combined your words with their pre-existing knowledge and eliminated everything they don't understand! You listen, and what can you do? He's a child—not a college student. So you affirm what he understands, without affirming his or her mistaken conclusions.

Likewise our understanding of the Bible's teaching about spirit reality. We can grow into it—resolute kings searching out His mysteries (Proverbs 25:2). Or we can remain juvenile in our spirits.

THEIRS IS THE KINGDOM OF GOD

So many Christians fixate on what the devil can do to them. They tiptoe through life to avoid rousing the dragons of darkness. If such a Christian musters up the fearlessness, they might charge in. Yet, they continue to define the primary influence as the kingdom of darkness. They refuse to give proper weight to the kingdom of God.

God Almighty lives in us. How could He ever be anything but the primary influence? By exercising our faith in Him, we accept our position in the unseen as the only spirits filled with Him. Can any spirit withstand us? or exact penalties from us?

The fallen, evil spirits are eternally bereft of the only source of spirit life—God. We, in contrast, have full access to Him; we are His home on the earth. He lives inside my skin; my body is His temple here, and so is yours (1 Corinthians 6:19–20).

In Matthew 16, Jesus' disciples first professed that He was the Christ. He then said this to the disciples: *"I will give you the keys of the kingdom of heaven, and whatever you bind on earth will be bound in heaven, and whatever you loose on earth will be loosed in heaven"* (Matthew 16:19).

He describes an authority that is supreme and unexcelled. Its trigger is faith in Him. He says He will give it to His disciples and all whom they represented. This incontestable authority is not a Christian commodity, skill, or position. To all who believe in Him, He gives the power to become children of God (John 1:12). Rebirth as a spirit is the gateway to this authority in heaven and earth.

To repeat: every Christian longing is obtained by maturing as a living spirit.

Spirit King

Something big, global, national concerned me in November 2020, and I asked You about it. You said, "Paul, you have the authority to ask it." Your "you" was singular, as if no one else need concur. "Paul, you have the authority, and the angels will serve you." Singular again, Lord? "No need to enlist anyone's agreement—you need only to ask. Only yourself is enough."

Your statements were sudden in my spirit—a packaged knowledge, not with words, and certainly not this many words. Like words of a coronation, the knowledge was full of respect and gravity. Am I a king? Yes—I am a king. By faith in the word of the Lord, I agree, and I activate.

Lord, where is this in the Bible? "In beatitude number one, Matthew 5:3, *'Theirs is the kingdom of heaven.'* Hey—it's possessive!

Then another knowledge packet appeared within me, a 1 John 2:20 kind. What did the people think about when he said, *"Theirs is the kingdom of heaven"*? David's kingdom, Solomon's kingdom, the emperor's kingdom. Suddenly I knew what Jesus meant in the first beatitude: a Christian's kingdom has greater authority than earthly ones. Ours is the kingdom of heaven because we are poor in spirit.

Lord, is this really you? *"If we know that He hears us, whatever we ask, then we know that we have the petitions we have asked of Him"* (1 John 5:15).

Do others need to see it? "No, just do it and be it. When you act under My anointing of kingship, then the ones meant to follow you will appear. Angels also have been waiting for you to rise into the intended authority."

Suddenly, I see my whole life as a forced march to this point. Everything makes sense. In fact, it makes more sense precisely because this kingship identity is not natural to me at all.

You say, "Paul, this fits the biblical premise: you and your race are the rulers of Earth. I created mankind and put you on Earth to replace the dark rulers whom I previously exiled there. Everything I'm showing you about being a king is a *sine qua non* ('without which, nothing') of the original authority I intended for all mankind.

"Each time I have taught you this, you plugged it into your head, but not into your identity. You conformed your thinking to it, but didn't believe it or yield to it. Instead, it always remained once-removed, and your identity remained servile."

Afterwards I read 1 Chronicles 17:8, which tells how You treat Your kings, such as David. *"I have been with you wherever you have gone, and I have cut off your enemies before you, and I have made you a name like the names of the great men of the earth.... [I] will build you a house.*

David's response was not servile, nor falsely modest, but obediently agreeable with the divine coronation. *"O Lord, for your servant's sake, and according to Your own heart, You have done all this greatness, in making known these great things ... Lord, let Your word be established ... that Your name may be magnified forever"* (vv 19, 24).

Jesus didn't just *say* ours was the kingdom. He *conferred* our kingship upon us in Luke 22:29. *"I confer upon you a kingdom, just as My Father conferred one upon Me."*

"Paul, I showed you the Paul-that-is and the Paul-that-does. The king is the first; the servant is the latter. Yes, in the natural you are a mover/doer, but in the spirit, you simply give the word. A king makes decrees. A king is obeyed for what he *says*, not what he *does*."

Exercising Your kingship? How do I do that? *"Come to me, that you may live. Listen to me, and you will eat the richest of fare"* (Isaiah 55:1–3).

"Paul, I made you with that Point-A-to-Point-B impulse to be efficient. You weren't made to work independently, but in concert with Me. In the spirit, everything is agreement. The real doing is in agreeing with Me. As a king in spirit, we agree, and we speak it."

Blessed are the poor in spirit, for theirs is the kingdom of heaven.

Coronation

How backward everything is from the world's expectation. You make the spiritually impoverished into its kings. Mary and Hannah both recognized it in their songs (1 Samuel 2, Luke 1).

Only one requirement, one sign of our destiny: the persistent pursuit of You. We mature and layer each beatitude quality throughout our lives. We yield to You all the more, all the time—ultimately overcoming every deterrent, every distraction, every self-reliance, every craving of the natural man.

> He who overcomes, and keeps My works til the end, to him I will give power over the nations. He shall rule them with a rod of iron, "they shall be dashed to pieces like the potter's vessels"—as I have also received from My Father. (Revelation 2:26)

> To him who overcomes, I will grant to sit with Me on My throne, as I also overcame and sat down with My Father on His throne. (3:21)

Both these statements presume the divine analogy: "As Father/Me, so I/you." This analogy with the Lord Jesus is replete in Scripture. He is our pattern. John 17 is full of it. He specifically stated it in many places, such as John 20:21, *"As the Father sent Me, so I send you."*

Angel Causation and the Economy of Authority

As I drive along to a potentially lucrative appointment, I'm praying. This unplanned opportunity suddenly sprang up after a morning enlisting the assistance of the Lord's angel partners.

And so I've become aware of the angels present to assist in this meeting. As I give attention to their function, the first one says, "We cause people to see you as a king—to see you as God has ordained you."

Then from the second angel: "You are a benevolent and kind king, a humble king who uses his power for the benefit of others and without regard for your own fame, power, or money."

After these statements, it suddenly dawned upon me: the more meekness, the more kingliness. This is how You allocate authority. In our earthly economy, supply and demand work hand in hand. These complementary forces cause goods to be distributed. Likewise, in heaven's economy for the distribution of authority, beatitude number three gives us standing. *"Blessed are the meek, for they shall inherit the earth"* (Matthew 5:5).

Four Blank Checks for Overcomers

Upon Moses's death, his protege Joshua (then over sixty years old) became the leader of Israel. Joshua would lead the conquest of Canaan, and had much on his shoulders. God spoke to him in the first chapter of the book by his name, where He gave Joshua four blank checks.

1. *Every place you set your foot I will give you.*
2. *No one will be able to withstand you.*
3. *You will be successful in all you do.*
4. *I will be with you.*

When God gave Israel these blank checks, He commanded faith. *Have I not commanded you?* He defined obedience as relying upon these promises.

In Joshua 7, Israel had a major setback. Although casualties were few, the defeat threatened their confidence. Joshua's faith also weakened, and he blamed the setback on the Lord. This broke agreement with the Lord. Joshua was now at odds with God's command to rely on the four blank checks. His prayer is faithless:

And Joshua said, 'Alas, Lord God, why have You brought this people over the Jordan at all—to deliver us into the hand of the Amorites, to destroy us? Oh, that we had been content, and dwelt on the other side of the Jordan!' (Joshua 7:7).

For this, God rebuked Joshua. Surrendering faith in God's promises is disobedience. *"Get up! Why do you lie thus on your face?"* (v 10). The events after this rebuke show that Joshua passed the test, overcame his despair, and believed the Lord's blank checks.

A later battle with five unified Canaanite kings is recorded in Joshua 10. There Joshua imparts his faith to his commanders. He cashes one of God's blank checks, in 10:13–14 and prayed,

"Sun, stand still over Gibeon; And Moon, in the Valley of Aijalon." So the sun stood still, And the moon stopped, Till the people had revenge Upon their enemies.

Is this not written in the Book of Jasher? So the sun stood still in the midst of heaven, and did not hasten to go down for about a whole day.

Such an event might inspire faith in God, yet leave questions behind. Many in Israel and among his commanders still needed reassurance to rely on the promises of God. For them, the issue was not simply who

God was, nor whether He was on their side. The issue that remained unresolved was who they were.

Joshua makes them resolve the issue in 10:24–25. Israel is victorious, the enemy flees, and in pursuit Israel captures the enemy kings at a place called Makkedah. There, Joshua imparts to his commanders the blank checks he received from God.

> So it was, when they brought out those kings to Joshua, that Joshua called for all the men of Israel, and said to the captains of the men of war who went with him, "Come near, put your feet on the necks of these kings." And they drew near and put their feet on their necks.
>
> Then Joshua said to them, "Do not be afraid, nor be dismayed; be strong and of good courage, for thus the LORD will do to all your enemies against whom you fight."

Jesus didn't make His disciples put their feet on people's necks, for their enemies were unseen. Jesus said His kingdom would advance and take ground from hell. The kingdom of darkness is who we crush under our feet, at His direction. Apostle Paul alludes to Makkedah in the final greetings of his letter to the Roman church: *"The God of peace will crush Satan under your feet shortly"* (Romans 16:20).

When Jesus gave Apostle John the prophecy we now call Revelation, His promises to each church were not addressed to every member. Within each church, He singled out individuals with the promise of unimaginable rewards. Those individuals, He referred to as overcomers.

May I be an overcomer, Lord Jesus. Reveal in me whatever You choose, and make me one of Your overcomers.

SPIRIT OF STEEL

The long-lasting moniker for Superman is The Man of Steel. After watching the 2013 movie, its parable inspired me: *"in the world, but not of it."* One theme is that the surrounding people cannot handle his true identity. The solution is to be mild-mannered—in other words, meek.

In Superman's case, he feigned meekness because he actually did have the strength. That's why it is a parable and not an allegory. In our case, however, there is no feigning. We actually are poor in spirit. Mourning and meekness are appropriate for us. Our inadequacy is real. But we can forget these and feign strength of our own.

The Scripture says we are strong. *"Let the weak say, 'I am strong.'"* (Joel 3:20). How do we reconcile the Beatitude meekness and the Pauline confidence, or even the confident identity that Jesus manifested about Himself?

When filled with the Spirit of God, we have a spirit of steel. We know it is not our own spirit, which is growing with far yet to go. Our spirit is not adequate for the worship God desires. We know that one day He will perfect us with His marvelous power.

In the meantime, along the way, my spirit is still a spirit of steel. The steely resolve of my spirit comes by no merit or device of my own. It's solely and entirely because the Spirit of Steel, the Spirit of Almighty God, the Spirit of all-surpassing power, has filled me. The only questions remaining is whether I believe it and act accordingly.

Our spirit of steel is an imparted steel, for the Spirit of Steel lives in me. I am a spirit of steel!

Conclusion

We have looked in depth at spirit.

God granted everything Christians want when we became living spirits by faith in Jesus Christ. Every longing you have is obtained by maturing as a living spirit. And every obstacle you face is part of that maturing process. Evil spirits try to obstruct you. God's Spirit develops, tests, proves, and confirms you.

The Bible presents the backing on the tapestry—the unseen world. Much remains to discover about the backing. It is the author's hope that you will wholeheartedly join him in pursuing Jesus Christ, maturing as a living spirit, and activating all that He intends on this earth.

Paul Renfroe

RESOURCES

About The Unseen Series

PARADIGM LIGHTHOUSE

The *Unseen* Series comes to you through the ministry of Paul and Diane Renfroe, named Paradigm Lighthouse. Their calling is to help you mature as a living human spirit—but what does that look like?

The undeniable fact is this: between you and God is an inexpressibly enormous difference in scale, being, and quality. The farthest star is closer to our sun than our mortal being is to God. He is an eternal Spirit who is both perfect love and perfect rightness—a severe contrast to us.

Yet for all this gap, He can adopt you as His intimate child. He does this when you are born as a spirit. The *Lighthouse* name expresses the explosion of lighthearted safety that His peace implants into every such person.

This quasar of His bursting love within you pulls your thinking and beliefs into agreement with Him. The *Paradigm* name identifies this process as profound, life-changing paradigm shifts. One perception of reality supersedes another, as He blows your mind with the unseen things He reveals. This experience of large-scale paradigm shifts has also characterized the history of His Church, a core observation of the Present Truth movement.

Further in and higher up to our Father God is a lifelong process, and well worth every sacrifice known to mankind.

The numbered books in this series are sequential. However, each contains the following series orientation and a summary of the preceding books—making any of the books a beneficial starting point. For your full benefit, read each book for its unique contribution to your paradigm of reality.

Each book of the series is available where you purchased this one, and if not, you may visit ParadigmLighthouse.com. There you can also contact us to receive ministry directly, both public and private.

YOU

In our days, a burgeoning number of people worldwide are perceiving unseen realities. The gap between seen and unseen, between natural and spirit, is narrowing. You were magnetized to this book and the *Unseen* series because you also feel the nearing of the invisible. You are not alone in this. I wrote this series to equip you and your friends for holy perception of that world.

Normal questions arise. How can you interpret what you are faintly perceiving? Are there rules? Guidelines? What's causing your growing awareness of the hidden world? Why you? Can you make your perception clearer? Can you make it stop?

Mankind's default is to control our perception of the unseen. The words *dread* and *terror* are often used because perceiving it threatens loss of control for us. We feel gravely unprepared for the accountability these perceptions impose upon us.

Well we should, because we are terribly ill-equipped for the invisible world of spirit. Its spirits which are holy can, if fully unveiled, intimidate and reduce us to quivering. Those which are unholy can trick us and take advantage of us. We are, in fact, defenseless against both as mere human beings—so poorly equipped that we can go through our entire lives without noticing they are pulling our string and jerking our chain.

The unseen world is rapping harder and faster on the windows of our souls.

RESPONDING TO THE SPIRIT WORLD

Most people endeavor to control their interface with the invisible world of spirit. The low intensity method is to control it by ignoring it. The high intensity method is to manipulate spirits. Its lasting name is sorcery, always destructive and divisive.

Between these two ends, people try to use the spirit world for gain. Religion, for instance, is a tit-for-tat effort to secure favor from God and obligate Him to us. When we complain about God's unfairness, we reveal the religion in us.

People try to use the unseen for gain in the seen world, and not just with religion. The list includes business, family, education, and government.

Deeds can be beneficial and character admirable, all the while treating the unseen as a mere tool for the natural world.

Today, the spirit world is becoming harder to ignore, manipulate, and use. There are many ways we try to limit it. All of them express our default reaction: "Stay in the place we assign you!"

But in our days, the unseen is refusing to stay there.

THE BEST RESPONSE

You can receive a welcome into the spirit world. God, a Spirit, revealed a specific protocol. No one can be a spirit without following it. The results are very desirable.

It begins simply: you admit to God your poverty for His world of spirit. Yet as simply as the protocol begins, its results defy imagination.

This admission brings an inward mourning over your poverty as a spirit. You recognize how distant you are from the true God, a Spirit. Drastically lower expectations follow as meekness arises within you. You mercifully respond to others after facing your own poverty.

Simultaneously, you have a growing hunger and thirst for the good that God wants. As you mature, old values become replaced with what God wants, and you are purified. You gain new abilities to create peace in relationships, both with God and among people. And you become loyal to God at any cost.

This summarizes nine qualities God likes to bless, which Jesus of Nazareth listed in the first book of the Bible's New Testament, Matthew chapters 5 through 7, together with the specific blessings God places on each quality. Their lasting name is the Beatitudes.

So how do you gain these desirable qualities? You become a living spirit with the following protocol.

THE PROTOCOL TO BECOME A SPIRIT

For anyone poor in spirit to become a spirit requires help—the help of the Head Spirit, God. He wants you to become a living spirit with Him! He has revealed the protocol so you can.

1. Admit that you are spiritually poor. You do not have what it takes to relate to God, who is a spirit, and holy. The lasting word for this situation is sin.

2. Admit the dire consequences of that spiritual poverty. These are distance between you and the God who would be your Father, slowness to honor and obey Him, damage to yourself and those around you, and hindrance to His good desires for mankind. The lasting word for this step is confession.
3. Admit that He solved this spirit gap. Jesus proclaimed that His death on the cross fully satisfied God in the spirit world, where we are so poverty-stricken. When you believe this and follow Jesus, God the Father gives you birth as a spirit. Immediately, God adopts you as His own child, just as Jesus was. The lasting word is faith, because your adoption is unsee-able, and is perceived by trusting the truthfulness of what God's revealing.
4. Admit those three things directly to Him. Here's one way to express it to Him.
5. *God, I admit You deserve much, yet I can only give so little. I want to follow Jesus so His death solves the spirit gap I have with You. So I ask you to forgive me. I put my trust in Jesus, that His death enables You to adopt me as your child. I don't know what to expect, but when You show me and help me, I will respond to You as my Father, with the best of my ability.*

THE PROTOCOL TO STAY A SPIRIT

After you admit these facts, the spirit world tests your genuine intent. The host of heaven observes your persistent commitments in this seen world. This includes angels who serve us, sent by God. Also included: spirits who hate people, including you. These evil spirits try to imprison your spirit. If they cannot, then these destroyers try to disrupt, discourage, dissuade, or deceive you. Jesus knew this would happen and provided a protocol for you to stay a living spirit.

1. Jesus started a protective group for people born as spirits after these admissions. Its lasting name is The Church, uppercase. Now it is globally huge, full of many churches, lowercase, in different forms. Not everyone in a church is the same. One quality is common: poverty of spirit and dependence upon God. In church, God trains and tests everyone born in spirit, to grow our ability to love others graciously.
2. There is a book He provided to everyone born as spirits. Jesus rose from the dead but did not remain physically in the seen world. To

see and hear Him with our spirit's "eyes" and "ears," He endorsed an authoritative collection of writings. It holds many yesterdays, written over 1,500 years and compiled in 397 AD. Its lasting name is the Bible and there are many translations available from its original, well-known languages. In it, you will find God and He will reveal the invisible to you. The Bible is an ancient book written by forty people distant in time and culture, both from each other and from us. That's why effort is required to understand this book—an effort that also trains and proves your spirit. The effort is amply rewarded because the Bible is a proven book; it contains many todays as well as yesterdays. By it, God grows your spirit for effective activity in many todays and tomorrows, in both the seen and the unseen worlds.

3. Other commitments—not mere behaviors—help us grow as spirits. One example is self-sacrificing thoughts and deeds, such as service to others. Another is giving money as tithes to our particular church group and offerings to others. Obedience to God's explicit commands governs all our commitments. Submission to the leaders He provides us trains us to lead others as well.

THE EVENT

The above admissions cause an unseeable event: you are born as a spirit for the first time. You are born into the unseen world. Anyone who sincerely follows the above protocol can have a newborn spirit. Jesus described it to someone in the fourth book of the New Testament, John chapter 3 verse 6: *"That which is born of the flesh is flesh, and that which is born of the Spirit is spirit."*

When we are born in this seen world, that's the limit of our being; we cannot participate in the spirit world. The Bible's word for this is the flesh. Every person is born in the flesh. But when we believe Jesus and follow Him, we are born into the unseen world. The Bible's word for that is the spirit. Only followers of Jesus are born in spirit.

THE MATURING

Your spirit begins as an immature spirit, just as your body was born immature. Likewise, either you feed it or it withers unnourished. Either you mature as a spirit, or you atrophy.

Church, the Bible, prayer, and obedience are good ways to nourish your spirit. Denying the cravings of the flesh strengthens your spirit, just as weight training strengthens your muscles. As your spirit matures, your spirit asserts its dominion over your natural self, as it should.

We also ask God to put His Spirit within us more every day. Holy is the adjective used to describe Him, so His lasting name is the Holy Spirit. Maturing as a spirit is impossible without God's Spirit within.

Some ask insincerely. Some try to limit the spirit and control the unseen. As your spirit matures, you may feel the pain and desperation in their futile effort. Yet upon them we always have mercy and desire their best; God is patient with us all.

YOUR UNSEEN SPIRIT

As a newborn spirit, the world of spirits immediately recognizes you as an active participant. They see you as a spirit born of God's own doing. The unseen spirits who are holy are angels. God assigns some to help you mature. Unholy spirits, including demons, are assigned to deter you by their chief, the devil.

The *Unseen* Series is a guide for every person born as a spirit by following Jesus Christ. You have entered this very active but unseeable world. Being a spirit being raises many questions we'll investigate in this series. How do you act? What actually are you capable of, as a spirit? As a spirit, do you hear, like you do in your body? See? Feel? Smell? Taste? Do you talk as a spirit?

How do you distinguish between your unseen spirit and the more immediate parts of yourself? How do you identify and respond to the spirits you encounter?

If you are adopted by God as your Father, how does that interaction occur? Surely you talk together—but how? What does He do, and what's your part? Do you have to forget old things? What new do you need to learn?

Take heart: Your Father will not leave you hanging. He may test your persistence. He may prove your sincerity by requiring patience—but you can count on Him.

THE FORGETTING

Even as a living spirit, everyone has some baggage from the old days. Parents and predecessors hand it down to us. Some baggage is from living by our own wits without full access to God's help and protection. There is also baggage that evil spirits tricked us into carrying. A constant experience of maturing spirits is shedding such baggage. Forgetting these hindrances is a welcome process.

That baggage includes our definition of impossible. When your spirit grows, you constantly see the falsity of limits which you once accepted without question. Forgetting these limits signals your growing intimacy with your Father.

A regular habit is to break agreements with old beliefs and habits in favor of what God reveals to us. Our area of agreement with God expands this way, while the dominance of the seen world wanes.

THE LEARNING

The Father of your spirit, God Himself, desires intimacy with you. It is a process over time; there is much to learn about one another. This is one reason He puts His Spirit into us, so we can understand His thoughts. Apostle John, one of Jesus' first four followers, described it in his first letter, chapter 2 verse 27: *"The anointing which you have received from Him abides in you [and] teaches you concerning all things."*

THE PAYOFF

This forgetting and learning process requires outside help. The guidance of mentors and leaders is indispensable; God will lead you to the right ones.

Most important is God's active, vocal presence within your skin. This occurs by the repeated filling of the Holy Spirit. Reliance upon Him is a constant need—as it should be for a meek, poor in spirit person.

He is a Spirit, and He will teach you to use your spirit senses. With His life inside you, you will be alive beyond imagination. You will surpass the discoveries of the *Unseen* Series. Your participation in the unseen world of spirit can only become more effective.

Welcome to the world of the spirit-born.

Works Referenced

1. Thayer, Joseph Henry. *Greek-English Lexicon of the New Testament.* Grand Rapids, MI: Zondervan, 1885; Second Edition 1981.
2. Bonhoeffer, Dietrich. *The Cost of Discipleship.* New York, NY: Macmillan, 1937; Second Edition 1980.
3. Renfroe, Diane. *The Bible: The Life of a Book.* Freeport, FL: Paradigm Lighthouse; Pending publication 2022.
4. Tozer, A.W. *The Knowledge of the Holy: The Attributes of God: Their Meaning in the Christian Life.* San Francisco, CA: HarperOne, 1961; Second Edition 2009.
5. Tournier, Dr. Paul. *The Healing of Persons.* New York, NY: Harper & Row, 1965.
6. Prince, Derek. *They Shall Expel Demons: What You Need to Know About Demons–Your Invisible Enemies.* Grand Rapids, MI: Chosen Books, 1998.
7. Hamon, Dr. Bill. *Prophets and Personal Prophecy.* Shippensburg, PA: Destiny Image, 2010.
8. Nee, Watchman. *Spiritual Authority.* New York, NY: Christian Fellowship Publishers, 2020.
9. Edwards, Gene. *A Tale of Three Kings: A Study in Brokenness.* Carol Stream, IL: Tyndale House, 1992.
10. Renfroe, Paul. *The Pains of the Christian: Desire, Glory, Joy.* Santa Rosa Beach FL: Christian International Publishing, 2015.
11. Lewis, C.S. *Mere Christianity.* New York, NY: Macmillan, 1952; Second Edition 1977.
12. Edwards, Gene. *A Tale of Three Kings: A Study in Brokenness.* Carol Stream, IL: Tyndale House, 1992.
13. Hamon, Dr. Bill. *The Eternal Church.* Shippensburg, PA. 1981; Second Edition 2005.
14. Hamon, Dr. Bill. *70 Reasons for Speaking in Tongues: Your Own Built-in Spiritual Dynamo.* Tabor, SD: Parsons Publishing House, 2010.

Topical Listing of Books for Your Spirit

TOPIC	TITLE	AUTHOR	WHERE TO OBTAIN
Beating doubt about the Bible	*The Bible: The Life of a Book* (new in 2022)	Diane Renfroe	ParadigmLighthouse.com
Becoming like Jesus	*You Can Be Just Like Jesus*	Luke Armstrong	Amazon
Building your local church	*Building Strong*	Robert Gay	highpraisepc.com
Checking with a Bible scholar	*Supernatural*	Dr. Michael S. Heiser	theunseenrealm.com
Cooperating with miracles	*Miracles Now! And Financial Miracles Now!*	Gale Sheehan	christianinternational.com
Finding your place in church	*I Belong*	Robert Gay	highpraisepc.com
Healing emotional hurts	*Restore My Soul: A 90 Devotional*	Kathleen Tolleson	kingdomlifenow.com
Healing sexual hurts	*Restoring Sexuality*	Kathleen Tolleson	kingdomlifenow.com
Hearing God's voice confidently	*God Speaks and You Can Hear Him*	Edgar Iraheta	christianinternational.com
Identifying globalism	*Globalists on Trial*	Sally Saxon	Amazon
Identifying spirits	*Discernment*	Jane A. Hamon	tomandjanehamon.com
Improving relationships	*Uprighting Relationships*	Linda Roeder	Dave-Linda.com
Interpreting dreams	*Dreams & Visions*	Jane A. Hamon	tomandjanehamon.com

TOPIC	TITLE	AUTHOR	WHERE TO OBTAIN
Leading as a woman	*Deborah Company*	Jane A. Hamon	tomandjanehamon.com
Receiving deliverance from oppression	*Passport to Freedom*	Sharon Parkes	christianinternational.com
Serving others spiritually	*How to Reach Your Highest Level*	Jimmy Kellet	christianinternational.com
Speaking what God says to others	*Prophetic Divergence*	Robert Paul	kaiembassy.com
Transforming your community	*Seven Anointings for Kingdom Transformation*	Tom Hamon	tomandjanehamon.com
Trials and Tribulations	*God's Tests Are Positive*	Evelyn Hamon	christianinternational.com
Updating worship	*The Tabernacle of God*	Dean Mitchum	christianinternational.com
Verbalizing victory	*Declarations & Decrees of a Warrior*	Marlene Babb	Amazon

Reflection and Discussion Questions

INTRODUCTION

1. In your encounters with the unseen world, what was the most creepy? What was the most reassuring?
2. Has religion helped you understand the unseen world? What obstacles made it hard to explore the topic?
3. Have you ever read a book that offered you a private readers' discussion group? Have you requested your login credentials?

THE BACKING

1. When have you sensed a uniform, unifying, wall-facing side to the tapestry of your life? What did you think it was? This book explains a backing you've not known in depth before. Is that appealing and hopeful? Perhaps some unpleasant responses arise. If so, jot them down for later comparison.
2. If agreement makes everything go in God's Creation, how would you assess your agreement with Him? Are you aware yet of areas where you have agreed with His enemies, who are yours as well?
3. Have you protected yourself against the threat of Jesus? Of the Holy Spirit? How?
4. Only you should pay for your sin, but only Jesus can. Have you accepted His invitation to that beneficial trade?

GETTING TO KNOW YOUR SPIRIT

1. Christians rarely understand body, soul, and spirit, and you may not have explored its usefulness. Beginning on page 250 is a protocol

for becoming and staying a living spirit. You can be intimate with God Himself in a pleasing, effective way. Do you want to? If so, review that protocol.

2. Usually, we know our weaknesses. Review them and identify where you are not in agreement with God. Then quickly ask God to forgive you and cleanse you. For better understanding, see Apostle John's 1st letter, chapter 1, verses 9-10.

3. If 1 is never, and 10 is always, what number would you give for your non-mental sense of His Father-love? What number describes your spirit's sense for His voice?

SPIRIT DEFINED

1. Given that understanding of our spirit is still growing, what words have you used in the past for your spirit?

2. If 1 is dead, and 10 is intense active desire, how active is your spirit presently? Without faith in Christ Jesus, there is no spirit. Re-affirm to Him your desire to be alive in spirit. Listen for what He says without being afraid. Follow His instructions when you pray that.

TOWARD GOD

1. You were dead in spirit. After becoming a disciple of Jesus, you are alive in spirit. Compare your present relationship with God with what you've read in this chapter.

2. Some people have faith in Jesus but don't see the effects of God's Holy Spirit filling them. Ask the Holy Spirit to make Himself unmistakable to you. Have you dedicated yourself to being receptive to Him?

3. When have you recognized your poverty in spirit? How did it come about? When have you felt reassured by your merits? Does your poverty of spirit seem threatening to you? Why is that?

THE CAPABILITIES OF SPIRITS

1. Review what changes when you have the point of view of a living spirit. Name a repetitive crisis or conflict that can benefit from your spirit's POV ability. How?

2. Over the years, has your sense for God grown more or less sensitive? What do you think about that? Which is more practical?
3. Give a number to your life as a spirit; let 1 be never and let 10 be often. Name one or two areas that will benefit by boosting that number.
4. Consider the troubling areas of your life, where your weakness and personal poverty are most evident. The Scriptures identify these as your spirit's most fertile opportunities. What are your present tricks to avoid dealing with those deficiencies? Using the Scriptures in this chapter, consider what would happen if you did not use those tricks and instead offered your personal poverty to God.

THE SPIRIT, THE SOUL, AND THE BODY

1. If you were born as a spirit prior to reading this book, what has ruled your spirit? Without knowledge of your spirit identity, have you deferred to the supremacy of your mind, emotions, or body? Have you deferred to physical limits, or pressure from others? What change would you want after maturing as a spirit?
2. If you are not a spirit yet, what dominates your view of life: your body, mind, will, or emotions? How does that domination manifest itself? If 10 is the most free, how free are you? What attracts you about regaining authority over these persistent dominators?

LIVING AMONG SPIRITS

1. Reflect on the times you've encountered the unseen world of spirits. If you have given yourself to Jesus, identify which encounters to repent about.
2. Because obligations and IOUs are a signal indicator for spirits, make a list of the ones influencing you. Identify those which are characterized by rigidity, inflexibility, or legalistic guilt. List them and break the agreements that make them active in your life.
3. What has God achieved in your life by His use of darkness?

DARKNESS AND YOUR SPIRIT

1. How do you feel about God leaving you imperfect on purpose?

2. The Garden of Eden held two trees right in the middle. One led to life; the other, to death. Are there two similar alternatives in your life—not trees, but a similar choice?
3. Remember an experience that was like deliverance from evil. Identify the evil left behind and the open doors it used to oppress you. After that deliverance, what benefits resulted?
4. List three people in your life that don't seem to fear hell. How happy is each one? Is that happiness genuine, or is it more like avoidance? Identify the benefits you enjoy because of fearing hell.

DISCIPLESHIP OF YOUR SPIRIT

1. List your most appealing benefits of being a spirit from this chapter. What elements of maturing spiritually had a magnetism for you?
2. Think of your life since you become a living spirit through faith in Jesus. Has spirit been easy, no cost? Why or why not?
3. If resistance has been God's way of training you, what has resulted?
4. Think about your exposure to praying in tongues. What was negative? What was positive? In this chapter, what made it more desirable to you?

CHURCH OF SPIRITS

1. Your church, a ruling body (ekklesia): is that a new understanding for you? Ask God how He is using the imperfections there to advance His plans.
2. Would you describe your church as discounting the Holy Spirit? Write out a repentance prayer about it, just for you to pray on behalf of your church. (Chapter 9 of Nehemiah, Ezra and Daniel all give good examples of such repentance.)
3. Pick out some examples of how measuring and status receive attention in your social circles. What would be different if everyone in them understood poverty of spirit and meekness?
4. The chapter identified a few mistaken church practices. Are any of them evident in your church? Can you add these to your prayer list—and talk only with God about them? Consider: can you simultaneously be under the leaders' authority and also part of the solution for these substandard church actions?

Reflection and Discussion Questions

SPIRITS IN THE WORLD OF THE DEAD

1. List the names of a few people that act threatened in your presence. Review the chapter for causes that result from the Holy Spirit in you. List one such cause by each person's name.
2. How do you feel about the us-them identity discussed in the chapter? If you disagree, try to defend your stance with Scriptures. Otherwise, consider why American Christians might have trouble with this.
3. Name the arenas where you bring influence. List some evidence that a living spirit is the superior influence there. If none, why not?

THE DAILY LIFE OF OUR SPIRITS

1. Review the conflicts that are in your life, and identify where God is offending you and wrestling you to help you mature. If 1 is poor and 10 is excellent, what number would you give your response so far? Give thought how you can boost that number higher—assuming you want to mature!
2. Your life as a spirit affects work, family, and church. Questions of time, fear, and death-time also arise. Which one of these struck home with you, and why? How can you progress as a maturing spirit?
3. After reading about speaking in tongues, what is your response? With honesty and candor, you can share that with the Holy Spirit. You won't be surprising Him. Consider how you can mature in this area.

THE REALITY FOR OUR SPIRITS

1. List some past puzzles that are easier to solve after reading about the comprehensive order that living spirits enjoy. Write out your new solutions. How did this book help find them?
2. The kingdom of heaven belongs to its royalty who are simultaneously poor in spirit. Ruling in the spirit is a learning process. Determine one or two substandard responses that you have had. Contrast those with one or two new responses that show both your poverty of spirit and your God-given authority.

Reader Engagement Resources

OBTAINING CREDENTIALS FOR THE ONLINE DISCUSSION GROUP

As an owner of this book, you can request login credentials for a secure online discussion group at ParadigmLighthouse.com, to share your meditations and your progress. The group is limited to readers of the *Unseen* Series. There, you can share your reflections and discoveries. I am growing also and treasure your discoveries as you walk through this book and meditate on the scriptural principles.

With the correspondence and reflections our readers share there, we can all see how God is speaking to us, His body, about our spirits. I'm sure we will find patterns in God's speech to us. Doubtless we can use this book from our discoveries together.

To obtain your log-in username and password, please visit ParadigmLighthouse.com and follow the instructions you see after clicking *Request Log-in Credentials*.

REVIEWS ON AMAZON

Every single review left by a reader helps someone else see and benefit from this Book One of the *Unseen* Series. As you know from your own online shopping, the number of reviews for a book shows that is interesting—whether the reviewer agrees or not. Short or long, general or specific, your review will make a positive impact.

Please visit Amazon.com to leave your review for *Nobody Sees This You: How to Live as a Spirit in the Unseen Realm.*

SOCIAL MEDIA

Neither the author nor publisher utilize social media. If you do, please mention the book by its title, *Nobody Sees This You.* Our ranking on Amazon is affected by people searching for the book by name.

You may also like to share the ParadigmLighthouse.com link, where people can purchase the books as well.

POSTER

To provide you a reminder of this book's central message, we have created a full color 11X17 poster. It summarizes this book pictorially. Post it to encourage yourself. You can also place it for conversational purposes with all who see and ask about it.

You can buy it for $4.99, but you can also get it for free. Learn how at *ParadigmLighthouse.com.*

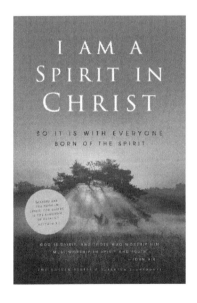

About the Author

Paul Renfroe is a Memphis native and Florida resident, with his wife Diane Renfroe of four decades. They have two sons and one grandson.

Through their business, Emerald Coast Financial Accounts LLC, they have served savers and investors who do not want to lose money. Their ministry and publisher is Paradigm Lighthouse, created to implement the mind of Christ in people born as spirits.

Paul & Diane are members of Vision Church at Christian International, in Santa Rosa Beach FL, and are graduates of The Ministry Training College. In their church journey they have served at every level of leadership and service except pastor. They are ordained to minister through Vision Church, under the leadership of Apostles Tom and Jane Hamon.

Paul's academic endeavors include a Bachelor of Arts with Distinction from Rhodes College (Memphis, TN), where he majored in Bible, Church History while minoring in Philosophy. After graduating, he and his wife served twelve years as campus staff and state directors for InterVarsity Christian Fellowship (Madison, WI).

He has also served as board chairman for several nonprofits and participated in the founding of one school and two churches. With his ability to see what others do not, Paul has been instrumental in several turn-arounds with nonprofits and ministries that were in decline.

His life includes many more encounters with death than is common. Seven times including his birth with a defect, doctors have diagnosed Paul with a fatal condition. He has received many healings, both with doctors and without them. Not surprisingly, Paul has also participated in healing many people from physical ailments—including death.

Paul's vision for the *Unseen* Series developed over five decades of following Jesus sacrificially. His reputation for knowledge of the Bible is rarely exceeded. With practice he has an acute ear for God's voice, and a sharp discernment of the topics people wrestle with.

In the *Unseen* series, this depth and breadth has been condensed for you to go even further. May God bless you as He has Paul—with lifelong hunger for intimacy with Him.

Made in the USA
Columbia, SC
08 February 2025

52929517R00157